Attribution of Advanced Persistent Threats

Timo Steffens

Attribution of Advanced Persistent Threats

How to Identify the Actors Behind Cyber-Espionage

 Springer Vieweg

Timo Steffens
Bonn, Germany

ISBN 978-3-662-61315-3   ISBN 978-3-662-61313-9   (eBook)
https://doi.org/10.1007/978-3-662-61313-9

This Springer Vieweg imprint is published by the registered company Springer-Verlag GmbH, DE part of Springer Nature.
The registered company address is: Heidelberger Platz 3, 14197 Berlin, Germany

Nothing made by a human can avoid personal expression—Hrant Papazian (typographer, April 2012)

Acknowledgements

Attribution is a team sport. The same is true for writing books. This book would not have been possible without the support and expertise of many people.

First, my thanks to Juergen Schmidt, who got the ball rolling with a request for an article on attribution methods for a German magazine. Martin Boerger came up with the idea to publish a whole book on the topic and provided encouragement. His support and dedication was also essential for this translated version. Dorothea Glausinger and Sophia Leonhard have made the editing and publishing process a productive and uncomplicated experience.

I thank my employer for the liberties in covering attribution and the related analysis processes.

Many thanks to Stefan Ritter for a wealth of suggestions regarding style and structure. Selma Jabour assisted in assessing the Vault 7 documents and pointedly pinpointed passages that were too heavy with subjectivity or whose presentation was not convincing. Gavin O'Gorman gave important insights into several analysis processes. I am grateful to Collin Anderson for the exchange of ideas on ethical questions of attribution. Michael Raggi deserves merit for digging up the Papazian quote and transferring it from the art of design to the art—or as I prefer: science—of attribution.

Finally, I thank the analysts and security researchers who shed light on their attribution work in research reports. These reports were the basis of the methods and frameworks covered in this book. These analysts will continue to progress the field of attribution each day with their work—beyond the snapshot covered in this book.

Contents

Acronyms

3PLA	Third Department of the PLA General Staff
ACH	Analysis of Competing Hypotheses
AD	Active Directory
APK	Android Package
APT	Advanced Persistent Threat
BfV	Bundesamt für Verfassungsschutz
BND	Bundesnachrichtendienst
BSI	Bundesamt für Sicherheit in der Informationstechnik
C&C	Command-and-Control
CIA	Central Intelligence Agency
CMS	Content Management Software
CSIS	Canadian Security Intelligence Service
DC	Domain Controller
DNC	Democratic National Committee
DNS	Domain Name System
GCHQ	Government Communications Headquarter
GDPR	General Data Protection Regulation
GSM	Global System for Mobile Communications
GUI	Graphical User Interface
HTTP(S)	Hypertext Transfer Protocol (Secure)
HUMINT	Human Intelligence
ICS	Industrial Control Systems
IDF	Israel Defense Forces
IoC	Indicator of Compromise
MICE	Money, Ideology, Coercion, and Ego
MICTIC	Malware, Infrastructure, Control Servers, Telemetry, Intelligence, Cui Bono
MPS	Ministry for Public Security
MSS	Ministry for State Security
NSA	National Security Agency
OSINT	Open Source Intelligence

PDB	Program Database
PE	Portable Executable
PLA	People's Liberation Army
PtH	Pass-the-Hash
RAT	Remote Administration Tool
RDP	Remote Desktop Protocol
RGB	Reconnaissance General Bureau
SIGINT	Signal Intelligence
SMB	Server Message Block
SQL	Structured Query Language
SSH	Secure Shell
SSL	Secure Sockets Layer
TAO	Tailored Access Operations
TLP	Traffic Light Protocol
TLS	Transport Layer Security
TRB	Technical Reconnaissance Bureau
TTP	Tactics, Techniques, and Procedures
VPS	Virtual Private Server
WMI	Windows Management Instrumentation

Part I

Introduction

Advanced Persistent Threats

Imagine your employer was hacked. You enter your office in the morning, turn on your computer and are informed by a pop-up message that the IT staff has re-installed the system and has reset your password. As you walk through the hallways to get your new credentials at the IT department, you pick up some gossip. The network had been completely compromised for several months and the attackers had accessed dozens of systems, snooping around on file servers and in databases. In the end they were able to steal hundreds of megabytes of carefully selected sensitive documents. If you are a technically interested person, chances are that one of your first questions is how the attackers managed to get into the network and what was necessary to kick them out. But most likely, soon after that you will wonder who the attackers are, what information they were looking for, and how they will take advantage of the stolen data. And probably you will think about these questions not because you are hoping for legal consequences or other forms of revenge. Instead, such answers would help you to make sense of the whole situation. Without an idea of who was behind the incident and what their motivation was, the fact that the network was cleaned up does not satisfy human curiosity.

That is where attribution comes in. Attribution is the analysis process that attempts to answer who was behind a cyber-activity and why they did it.

Most victims of computer crimes will have to accept some day that the criminals will never be identified nor indicted. It is too easy for hackers to hide in the anonymity of the internet, because law enforcement is effectively impeded by anonymization services or by the hackers using compromised computers of unwitting innocents. If the crime was credit card fraud or an ATM jackpotting, the bank will likely settle the damage out of goodwill (or rather a well-calculated trade-off of costs and security). The police investigation will be closed and will remain an entry in the crime statistics.

In contrast, when it comes to targeted cyber-attacks, so-called *Advanced Persistent Threats (APTs)*, IT-security companies and government agencies often claim to know who ordered the attacks. For example, the German Federal Office for Security in Information

T. Steffens, *Attribution of Advanced Persistent Threats*,
https://doi.org/10.1007/978-3-662-61313-9_1

Technology (BSI) had not even fully remediated the incident at the Bundestag in 2015, when media reports named a presumably Russian group called APT28 as the likely culprit. The President of the German Federal Office for the Protection of the Constitution (BfV) Hans-Georg Maassen was later even quoted with an even more concrete attribution, stating that the group was part of the Russian military secret service GRU.

The Bundestag case is not the only noteworthy network compromise that was attributed to a country's government. According to public reports, hackers working for or sponsored by the Iranian government destroyed tens of thousands of computers at the oil company Saudi-Aramco (2012). The IT-security firm Mandiant released a report accusing a unit of the Chinese People's Liberation Army (PLA) of being involved in computer espionage in dozens of countries (2013). The US government has accused North Korea of sabotage attacks against the entertainment company Sony (2014). And again, it was the Russian GRU that was accused by US officials of attacking the network and mailboxes of the Democratic National Committee (DNC) (2016). Just as similar attacks against the World Anti-Doping Agency and the leaking of stolen documents of the En-Marche movement in the French presidential election campaign (2017).

Just a few years ago, the question who was behind attacks like these was relevant only for technical experts. But the meddling in election campaigns showed clearly that attribution was also important for political, social, and strategic reasons. Citizens and voters need to know whether sensitive data of presidential candidates were published by individual criminals because of personal preferences or whether a foreign state ordered such an operation with a strategic intent that may try to maximize the political, social, or economical damage for the affected country.

Yet, evidence that supports attribution statements is rarely presented or at least not addressed by the media. Therefore, the public and even IT-security experts may be left with a sense of skepticism. These doubts do not only concern specific cases, but also the general question of whether it is possible to identify the origin of professional hacker attacks at all.

To this day, the book 'The Cuckoo's Egg' by Stoll [1] is arguably the most influential work that shaped the public's view of attribution. It is the story of an employee of an American university that tracked hackers who attacked the Pentagon and the NASA on behalf of the Soviet intelligence service KGB in the 1980s. The perpetrators had used the university's computers as intermediate jump servers to hack into the actual target's systems. Over the course of many months, Stoll analyzed connection data to identify subsequent jump servers and contacted the unwitting owners of these compromised computers to find additional connection details that led to the next jump servers. In the end, in cooperation with police and intelligence services he managed to track down German hackers in Hanover who had been hired by the KGB .

This scenario of tracking hackers via connection data from one server to the next is repeated time and again in movies and TV series. However, in reality anonymization networks such as The Onion Router (TOR) and similar services often render this investigation method hopeless. Fortunately, the tracking and attribution techniques have evolved fundamentally since the 1980s. As we will see later, many attribution methods have become possible just because - counter-intuitively—the attack methods have become more complex and varied.

In the following, we will explore how IT-security firms and government agencies track down and identify hackers. For this, we need to understand how the perpetrators work and which methods they use. While the Hanoverian hackers were successful just by guessing and stealing passwords, today's Advanced Persistent Threats have a large arsenal of malicious software and techniques at their disposal. They are the premier class of hackers—and arguably the most important to track down.

1.1   Advanced Persistent Threats

The above examples of cyber-attacks all belong in the category of Advanced Persistent Threats (APTs). This term was first introduced by the military and was quickly adopted in the civilian IT-security community. However, the day-to-day usage of the term led to a certain blurring and reinterpretation over time.

The inaccuracy of the term is due to the purpose for which it was invented in the beginning. In 2006, the US Air Force faced the challenge of discussing hacker attacks against its network with civilian experts. They wanted to avoid revealing their findings about the origin of the perpetrators. At the same time, they had to tell the experts that they were not run-of-the-mill attacks. So they came up with the notion of Advanced Persistent Threat.

Advanced means that these attacks are more sophisticated than—for example—those scans and probes that every computer is exposed to within 15 min of connecting to the internet.

Persistent means that the attackers deliberately select their target and—if necessary— repeatedly try to attack it over a long period of time. If an attack technique fails or is not applicable to the victim, the perpetrators do not move on in search of a simpler target. Instead, they adjust their techniques and try again.

Threat is the term that specifies that the actor behind the attacks is relevant. An APT is not a technique or certain class of malware, but an actor with strategic motivations.

At the time, the American military was mostly concerned about hacker groups which they believed to be based in China. Later, when the term APT had also become common in the civilian sector and IT-security industry, it was used to refer to entities on different abstraction levels. A hacker group with a fantasy name, a country, or a specific government agency could be named an APT. For example, according to a series of diplomatic cables published by WikiLeaks in 2010, the US Department of State referred to attackers belonging to the Chinese People's Liberation Army (PLA) as *Byzantine Hades*.

In day-to-day language, the term APT overlaps with the terms *targeted attack* and *cyber or computer espionage*. However, these are different concepts even if we ignore that the

Fig. 1.1 Distinction between targeted attacks, activity by APTs, and cyber-espionage

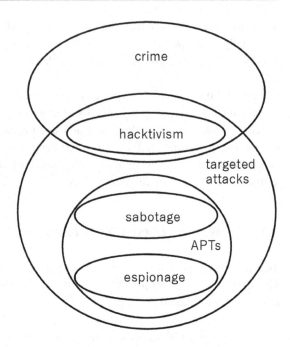

first refers to actors and the latter to actions. Attacks are targeted if the victims are not selected opportunistically or by chance, but deliberately and intentionally. Thus, targeted attacks are a superset of those executed by APTs, because they also cover phenomena such as hacktivism. Hacktivists are politically motivated and deliberately pick companies that they accuse of moral misconduct. Their typical goal is to place a political message on the company's website or to disrupt the website by overloading it with requests. Computer espionage, in turn, is a subset of APT activity, as the latter may also include sabotage (see Fig. 1.1).

Throughout the book we will refer to APTs as attacks as they are purposeful violations of IT-security policies and this word is rather established in the infosec community. In the realm of policy-makers, the term *attack* is reserved for incidents that include sabotage or even violate international law, but we will not make this distinction.

Curiously, in the first reports about these kind of attacks the acronym APT and its long form do not appear at all. The *GhostNet* report by the University of Toronto (2009) and the *Operation Aurora* report by Google (2010) used the terms computer espionage or targeted attack. While media reports were already talking about *APTs* at the time, this term was used only in reports by Trend Micro and McAfee in 2010. Only after Mandiant published their groundbreaking report about the attacker group *APT1* the term APT was established and used by everyone. This report can also be seen as milestone for attribution, as Mandiant presented a wealth of detailed and comprehensible evidence that suggested that APT1 was a particular unit of the Chinese People's Liberation Army.

Since then, IT-security companies have published hundreds of reports about such attacks. More than 130 APT groups have been named and described publicly in varying levels of detail. However, unlike the military and intelligence services, after 2010 security firms did not focus much on the perpetrators behind the attacks, but rather on the malicious programs that were used. In the same vein, the sales people of anti-virus vendors bombarded their potential company customers with presentations about advanced or so-called sophisticated malware. The result was that for some years the term APT was used inflationary for malware that could not be detected by traditional security products. During this time, the term lost its reputation and was ridiculed in the IT community. Particularly the first part of the term led to scathing controversies, because many malicious programs used in these kind of attacks were no more advanced than widespread run-of-the-mill banking trojans.

And indeed, as we will see later, the *Advanced* part of the term remains only for historical reasons and out of habit. Many APTs (and we use the term to denote the actors behind the attacks) are clearly less competent than the developers of banking trojans such as Zeus or Ursnif. The real challenge for IT-security companies and their products and the reason why the malware families of APTs remain under the radar for so long, is that they are used against much fewer targets. So there are less opportunities to discover them.

As marketing and sales trends evolved over time, the next product innovation focused on a characteristic method used by APTs, the so-called *lateral movement*. This refers to the way the hackers move from one system to the next in the compromised network. Security products now promised to detect such activity. This had the effect that the term APT was now used to denote attacks that included lateral movement.

Since about 2015, a service called *Threat Intelligence* gained relevance in the IT-sector. Under this product name security companies offer information about attacks and groups of perpetrators so that customers can configure and harden their systems against specific APTs. With this information, enterprise customers are increasingly developing a sense about which attacker groups are relevant for their industry sector. This completed the circle in the meaning of APT: Finally it refers to the actors behind attacks again. Today, by using the term APT the following characteristics are emphasized: An Advanced Persistent Threat is a group that is not purely financially motivated, but tries to obtain data that can be used strategically or politically. This usually excludes a petty criminal background. Instead, it is assumed that the group either belongs to a government organization or acts on its behalf furthering a strategic intent.

1.2   Phases of Attacks by APTs

As explained earlier, in order to understand why attribution methods work it is necessary to know how APTs operate. The techniques of attackers have increased in variety and complexity since the days of 'Cuckoo's egg' [1]. Compromising a system back then was pretty much just connecting to it over the Internet, hacking a vulnerability or guessing a password,

Fig. 1.2 The killchain is an idealized model of the typical phases of an APT attack

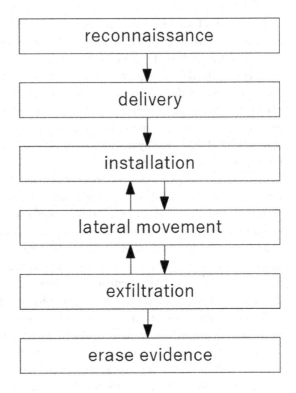

and then copying data. Nowadays an APT attack is a multi-layered and—above all—time-consuming process that can take several months. In order to systematically categorize the different aspects of such an attack, the concept of a *killchain* has been established. It abstracts away some details and idealizes the sequence of events, but it is a helpful concept when discussing the activities of attackers. Just like the term *APT* the concept of a killchain originated in the military world—which explains the martial connotation. The killchain (see Fig. 1.2) describes the stages that attackers typically go through. These phases are briefly explained below, and afterwards each phase will be covered in more detail with examples.

Reconnaissance The attackers do not target random systems but pick networks of organizations that may contain the information that the APT's sponsor wants. In this phase suitable companies, agencies, or other organizations are researched and information is collected that can be used to facilitate the later phases.

Delivery In order to get malicious code onto the target system, the attackers need to find a way to deliver it. A common method is to embed the malicious code into a document which is sent to a target recipient via mail. Another way is to scan for poorly maintained servers and send an *exploit* which is code that takes advantage of a programming mistake—called a vulnerability—in a software.

Installation Delivering the malicious code alone is not sufficient, since the operating systems of computers are designed to prevent execution of unauthorized code. Depending on the method that was used for delivery, the attacker needs to devise a way to execute his code. If attacking via email, the most common method is to use psychological or social tricks to manipulate the recipient to open a malicious mail attachment or click a malicious link. Often this leads to execution of an exploit or a macro that drop the code to the hard disk and install the malware.

Lateral Movement If the execution of the code succeeds, the attacker has infected the first computer in the organization's network so that he can control it. Yet, this is usually not a system that contains the information that he is looking for. Central servers with sensitive information usually cannot be attacked directly over the internet, and the attackers usually do not even know exactly where the relevant data is stored. But having a computer under their control they can use it to start looking around and spreading to other systems in the internal network. This phase can last for several days or weeks until the attacker finally finds the information he is interested in.

Exfiltration Most APTs engage in espionage. At this point in the killchain, the attackers have almost reached their goal. Now they only have to transfer the data from the victim's network to their own systems. This is usually done by upload functions that are built directly into the malware. There are also cases in which data is sent by email or uploaded using legitimate tools that are already present on the compromised system.

Erase Evidence Just like classic espionage, spying in the cyber-realm aims to stay undetected. Even the most sophisticated APTs cannot completely avoid generating suspicious events and traces on compromised systems. Therefore, the more careful APTs expend some effort in the final phase (or sometimes throughout the whole attack) to erase traces as much as possible. This includes deleting log data and removing the malware when it is not needed anymore.

In the following we will look at each phase in more detail and discuss examples from real cases. Several real APT groups will be introduced. For reference during the presentation of

Table 1.1 Non-exhaustive list of typical techniques used by various APT groups in the phases of the killchain

Phase	Desert Falcons	Deep Panda	Lotus Blossom	Snake
Reconnaissance	Facebook	Acunetix	Web-research	Unknown
Delivery	Chat	Direct access	Mail	Watering-hole
Installation	APK	server-exploit	Office-exploit	Browser-exploit
Lateral movement	None	WMI	Unknown	Mimikatz, WMI
Exfiltration	Backdoor	Backdoor	Backdoor	Mail
Erase evidence	Unknown	Unknown	Unknown	Unknown

the examples, the groups and their typical techniques in each phase are listed in Table 1.1. In the infosec community it has become a habit to give these groups rather colorful names. This has the useful side effect that memorizing them becomes easier.

1.3   Reconnaissance

The phase in which the actors collect information about their targets is one of the least understood, because these activities usually take place long before the actual attack. Even worse, the traces of reconnaissance are not necessarily generated in systems that the victim and its incident responders have access to. Information can be gathered in social media, on news sites, or other external web sources. Only in rare cases some insights into the reconnaissance approaches of the actors can be found.

One can only speculate how and why actors select a specific target. It is widely assumed that the hackers receive their tasking from a customer like an intelligence agency or—if they work directly at an agency—from a specialist department that is not comprised of cyber-operators but of analysts reporting to decision makers. Tasking can be done in a rather general way like communicating an interest in research in the field of, say, renewable energies, or very concretely, such as obtaining strategy documents about a specific merger of companies. Whether APT groups receive general or specific tasking heavily depends on the bureaucratic culture in their country. For example, in democratic societies for effective accountability offensive cyber-operators receive very specific tasks along with rules of engagement [2]. Non-democratic governments are more likely to lack oversight so that APT groups are kept on a looser leash. However, even within a country the intelligence agencies may differ in their bureaucratic policies.

In the case of general tasking, the actors first need to identify relevant companies or organizations. This can be done in a variety of ways, such as a simple web search, or evaluation of patent applications, or via poring through conference proceedings. If the APT group is part of an intelligence agency, relevant information can also be requested from the traditional espionage departments. It is a common practice that intelligence officers establish contacts to individuals working at relevant organizations, agencies, and companies, sometimes under the cover of working at an embassy. These contacts may knowingly or unknowingly provide information about people to target or interesting projects.

If the tasking is more specific or once one or more organizations have already been identified as promising targets, the actors need to find vulnerable systems in the target network or suitable employees. Often it is assumed that APTs target VIPs for their alleged access to privileged information. While this does happen every now and then, more often than not attackers target employees who receive mails from unknown persons as part of their daily job. For example, Human Resources staff that evaluate job applications or Public Relations agents are frequent targets. For their work it is necessary to open mails with document attachments from unknown senders. These people are also particularly exposed because usually their contact details are visible on the company website or in internet portals and business networks.

An even better example of targets that are exposed and repeatedly exchange emails with new contacts are investigative journalists. It is part of their job to be visible and public figures and the topics they are interested in are trivial to identify. According to an evaluation of the German BSI the media sector is one of the most targeted by APT groups [3], right after government agencies, defense contractors, and energy companies.

But if necessary APT groups also take their time to identify targets that are not publicly visible. The group *Desert Falcons* is particularly skillful at this. According to an analysis by the IT-security company Kaspersky Labs, this group has started as cyber-criminals in 2011. But in 2014 their behavior changed, and their targeting switched from random individuals to government agencies and military organizations in the Middle East. The information stolen from these targets is monetizable only if it is sold to a customer like an intelligence agency. Therefore, the Desert Falcons are now considered a special kind of APT called cyber mercenaries. In other words, the members of the group are most likely not directly employed as civil servants, but are contracted by a government agency.

In the summer of 2016, the Desert Falcons attacked the Android smartphones of soldiers of the Israeli Defense Forces (IDF) [4] in an elaborate *social engineering* campaign. Social Engineering means manipulating people into carrying out an act desired by the perpetrator, usually by psychological or social tricks. In this case, the attackers created fake profiles of young women on Facebook and joined user groups which were also used by Israeli soldiers. Apparently the perpetrators sifted through the list of group members to find those whose profiles indicated 'Gaza' as location and featured avatar photos with uniforms. The pretended women then contacted these soldiers via the Facebook messenger and invested time and effort to built up a relationship of trust. In order to lure the soldiers to give up information, the women seemingly revealed a lot of information about their own lives. They pretended to come from foreign countries and to be interested in Israel and its history because they took college courses in Arabic or Political Studies. They also often talked about their plans to visit Israel and that they would like to meet locals who can show them around the area. When enough trust was built up, they managed to make the soldiers install apps on their Android devices, which of course were trojanized. We will come back later to this case to look at the other killchain phases of this attack.

Another particularly brazen example is a campaign run by the group *Lotus Blossom* [12]. Typically, this group focuses on government and military facilities in Southeast Asia. In 2016, however, they expanded their targeting to include IT-security researchers—of all people! It is unclear how they compiled the list of targets. Likely, they searched the websites of security conferences for the names of speakers. Another possible source are the blogs of these researchers that often contain their email addresses. Finally, it is often possible to guess the addresses, since many companies use a predictable pattern like firstname.lastname@company.com.

In this campaign the attackers sent fake invitations to a IT-security conference by the company Palo Alto. Attached was a Word document that exploited a known vulnerability. When the recipient opened the document, the *Emissary* was installed. This malicious program had previously only been observed in a low number of attacks against targets in Hong Kong and Taiwan [13]. Apparently, the actors had assumed that this trojan was not yet known to the researchers and their security softwares.

Completely different preparations are necessary for attacks that do not use email for delivering malware, but exploit vulnerable servers that are directly accessible from the internet. Poorly maintained web servers or forgotten test systems that are no longer administrated by security teams are opportunities for hackers. One of the groups looking for such servers is called *Deep Panda*. They use tools such as the Acunetix vulnerability scanner, which is a legitimate software also used by IT-security teams. Its purpose is to find outdated software versions of web servers, databases, or other systems. These versions typically contain vulnerabilities that the security teams want to find and fix. Deep Panda uses Acunetix in the same way, but with the aim of exploiting these vulnerabilities in order to install *webshells* [14]. These consist of a few lines of code that allow the attackers to execute commands remotely over the internet.

The attackers used the Acunetix scanner to consecutively connect to all of the target organization's servers that are reachable from the internet. Each of these servers is tested with a large number of pre-configured requests that provide hints about the installed software and their version. This is a rather noisy approach as it generates large amounts of log data on the target computers, which can be detected by security teams. Unfortunately, similar tools are also used by less professional attackers and every server connected to the internet is subjected to such scans several times a day. These run-of-the-mill scans fill up the log files of organizations so that the traces of targeted attacks are drowned in unrelated data. This way Deep Panda can find vulnerabilities in corporate networks without being noticed. Often they take their time before taking advantage of the vulnerabilities they discovered—poorly maintained servers typically remain vulnerable for a long time.

Several steps of reconnaissance are required if the attackers use *watering-holes*. These are web sites that are visited by employees of the target organization with a high probability. The term is a metaphor referencing the waterholes in Africa that attract many different animals, which makes them preferred areas for predators to prey in the bushes. Similarly, APT groups use such watering holes to prey on their victims by placing malicious code on these websites, exploiting vulnerabilities in the browser or its extensions. Then the attackers only need to wait for an employee of the target organization to visit the website and let the exploit install a malware.

Not much is known about how the attackers identify the websites that are relevant to target organizations. But once they have identified and compromised a promising site, they usually analyze what kind of visitors view the pages. So at first they do not install malicious code but run extensive data collection scripts. This process is referred to as *fingerprinting*, because it profiles visitors based on their IP address, browser settings, and installed software. In the

Witchcoven campaign the *Snake* group collected and examined the IP addresses of visitors and checked which organizations the addresses were registered for [15]. This way they identified interesting address ranges that belonged to government and embassy networks. These addresses were put in a configuration file on the watering hole in order to serve like a whitelist. When visitors from the corresponding organizations accessed the website, malicious code was delivered only to them. Visitors whose IP addresses were not in the whitelist were ignored by the attackers' exploits. With this technique the group prevented the malicious code from being distributed widely, making it less likely that security companies discovered it.

1.4   Delivery

The reconnaissance phase is closely related to the delivery phase. Either one can determine the other. For example, in some cases the actors may have already decided that they will use email attachments as delivery method. This means reconnaissance has to identify suitable persons and their email addresses. In contrast, for groups that have different delivery techniques at their disposal, the reconnaissance phase will be more varied. At first, the attackers may scan for vulnerable servers, and only if they do not find exploitable vulnerabilities they will reconnoiter mail recipients.

If the attack vector is email, the identification of suitable target persons and their email address is followed by creating a lure document. For tailored attacks, the document deals with a topic that is relevant for the target person. If the attackers did not reconnoiter the target's field of interest or if they want to reuse the lure document, they select a generic topic such as recent news. Lure documents are often based on legitimate files that the actors download from public websites or steal from already compromised networks. Finally, an exploit is added and the document is attached to an email. Groups that attack large numbers of targets sometimes develop tools that insert exploits into documents with easy-to-handle interfaces.

When Lotus Blossom prepared the aforementioned fake conference invitations, apparently they only had an exploit for Word documents. But they were not able to find a suitable legitimate document to serve as lure. So they resorted to creating screenshots of the conference website and inserting them into a Word document. It was attached to an email with a few introductory sentences. The sender address was faked to appear as if it was sent by the conference organizers at Palo Alto.

This attack vector is the most common one for cyber-espionage. The IT-security company Symantec observed an average of 141 targeted attacks via mail attachments against their customers per day [5].

However, APT groups are also notorious for their ability to adapt their methods if these are no longer effective against their targets. The following example illustrates the cat-and-mouse-game between attackers and targets. After the community of exiled Tibetans had experienced several attack campaigns using malicious attachments, they avoided sending documents via email [6]. Instead, they moved to use Google Docs, which allows to share content on password-protected websites and provides mechanisms that prevent malicious code in documents. This change of user behavior made any mails with attachments look suspicious. When the attackers noticed that their attacks turned increasingly unsuccessful, they adapted their tactics very quickly. They created fake emails that looked like Google Docs notifications in order to trick recipients into entering their credentials on websites under the control of the attackers. With the stolen credentials the attackers had access to the victims' Google Docs documents—without installing any malicious code at all.

In contrast, the Desert Falcons used a different method with significantly more effort in order to deliver malicious code to the Israeli soldiers. This is an example for the delivery phase defining requirements for the reconnaissance phase. The group had developed Android installers (called *droppers*) that carry the malware and can install it on the targeted device. These droppers used the common format of APK files just like legitimate apps for Android smartphones. Still, they could not be uploaded to the official Google Play Store, because apps containing malicious code get deleted by automatic scans. So the perpetrators simply put the installation files on their own server. The whole aforementioned effort of creating fake women's profiles and finding soldiers via Facebook was to win the trust of the soldiers through chat conversations so that the women could persuade the targeted men to click on a link and manually install the dropper. The ploy was to suggest moving to another chat program which supposedly made exchanging photos more convenient. Many soldiers followed this suggestion and installed the chat program along with the malware.

If an APT uses a watering hole like Snake did, they actually have to deliver malicious code twice. First, they need to get access to the website that they want to turn into a watering hole. This is easy if the web server runs outdated software. Snake has a habit of exploiting vulnerable versions of content management software (CMS) like Joomla or Wordpress. These programs allow website owners to comfortably maintain the content on their sites. Unfortunately, time and again new vulnerabilities are discovered in CMS and exploits are published. Snake is known to use such exploits (called server-side exploits) to compromise websites. They deliver these exploits via the same HTTP protocol that the website owners use to interact with the CMS. Once Snake has gained administrative access to the website, they upload a different exploit (called a client-side exploit), this time for browsers or extensions that are likely to be used by the visitors they want to target. The delivery of the client-side exploit to their actual targets is now performed by the compromised web server. Snake just needs to wait for the employees of the targeted organization to visit the watering hole and being served the malicious code.

Even though many APT attacks are described in detail by IT-security companies such as Kaspersky, Symantec, Palo Alto, and Trend Micro, for people investigating a network compromise (called incident handlers) it is often impossible to ascertain how the attackers got into the network in the first place. This is because in many cases the hackers roam many months in the network before they are detected. In 2016, the security company FireEye reported attacks go undetected for an average of 146 days [7]. So the attackers have enough time to erase traces. And even if they do not, many organizations delete log files after a few months anyway—for data privacy reasons or to save disk storage.

1.5 Installation

At first glance it seems over-complex that the killchain distinguishes between the delivery of the malicious code and its installation. But in fact these two phases are the main challenges for the attackers. Most IT-security measures are designed to prevent exactly these steps that the attackers need to make to gain a foothold in the network. Once the first computer is compromised, propagation in the internal network is often rather easy. As already mentioned, the subsequent activities often go undetected for months. In contrast, unsuccessful attacks typically fail already in the first phases—when trying to gain access and establish a virtual bridgehead in the target network. Therefore, APT groups came up with various techniques in order to evade security products. As we will see later, the differences in these techniques provide important hints for attribution.

The goal of this phase is to take control of a target system so that the attackers can execute commands. Since access to a computer from the internet is usually prevented by a firewall, the perpetrators usually install a *backdoor*. This is a type of malware that establishes a connection from within the network to a *control server*. This server is under the control of the attackers. By placing commands or additional malware on it, they can control the backdoor or load additional components onto the compromised system. In order to remain undetected, the backdoor camouflages its network traffic as legitimate web traffic.

If the delivery method is a mail attachment, the most convenient method for installation is to exploit a vulnerability on the recipient's computer. The most sophisticated APTs may use *zero-day exploits*, which target vulnerabilities that are not yet publicly known. Such exploits are rare and developing them takes a lot of skill and effort—or cost a lot of money if they are purchased. Many APTs do not have the necessary skills or financial resources despite their reputation of sophistication. And even groups that have zero-day exploits at their disposal often prefer to use older and well-known exploits. This is because they want to minimize the risk of their precious zero-days being discovered. In addition, often enough old exploits do the trick, because in most organizations there exist at least a few systems that run old software.

In recent years even the use of old exploits is rarely seen. Modern office software offers so many features for automation and interaction that attackers do not even need exploits. Instead, they make use of macro and script features that software vendors had designed to cover repetitive tasks. Unfortunately, these features were extended to even allow writing or executing files. For security reasons, in the default configuration users need to confirm running macros, but as we will see the attackers often succeed in tricking users to run malicious code.

So once the attacker has figured out or guessed which software versions are used in the target organization, he selects a suitable exploit or develops a macro. Now all he has to do is to make sure that the recipient opens the attached document and confirms any security alerts. So the mail needs to appear trustworthy and relevant. Both of these requirements were met rather well by the previously mentioned conference invitations by Lotus Blossom. As soon as the recipient opens the attached document, the exploit executes and downloads a dropper, which writes malicious code to the hard disk. This is called a *multi-stage malware*, as the individual components are consecutively downloaded from servers under the control of the attackers. Since every component in this sequence can be changed easily, it provides a high degree of flexibility. This also gives the attackers an edge in the cat-and-mouse-game with security researchers, as getting hold of all components in the attack sequence becomes more difficult.

The IDF soldiers had to confirm several security warnings for installing the chat app from a non-official website. If the attackers had not built up a trust relationship using the fake profiles, their success rate for getting their malware installed would have been much lower.

For compromising web servers social engineering and user interaction are not applicable. So Snake needed a server-exploit to take control of their watering holes. And since several international organizations lack the resources to secure their web servers, Snake was able to find websites that were vulnerable for exploits. Because web servers are directly reachable from the internet, Snake sometimes does not install a backdoor (that opens a connection to a control server from within the network), but a webshell. These tiny programs can be accessed remotely via browsers or simple tools without the need to bypass firewalls.

The next step in setting up a watering hole is much more difficult. Its purpose is to compromise the computers of relevant website visitors. A few years ago, this was easier because browser extensions such as Java and Flash produced vulnerabilities faster than users were able to update their software. For this very reason website developers started to avoid Java and Flash, so that nowadays most users do not even have these browser extensions installed. Additionally, most browsers download and install security updates automatically now. As a result, watering holes have become much rarer. When watering holes are detected these days, they typically make use of zero-day exploits [8].

1.6   Lateral Movement

Lateral Movement is one of the characteristics that sets APT attacks apart from crime cases. In the latter the perpetrators usually compromise only individual computers in order to steal online banking credentials or to send spam. As explained earlier, for APTs lateral movement is necessary in order to find sensitive information inside large company or government networks.

Modern operating systems define a set of privileges for each account. One of the most important differences between user and administrator accounts is the privileges of the latter to install software—an effective security measure against malware in user accounts. If attackers send malicious mails to a recipient that only has user privileges, they may not be able to install malware. Therefore, the attackers' first step is to do a *privilege escalation* in order to gain extended privileges such as writing files into arbitrary locations or installing software. Usually the attackers aim to gain privileges on the level of a system administrator. There are special exploits for this very purpose—in contrast to code execution exploits we have discussed above. In the IT-security community privilege escalation vulnerabilities are assigned less priority than those allowing the execution of arbitrary code. So software companies wait longer before fixing the vulnerabilities and IT-administrators often postpone installation of security updates.

Once the hackers have obtained administrative privileges with an exploit, they search the computer memory for credentials of other users and services that have logged into the computer. Even administrator credentials may be present in memory if he or she has logged into the computer to install software or change a configuration. Also automated backup services log into computers with high privileges. The operating system handles these services just like user accounts, along with credentials and privileges. With penetration test tools such as Mimikatz the perpetrators can dump the credentials from memory. This is the first step of *pass-the-hash* attacks. Strictly speaking, the attackers do not dump passwords from memory, but cryptographically derived hashes. However, with the appropriate tools these hashes can be used in pretty much the same way as passwords. With these collected credentials the attackers can log into any computer on the network as administrator—using legitimate tools that are part of the operating system. There is no need for malware at this point.

As they move from one computer to another, they gather more information about the structure and architecture of the victim's network. Gradually they learn whether the organization's departments are internally separated into different networks, whether sensitive servers are secured differently than other systems, or which users have access to interesting documents. The attackers always keep their eyes open for interesting data, searching for certain keywords, or copying directory listings of document filenames. In parallel, they identify suitable systems where they can install additional backdoors. Theoretically, a single backdoored computer is enough for the hackers to return into the network at any time they want. However, the backdoored computer may be replaced due to hardware defects or for performance reasons, or because the infection was detected by network administrators. So the attackers usually install additional backdoors on tactically selected systems. Good candidates are decommissioned servers that are no longer maintained but are still online.

In most incidents, one of the first servers the attackers specifically search for is the *Domain Controller*. This is a server that stores all user privileges and credentials and is used by many systems and software to verify that a user is authorized to log into his or her desktop or that certain directories on a file server may be accessed. As soon as the attackers have compromised the domain controller, they can copy the credentials of all users. Even worse, they can then add additional accounts, grant themselves arbitrary privileges, or can cause havoc by modifying the complex configurations. So once the domain controller is compromised, the effort necessary for remediation of the incident increases enormously.

This was the case when Snake compromised the Swiss defense company RUAG [9]. The group roamed through the internal network and created a list of employees, installed software, and server configurations. Then—using the aforementioned Mimikatz tool they even managed to gain a *Golden Ticket* on the domain controller—comparable to an all-access pass with unlimited validity.

Since at least 2016 many APT groups turned to living-off-the-land methods for lateral movement. Instead of installing their own tools or malware they use the administration software that is already present on the target machines. *WMI (Windows Management Instrumentation)* and *PowerShell* are particularly comfortable tools that allow for moving through the network or executing code at arbitrary times. DeepPanda and Snake were among the first to use these tools and seem to have grown fond of them [10].

In the killchain lateral movement is depicted as a loop, since the attackers continue to move around the network during the whole network operation. So strictly speaking this phase overlaps with the next two phases.

1.7 Exfiltration

In cyber espionage, the exfiltration of documents and data is the ultimate goal of the perpetrators. All the other killchain phases are only means to an end. Therefore, most APT malware has functionality to collect documents on compromised machines and transfer them to servers under the control of the attackers.

One of these malware functionalities is to compile a list of files available on the compromised computer. Often a set of keywords is used to identify interesting file and directory names. Another method is to define a list of file extensions that the perpetrators are interested in. For example, some APT groups were looking for files that were encrypted by specific software.

These methods show that APTs do not pilfer random documents. Apparently their customers—which are often intelligence agencies—also do not encourage to grab everything on a computer in order to sift through it later. One reason for this is that exfiltrating data generates suspicious amounts of network traffic that might alert security teams. Another reason is that these groups regularly attack several dozen organizations at the same time. It takes a lot of effort to evaluate stolen documents. Intelligence agencies have entire departments of translators, linguists, and subject matter experts for this task. Nevertheless, they too must manage their resources. Therefore, the attackers already prioritize and filter the documents to steal.

But first the documents must be uploaded undetected from the victim network. For this purpose, the selected documents are copied from their various source folders and computers to a *staging server*. This is usually a server that is accessible from within the network, but also has connections to the Internet. The actors copy the documents into a directory on that server and then bundle them into a password-protected, compressed archive. In most cases they use the RAR format and, if necessary, even download the necessary software first. While other compression formats allow to encrypt files, RAR has the advantage that not even the list of the bundled files can be viewed without the password. So even if the security team detects the exfiltration activity, they cannot determine which documents the culprits were interested in.

From the staging servers the data is uploaded to servers under the control of the attackers. In rare cases this is done with legitimate tools like FTP. But as already mentioned in most cases the malware functionality is used to transmit data via the HTTP or HTTPS protocol. These protocols are mainly used for legitimate web browsing, so they are not blocked by firewalls and do not raise suspicion in network logs. Typically, the malware encrypts the traffic. Many APT groups develop the encryption functions themselves, even though this is very time-consuming and error-prone. Fortunately for us, attribution can benefit from this. The subtle differences in the implementation of cryptographic algorithms are used heavily in attribution, because they help to assess whether different malware families were created by the same developers. For example, Snake is notoriously known for developing the encryption algorithms CAST128 and AES on their own, even though there are publicly available libraries.

Yet, Snake is very versatile and employs various methods for exfiltration. When compromising the German Office for Foreign Affairs in 2018, public reports state that they sent data via email to specially registered email addresses [11]. In other cases when they needed to upload large amounts of data, they split the RAR archives into parts of 20 MB and sent them as mail attachments. Exfiltration via email is preferable in networks where HTTP (for web browsing) is uncommon, prohibited, or heavily monitored.

The stolen data is never transmitted directly to the attackers' own networks but to intermediate servers. The culprits may rent these servers with fake or stolen identities, or they may hack servers from uninvolved third parties. Usually there are several layers of such servers, and the attackers transfer the data gradually from one server to the next. For this purpose, many APT groups manage dozens or even hundreds of servers. The more countries these servers are scattered across, the harder it is for investigators and law enforcement to follow their track.

1.8   Erase Evidence

Very few reports cover the last phase of the killchain, in which the culprits erase their tracks. This is partly because this phase is an idealization of APT attacks. Many of the well-known groups show surprisingly little *Operational Security (OpSec)*. This term refers to methods and practices to protect the attackers from detection. As a rule of thumb, the technological sophistication of a group correlates strongly with their OpSec. Another reason for this phase not being covered in many reports is also due to the idealized concept of the killchain. Often, traces are not erased at the end of the whole operation, but attackers delete tools as soon as they do not need them anymore. For example, if the delivery was done by multi-stage malware, the dropper components are deleted once the malware was installed successfully.

Nevertheless, the killchain is useful to illustrate the overall attack process and to develop security measures. Some detection mechanisms of security products alert on any processes that delete log data. This is possible because operating systems even log the deletion of logs!

At the top end of the scale for OpSec are groups that were reported to be part of the NSA and CIA. In 2016 and 2017, a number of manuals and guidelines for the offensive cyber units of these two intelligence agencies were published. These contained detailed instructions how logging of some events can be avoided. So traces were not even generated in the first place. If logging was inevitable, the manuals explained when and how to delete log data on routers or security events on servers. There were even strict rules when to abort an operation and delete all the tools that were downloaded.

However, these groups are technically very advanced compared to other APT groups. In almost all economic espionage cases, many traces can still be found after the attackers left the network. As mentioned before, more traces are deleted by normal log-rotation processes of the targeted companies than by activities of attackers. To be fair, there are operational reasons for deleting logs. Domain controllers and DNS servers produce several Gigabytes of logs every single day. Therefore, they are overwritten after a very short time—sometimes after 24 hours or less. Another reason is data protection compliance, which restricts the collection of data if it can be used to profile employees.

Still, the fact that many APT groups lack systematic OpSec for erasing their traces provides opportunities for attribution. We will shortly see that attribution does not depend on mistakes alone (though they are always a bonus), but that most attack methods inherently leave traces behind that can be used for tracking and identifying the perpetrators.

References

1. Stoll, C.: The Cuckoo's Egg: Tracking a Spy Through the Maze of Computer Espionage, 1st edn. The Bodley Head Ltd (1989)
2. Maurer, T.: Cyber Mercenaries-The State, Hackers, and Power. Cambridge University Press (2018)
3. Federal Office for Information Security: The State of IT Security in Germany 2017 (2017). https://www.bsi.bund.de/SharedDocs/Downloads/EN/BSI/Publications/Securitysituation/IT-Security-Situation-in-Germany-2017.pdf Accessed 22 Oct 2019
4. Naor, I.: Breaking the weakest link of the strongest chain. In: Securelist (2017). http://web.archive.org/web/20170718171625/https://securelist.com/breaking-the-weakest-link-of-the-strongest-chain/77562/. Accessed 18 July 2017
5. Symantec Corporation: Symantec intelligence report 2015. https://www.symantec.com/content/dam/symantec/docs/security-center/archives/intelligence-report-jan-15-en.pdf. Accessed 18 July 2017

6. Dalek, J., Crete-Nishihata, M., Scott-Railton, J.: Shifting tactics-tracking changes in years-long espionage casmpaigns against Tibetans. In: The Citizen Lab (2016). http://web.archive.org/web/20170718174137/https://citizenlab.ca/2016/03/shifting-tactics/. Accessed 18 July 2017

7. FireEye: M-Trends 2016 EMEA-Edition (2016). http://web.archive.org/web/20170718174718/. https://www2.fireeye.com/WEB-RPT-M-Trends-2016-EMEA.html. Accessed 18 July 2017

8. Google Project Zero: A very deep dive into iOS Exploit chains found in the wild. https://googleprojectzero.blogspot.com/2019/08/a-very-deep-dive-into-ios-exploit.html. Accessed 19 Oct 2019

9. GovCERT.ch: APT case RUAG-technical report (2016). http://web.archive.org/web/20170718174931/https://www.melani.admin.ch/dam/melani/de/dokumente/2016/technicalreportruag.pdf.download.pdf/Report_Ruag-Espionage-Case.pdf. Accessed 18 July 2017

10. MITRE: DeepPanda, ShellCrew. In: ATT& CK (2016). http://web.archive.org/web/20170718180111/https://attack.mitre.org/wiki/Group/G0009. Accessed 18 July 2017

11. Tanriverdi, H.: So schleusten die Hacker Daten aus dem Auswärtigen Amt. https://www.sueddeutsche.de/digital/exklusiv-so-schleusten-die-hacker-daten-aus-dem-auswaertigen-amt-1.3894534. Accessed 21 Oct 2019

12. Falcone, R.: PSA: conference invite used as a lure by operation lotus blossom actors. In: Palo Alto Networks Blog (2016). https://web.archive.org/web/20170718172201/https://researchcenter.paloaltonetworks.com/2016/10/unit42-psa-conference-invite-used-lure-operation-lotus-blossom-actors/. Accessed 18 July 2017

13. Falcone, R., Miller-Osborn, J.: Emissary trojan changelog: Did operation lotus blossom cause it to evolve? In: Palo Alto Networks Blog (2016). https://web.archive.org/web/20170718172339/https://researchcenter.paloaltonetworks.com/2016/02/emissary-trojan-changelog-did-operation-lotus-blossom-cause-it-to-evolve/. Accessed 18 July 2017

14. Tilbury, C.: Mo shells mo problems-web server log analysis. In: CrowdStrike Blog (2014). http://web.archive.org/web/20170718173120/https://www.crowdstrike.com/blog/mo-shells-mo-problems-web-server-log-analysis/. Accessed 18 July 2017

15. FireEye: Pinpointing targets: exploiting web analytics to ensnare victims. In: FireEye Blog (2015). http://web.archive.org/web/20170718173610/https://www2.fireeye.com/rs/848-DID-242/images/rpt-witchcoven.pdf. Accessed 18 July 2017

The Attribution Process

For investigating the culprits behind criminal cases the term *investigation* is commonly used. In contrast, *attribution* is usually reserved for the tracking of APTs, that is, cyber-espionage. A fundamental premise is that APT groups are either directly embedded in intelligence agencies or are at least directed by them. Thus, the term *state-sponsored* attacks has been coined and is more or less synonymously used with *APT* attacks nowadays.

For several years the majority of public attribution statements originated from IT-security companies—with varying degrees of explicitness. The APT1 report by Mandiant was the most specific and outspoken, naming individuals and—politically most relevant—concrete military units. The government affiliation of the hackers was obvious. As we will see later, several other reports also contained names and even photos of individuals that were believed to be likely perpetrators and working for the military (e.g. [1, 2]). Other reports limited their tracking to countries of origin, avoiding to point a finger at the respective government (e.g. [3]). This of course is mostly a formal technicality, since the assumption is that APT groups are state-sponsored. Another flavor was to show that the groups were likely native speakers of certain languages [4]. These differences in attribution statements are partly due to the level of detail that the researchers were able to dig up. But partly these differences are also due to the policy of the respective IT-security company. Some do not name individuals for ethical considerations, some avoid naming governments for legal or political reasons. We will discuss ethical and political consequences of attribution in Chap. 13. For now, it is noteworthy that attribution can be done on different levels of detail—abstractly named groups, countries, organizations, and individuals.

Since 2016 the number of attribution statements that were published by government agencies is steadily increasing. Particularly, the United States Department of Justice has unsealed a remarkable amount of indictments against hackers from Russia, China, Iran, and North Korea [5].

In public discourse, the main difference between attribution by governments and by IT-security companies is often stated as a political one. While this is certainly true, there are

© Springer-Verlag GmbH Germany, part of Springer Nature 2020
T. Steffens, *Attribution of Advanced Persistent Threats*,
https://doi.org/10.1007/978-3-662-61313-9_2

also at least three clear differences in methodology. First, indictments and official statements cover specific attacks or incidents, whereas industry attribution focuses on APT groups and their activity over longer periods of time. Second, indictments need to name legal persons and official statements usually name a foreign government for political effect, while reports by security companies come in different flavors and may be limited to the granularity of a country of origin. Thirdly, official attribution is often based on data from intelligence agencies, which cannot be disclosed. In contrast, security companies are often very transparent in their sources and methods in order to increase transparency and trust in their assessments.

2.1   Why Attribution at All?

Considering the fact that governments traditionally publicly deny their involvement in cyberattacks and protect their own people from prosecution, it is a valid question what attribution is good for at all. Is it just a pastime for curious security researchers and over-active intelligence services?

The weakest reason for attribution—but still an important source of motivation during the lengthy work of analysts—is that it is in our human nature to want to know the culprits. You can see the same pattern after any terror plot or assassination attempt: One of the first questions that come to mind is about the identity of the attackers. This is not necessarily for revenge or prosecution, instead knowing who the perpetrators are provides indications for their intentions and thus a reason for the attack. Psychologically, it is unsatisfactory to think that attacks (or any other negative event such as accidents) happen arbitrarily or by chance. It is knowing the likely identity of the culprits that lets us deduce why particular targets were selected and whether there will be similar incidents again.

Still: Satisfying human curiosity alone cannot justify the effort necessary for attribution.

In the IT-security community there is the oft-repeated mantra that it is irrelevant who is behind an attack because IT-security measures are always the same, irrespective of the origin of the perpetrators. On a purely technical and operational level, this position is absolutely correct. If you can hermetically seal off your network, you are protected against random criminals as well as well-motivated intelligence services of any origin. In practice, however, there is hardly any company or organization that can implement all existing and recommended security measures. IT-operation and IT-security are a cost factor for any organization. Government agencies are committed to their taxpayers, and companies are committed to their shareholders, each limiting the financial resources. After all, IT-security measures are bound by the law of diminishing marginal utility: At a certain point, increasing security will lead to less and less benefits. So any manager in charge of the budget will have to decide how much security is enough.

So from the plethora of available security products those are selected which are most cost-effective. Processes such as installing security updates and monitoring network alarms are designed and set up depending on the number and skills of available IT-personnel. Even in the day-to-day business each IT-administrator needs to prioritize and decide between basic—but time-consuming—tasks.

Knowing whether and which APT groups target a certain industry sector can provide information which security measures are to be prioritized. For example, a few years ago a company that works in the defense sector may have been motivated to take the huge effort of switching its default browser to a new brand with a better sandbox, maybe even reducing usability for its employees by deactivating scripting and other active content. This could have been justified by Snake targeting that sector and using watering-holes in the Witchcoven campaign. If these instances of compromised websites had not been attributed to Snake and if the group's targeting had been unknown, these website compromises would have remained unrelated single events and the defense company might not have realized their relevance.

On a more strategical management level, announcements of the Chinese government about which research topics will be prioritized may help to decide about the company's security budget for the corresponding research departments. This is illustrated by the fact that in the past many cyber-espionage cases in sectors highlighted by Chinese strategic initiatives like the Five-Year Plan have indeed been attributed to the land of the dragon. Without attribution there would be no difference between the research strategies of China and those of, say, Germany with regards to their relevance for IT budgets.

Also at the diplomatic level a well-founded attribution is an important prerequisite for exerting pressure on governments directing cyber attacks. For years, the USA had accused the Chinese government of computer espionage against American companies. Always without providing evidence—always without success. The Chinese representatives had vehemently denied any accusations with reference to missing evidence [6]. Only when in May 2014 a court in Pennsylvania sentenced five officers of the PLA for computer espionage [7], the USA gained a point of leverage. The evidence presented in the court proceedings was so convincing that US diplomats were able to increase the pressure on their Chinese counterparts. In August 2015, a few weeks before a meeting between Presidents Barack Obama and Xi Jinping on cyber-policy, the US publicly considered imposing sanctions [8] against Chinese companies for cyber-espionage. This announcement seemed to have made the difference, because at the meeting China agreed to an agreement between the two states, which prohibited hacking for the purpose of stealing intellectual property. Since then the observed activity of China-attributed APT groups in the USA decreased noticeably [9]. However, attribution is no silver bullet. According to a later US indictment, Chinese hackers continued cyber-espionage against US companies shortly after the agreement [10]. And Russian groups like APT28 never slowed down at all after being outed by several Western governments.

Still, these indictments and public attribution statements show that the myth of anonymous hacking is wavering. Previously, computer espionage had offered states a good risk-benefit ratio. For developing and emerging countries the investment of a few million dollars in the development of APT tools may have been more promising than lengthy and expensive research projects. Stealing technical know-how can jump-start a nation's development plans tremendously. Considering this opportunity, it is not surprising that according to reports by security companies several APT groups have been attributed to India, Pakistan, Iran, North Korea, and China.

Without attribution, APTs would be a low-risk tool also for the military. The ability of plausible deniability might drastically lower reservations against placing implants for sabotage into critical infrastructures—such as power and telecommunication networks—in peacetime. In the event of a conflict, these strategically placed implants could be used for coercion or could even cause considerable damage to the opponent. Therefore the ability of a state to attribute—and prior to that the ability to detect implants before they are used for sabotage—is an important deterrent.

Even if governments do not employ hackers themselves but contract cyber mercenaries as proxies, attribution is effective. After the hack-and-leak attacks against the Democratic National Committee (DNC) the US White House sanctioned not only Russian intelligence agencies and GRU officers, but also two individuals [11]. These two persons were not explicitly linked to Russian authorities, but nevertheless sanctioning them can be seen as a means to drain the market for hackers. If a hacker has to consider that he or she can be identified, sanctioned, refused to enter countries, or even put on an international arrest warrant, his willingness to participate in cyber-attacks is likely to decline accordingly.

Finally, attribution also has an impact on the public opinion. During the US and French presidential election campaigns in 2016 and 2017, hackers stole emails and documents from politicians and published them. While in the US these leaks led to the resignation of the DNC chairman Debbie Wasserman Schultz, no effect was noticeable in the French election campaign. This was likely due to—among other things—the fact that the French public and media had expected such leaks after the incidents in the US. The effect of hack-and-leak operations depends strongly on the interpretation and reaction of the public. If attribution can help to show that the hackers are no selfless Robin Hoods but are directed by a foreign state with strategic intent, the leaked information is assessed more sceptically. Also the attention is directed at the mischievousness of the hackers and not at the leaked alleged wrong-doings of politicians.

2.2   Terminology for Describing Cyber-Attacks and Actors

The term attribution originated in psychology and describes how causes for behavior are explained. Fritz Heider characterized the corresponding psychological processes in 1958 [12]. A certain behavior can be caused by individual characteristics of a person or by the external situation. For example, athletic success could be attributed to the athlete's own physical and tactical abilities, to the support of the trainer, or to lucky coincidences.

In the cyber-domain the concept of attribution is abstractly similar to that in social psychology. In the broadest sense, in both disciplines the question is who is the cause or has the responsibility for an action. However, the events under consideration and the attribution goals are of course discipline-specific and have become very differentiated. In the following this differentiated terminology for the cyber-domain is introduced.

Attack and campaign So far we have coined attribution as assigning attacks to a country or a government. However, in every-day language the word 'attack' does not differentiate well between different categories of cyber-activities and events. A definition is in order.

In the following we use the term *attack* for a violation or attempted violation of IT-security policies. This term is very broad and covers the sending of large numbers of unsolicited emails, connecting an unauthorized device to a network, as well as the installation of malware. In the research community for cyber-norms and international law, 'attack' denotes incidents with disruptive effects. In the technical community, the term is used more broadly and we adopt this broader meaning.

A *campaign* is a series of similar attacks that occur in a narrowly defined period of time. This similarity is mostly based on technical characteristics, but can also be based on the context like the targeted industry sector. One essential assumption is that the attacks in a campaign were carried out by the same perpetrators. An example of this are several attacks on energy companies and nuclear power plant operators in 2017 [13]. Employees received fake job application emails from alleged engineers. The attached Word documents contained code that transmitted the user's Windows credentials to remote servers. Apparently, the goal of the perpetrators was to obtain sensitive information about power grids and the security mechanisms of nuclear power plants. Within a few weeks, companies in the US, Canada, Ireland, and Norway were attacked. Each company initially handled these attacks on its own and was unaware of the incidents at competitors or abroad. It was not until IT-security companies observed these attacks against several of their customers and realized their technical and contextual similarities that the attacks were grouped into a campaign.

Indicators For describing technical artefacts used in attacks and to give security teams the ability to check their own networks, security companies and agencies provide *indicators*— also known as Indicators of Compromise (IoCs).

An indicator of compromise is a technical characteristic that—if found in system or network logs—is evidence for malicious activity. An example is the IP address of a server used by an APT group. In the afore-mentioned campaign against energy companies, the stolen Windows credentials were sent to the IP address 5.153.58[.]45 [13]. (Whenever addresses that contain or contained malicious code are mentioned in this book, these domains or IPs are defanged by a dot surrounded by square brackets. Such addresses should not be typed into browsers and should not be connected to.) If this address is found in the log data of a firewall, there is a high probability that the perpetrators are active in the network. Other examples for IoCs are file names of mail attachments that can be useful as indicators if the perpetrators use the same name in several attacks. In the same campaign the fake application emails contained a Word document named *Controls Engineer.docx* (see Table 2.1).

IP addresses and file names are examples of atomic, i.e. simple, indicators. There are also complex combinations of several technical features. For example, the exfiltration technique

Table 2.1 Examples of indicators of compromise (IoCs)

Type	Category	Example value	Description
IP	Atomic	5.153.58[.]45	Server that stolen credentials were transferred to
File name	Atomic	*Controls Engineer.docx*	Name of an email-attachment
Mail address	Atomic	Chancery@indianembassy[.]hu	Sender address of an email
MD5	Computed	5a89aac6c8259abbba2fa2ad3f cefc6e	Hash of a malware file
Technique	Complex	Sends files in chunks of 20 MB via email	Exfiltration method

via mail used by Snake is captured by the indicator to check for a large number of mails with 20 MB attachments within a short period of time.

The basic idea behind using IoCs is to take advantage of the fact that the perpetrators were discovered during an attack on an organization. By describing the attack technically and precisely, also other affected companies and organizations can detect these activities— on the (empirically often confirmed) assumption that the attackers do not vary their methods much.

Security companies offer subscriptions to indicator feeds for current campaigns. This service is part of so-called *Threat Intelligence*. Large companies and government agencies regularly check their networks and computers for the existence of such purchased indicators.

Although indicators are mainly useful for IT-administrators to be applied in sensors to detect attacks, they can also be used by analysts to describe the malware and control server infrastructures of APT groups. In attribution reports this is a useful way to precisely document which attacks and resources are the object of the analysis.

Tactics, Techniques, and Procedures (TTPs) Hackers are creatures of habit, especially when they attack many targets over a long period of time. Then efficiency is more important than creativity, and methods that have proven successful are applied again. So a useful approach in IT-security is to describe these habits and repeating methods.

Indicators are useful for detection and analysis tasks that can be automated. However, most typical actions and habits of attackers cannot be represented by purely technical characteristics. The method of the afore-mentioned Desert Falcons to chat with target persons via Facebook is an example of such an approach that cannot be described with indicators. Also the use of the encryption algorithm CAST128 by the group Snake cannot be specified in its generality suitable for machines. For use in natural language *Tactics, Techniques, and Procedures (TTPs)* were introduced as analytical concept and to describe the typical behaviors that the perpetrators repeatedly exhibit.

Just like IoCs, TTPs are an integral part of Threat Intelligence. Still, there is no exhaustive list of TTPs. The ATT&CK framework of MITRE defines an extensive set of relevant tactics and techniques [14], but since TTPs can cover all attacker methods that can be described in words, creating a complete catalog of them is infeasible. For the same reason, TTP definitions are not necessarily machine-readable. The skills and creativity of human analysts are necessary to recognize recurring patterns in attacks and document them. IT-security experts can then write detection rules for the traces that some of these behaviors generate on computers. A popular tool for this is Sigma [15]. But generally speaking, not all TTPs are meant to be cast in code but rather to be communicated to network defenders and analysts.

Intrusion Set When security researchers analyze attacks, they often observe certain indicators and TTPs being used together repeatedly. Even though the public discourse usually only uses the term *APT groups*, a more precise term for such co-occurrences is *intrusion set*. This difference is necessary because an APT group can employ different approaches depending on the situation. For example, Snake does not always use watering holes, but also sends mails with malicious attachments. These two attack methods differ in exploits, malware, and control servers. Describing these attacks with indicators and TTPs results in at least two intrusion sets. A well-defined intrusion set is assumed to apply to only one group. However, the group can choose between several intrusion sets or develop new ones over time.

Security researchers generate a catalog of intrusion sets, which they can compare to specific attacks. If the TTPs and indicators match, there is a high probability that the same culprits are behind the specific attack and the intrusion set.

For illustration, the above-quoted campaign against energy companies did not match any known intrusion set. Therefore, US authorities defined a new one and named it Palmetto Fusion.

Note that the term is sometimes used to denote the attackers instead of the attack descriptions. This is unproblematic as an intrusion set refers to an (assumed) unique actor—even if its identity in the physical world is unknown.

Threat Actor As soon as a name for any cyber-phenomenon is used publicly, there is a high chance that it gets adopted in the media and IT-security community. Even if it refers to a malware, an intrusion set, or a campaign, it may get used like a name for a group of attackers. The difference between an intrusion set and what the infosec community calls *threat actor* is hard to convey outside of professional publications. Strictly speaking, a threat actor is a person, a set of persons, or an organization that supports or carries out attacks over a long period of time. The term can refer to a loosely organized group of hackers who offer their services like mercenaries, as well as to a formally defined unit in an government agency.

In this book we use the term *APT group*, or *group*, for entities that are given fantasy names like Deep Panda or Desert Falcons. These names are created because often security analysts deal with abstract descriptions of recurring intrusion sets that may be used by the same threat actor, but the real persons behind them are unknown.

Security companies such as CrowdStrike, FireEye, Kaspersky Labs, and Symantec assign their own names to intrusion sets and groups they observe. In some cases, they use characteristic naming conventions. For example, FireEye numbers its groups from APT1 to—currently—APT41. This naming scheme was chosen deliberately, because when FireEye started their APT research, they focused on a purely technical perspective and saw no value in attribution. Using numbers they wanted to avoid associations and hypotheses about the perpetrators. However, since then the expectations and requirements of customers have changed, and when introducing their then newest group APT32, FireEye stressed that the attacks are consistent with Vietnam's political interests [16]. Although this is a cautious wording, it is only chosen if the analysts are sufficiently sure about the attribution.

Similarly, Kaspersky Labs also avoid references to the real perpetrators in their group names. They often cluster groups around their characteristic malware, so that the name of the malware becomes synonymous with the group. In other cases they use movie titles. The name 'Red October' was given to a group they analyzed in October 2012 in a cramped and hot—metaphorically red-hot—office. 'Cloud Atlas' is a group that used cloud services for exfiltrating data [17]. Kaspersky Labs emphasizes being non-political and fighting malware of any origin equally. Therefore, the official company policy is to refrain from attribution. However, this does not prevent their analysts from documenting the likely native language or country of origin of malware developers in their reports.

Other security companies, such as Symantec, ESET, or PaloAlto, often assign names based on strings found in malware or domains that act as control servers.

The most attribution-friendly naming scheme was introduced by CrowdStrike. The names of their groups consistently contain a reference to their country of origin. Russian APTs will be called 'Bear', as in 'Venomous Bear', which is CrowdStrike's name for Snake. Chinese groups are named 'Panda' as in 'Deep Panda', Iranian groups 'Kitten', and North Korean groups 'Chollima'. The latter is a Korean mythical creature that looks like a winged horse.

Since the same threat actor may be referred to by different abstract names from security companies, there exists some confusion among researchers and network defenders. Assume the security teams of two organizations are customers of different security companies and want to exchange information about APT groups. They need something like a translation table for the group names, a kind of Rosetta stone, similar to the stone tablet found in Egypt, which contains the same text in three languages. Some examples of the different names used by security companies are given in Table 2.2.

Still, there are comprehensible reasons why security companies come up with their own names for APT groups. One is very practical: Contrary to general belief, when a report about an APT group is published, this does not mean that the group has been only recently discovered. Instead, security companies track a large number of intrusion sets or even groups without publishing them. In this time frame there is no (or not much) information exchange between the different security companies, but the analysts of each security company need to use names for their groups, so they have to create them on their own. Granted, a solution could be to switch to the name that was published first. However, there is also a systematic reason why group names need to be different: The group definitions in terms of IoCs and TTPs differ between security companies. Each of them has different customers and thus observes different attacks. Furthermore, each analyst team may focus on different aspects of a set of attacks, which can lead to different definitions of intrusion sets. As we will see later, the attribution to countries is rarely contested between security companies. Yet, the exact grouping of attacks into intrusion sets is rarely identical. So it makes sense that security companies keep their own names for their proprietarily defined APT groups.

Therefore, Rosetta stones like the Table 2.2 are inherently imprecise as the intrusion sets that the names belong to will never be identical between different analyst teams. Even more pronounced are differences between security companies due to the granularity that they prefer. Some partition the set of observed attacks into many small groups and are very hesitant before adding attack campaigns or intrusion sets to form a larger group. Some of their competitors are less cautious (or less 'conservative' in scientific terminology) and combine attacks to form larger intrusion sets (and thus, groups). For example, the group DeepPanda defined by CrowdStrike breaks down into the groups Black Vine, Iron Man, and Technetium at other security companies.

A particular challenge arises if the name of a malware has been established to also refer to the group that uses it. Over time, it can happen that the culprits share their malware with others, or it may even be the case that the malware was developed by a contractor that had several different customers. Something similar seems to have happened with the backdoor Winnti. For years it was used by criminals to attack game companies and steal virtual currencies. Since around 2016, however, espionage attacks against manufacturing companies have also been observed [18] using that malware. However, the TTPs of the newer campaigns differ from the earlier criminal ones. In addition, Winnti has since been

Table 2.2 Examples of names for APT groups by security companies. Security companies do not necessarily cover all existing groups

Kaspersky labs	CrowdStrike	FireEye	Symantec
Unknown	CommentPanda	APT1	CommentCrew
MSUpdater	PutterPanda	APT2	Junebug
Unknown	GothicPanda	APT3	Buckeye
Sykipot	Maverick/SamuraiPanda	APT4	Hornet
Sofacy	FancyBear	APT28	Sofacy
Turla	VenomousBear	Snake	Epic/Waterbug
Newscaster	CharmingKitten	Newsbeef	Unknown
CloudAtlas	Unknown	Unknown	Inception
RedOctober	Unknown	Unknown	Rocra
Project Sauron	Unknown	Unknown	Strider

used in conjunction with other malware that is regarded as the trademark of other espionage groups. Therefore, the current hypothesis in the IT-security community is that several actors use Winnti nowadays. In such situations, using malware names for APT groups is not only confusing, but clearly incorrect.

Diamond Model Intelligence agencies have invented a concept that distinguishes between four aspects of an attack. The *Diamond model* specifies the technical capabilities, the infrastructure, the victims and the information about the adversary [19] (see Fig. 2.1). The aspect 'capabilities' includes the malware and TTPs that are observed during an attack. The 'infrastructure' describes the control servers used, while the 'victim' aspect includes, among other things, information like the nature, the industry sector, or region of the affected organization. Finally, the aspect 'adversary' covers information about the identity of the perpetrators.

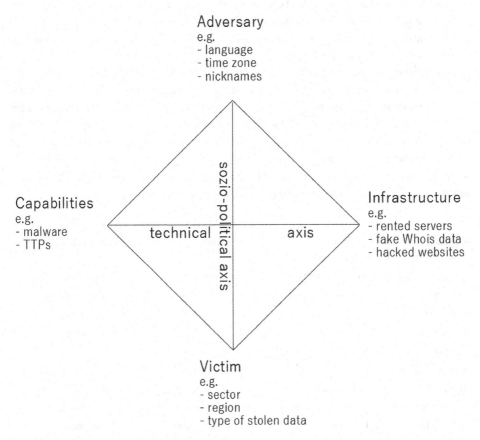

Fig. 2.1 The diamond model describes attacks using the aspects of capabilities, infrastructure, victims, and adversary

The diamond model is a useful concept to structure the data for the analysis process. For example, the name of malware such as Winnti clearly belongs to the aspect of technical capabilities and not to the aspect of the adversary, thus preventing confusion as mentioned earlier.

In later chapters we will encounter the model again.

2.3   Levels of Attribution

Attribution can be performed on several levels of granularity. The assignment of an attack that was observed in a particular company's network to an intrusion set is the first (but non-trivial) kind of attribution. Even if the assigned name is only an abstract construct like 'Deep Panda' or 'Palmetto Fusion', the definition of the group can already provide valuable information like related TTPs and IoCs to the security team. So, a basic and rather informal way of attribution is matching the IoCs observed in an attack to the IoCs of known intrusion sets. For example, the IP address 5.153.58[.]45 mentioned above can be a first hint that the attack is part of the 'Palmetto Fusion' intrusion set, which is targeting the energy sector. The corresponding diamond model for that intrusion set specifies a certain TTP in the 'capabilities' aspect: Windows credentials are stolen via a specific protocol called SMB (Server Message Block). So the security team can check their firewall logs for such network connections. Additionally, the administrators in the Human Resources department can search for incoming malicious emails with attachment name *Controls Engineer.docx* (see above). The 'victim' aspect of the model suggests that the attack is probably targeted at the company's energy division and not at its electronics division. Administrators can therefore focus their attention efficiently on specific parts of the network. If the diamond model even contains some information about the perpetrators, management may be able to deduce whether the attack is due to, say, business activities in certain regions.

The step of assigning attacks to a group is greatly facilitated if threat intelligence is available. Even if the data is not provided in the form of the diamond model, the general methods like comparing IoCs and TTPs are the same. Granted, a few matching indicators are only a weak initial indication. However, the more indicators and TTPs match, the more substantial the attribution to a group becomes.

The next higher granularity level of attribution is much more complex and is usually not performed by the security teams of an affected company, but by analysts at intelligence services or security companies. A lot of information is required to derive the country of origin of the actors behind an attack. A single attack usually does not provide enough data for this analysis endeavor. More data from more attacks means there is a higher probability of mistakes of the attackers and more statistical power to identify recurring patterns like the specific target selection. This is why in most cases it is necessary to group data from several similar attacks into an intrusion set before the attribution to a country is feasible.

The identification of the country of origin is the most common level of attribution. Of the approximately 130 groups for which public analysis reports exist, about 85% have been assigned to a country. Only a fraction of them was attributed to a particular organization or to individuals.

In the early days of APT publications—from 2009 to 2013—almost all reported groups were attributed as Chinese. (Which is really no surprise, considering the context in which the term APT was invented.) This cliche was the reason why attribution was long regarded as pseudoscience, guessing, or political propaganda. In the Internet culture, the meme of the attribution dice became famous. It showed the result 'China' on all six sides. At last in 2013, publications by Kaspersky Labs about Red October and MiniDuke brought Russia (or more precisely: Russian-speaking actors) into play. There are now many countries which were reported as likely origin of APT campaigns, including North Korea, South Korea, India, Pakistan, Iran, France, Israel, the USA, Great Britain, Uzbekistan, and Turkey—and the list is growing.

These attributions are almost never done in a manner that will stand up in court and usually leave room for alternative hypotheses. The perpetrators are usually not caught in flagrante, instead the attribution is based on a multitude of small clues such as language settings in the malware, the geopolitical analysis of which country is interested in the targeted victims, or working hours of the attackers. We will discuss these analysis methods and how to evaluate their validity in detail in later chapters.

Another level of attribution is routinely performed by analysts and covers the question whether an attack is state-sponsored or criminally motivated. The number and distribution of victims, as well as the functionality of the malware provide some useful clues. If, for example, a malware is distributed thousands of times by spam mail to random Internet users and the malware has the functionality of stealing credentials for online banking, the culprits are very likely criminals. If, on the other hand, the malware is placed on the website of a semiconductor conference and delivered only to visitors from two specific research institutions, and the malware gathers administrator credentials for lateral movement, then the motivation of the attackers is most likely espionage.

The most advanced level of attribution is the identification of specific organizations and individuals. This is only possible in rare cases, like in the case of Chinese PLA officers that were convicted of computer espionage by an US court [7]. They were found guilty of hacking networks and stealing trade secrets as part of the group APT1. Often the attribution to particular organizations comes together with insights into the internal setup of the team. An indictments of the US Justice Department not only attributed APT28 attacks to the Russian GRU, but also revealed that malware like X-Agent was developed inhouse, and a different unit was responsible for renting and maintaining server infrastructure [20].

2.4   Attribution Phases

The court verdict regarding the five PLA officers was preceded by a publication of the IT-security company Mandiant about the group APT1 [21] in 2013. The company stressed that it did not use any information from law enforcement or other government agencies for their analysis. There is no statement about the reverse flow of information, i.e. it is unclear to what extent Mandiant's findings were later used for law enforcement investigations. Since the investigative means of the FBI in the APT1 case are not publicly described in detail, we use Mandiant's publication to illustrate the phases or steps of the attribution process. Although the APT1 report was a remarkable milestone in APT research and attribution, it is worthwhile to state that it is just one example of the analyses that IT-security companies produce nowadays. The methods of attribution that are used throughout the infosec community are usually similar. Mutatis mutandis, this also applies to the work of intelligence agencies. We will discuss the differences in the methods of law enforcement and other government agencies in Chap. 8. In the remainder of this chapter the steps of the attribution process are covered. In later chapters we will look at the various analysis methods applied in each phase in more detail.

Phase 1: Collect data The first step necessary for attribution is something that IT-security companies do anyway. Their actual business model is selling anti-virus software or other security products, and continuously adapting them to new malware evolutions. To this end, they collect huge amounts of data about new exploits, malicious emails, compromised websites, and other information that their software products pick up. Most anti-virus programs act like sensors that send information about detected attacks back to their vendor—if the user did not opt out of this functionality. This information collection is essential for security companies in order to keep their virus definitions relevant and effective. We will look into these methods in more detail later, for now it is relevant that data is not only collected about malware, but—among other things—also about malicious websites. The main purpose for collecting this latter information is to maintain indicators for web filters and other protection products, but the data comes in handy for attribution, too.

In terms of volume and frequency, the largest part of the collected data is about run-of-the-mill malware, which is technically of little interest and is processed automatically on a massive scale. It is as much an art as a science for human analysts and statistical algorithms to find interesting—e.g. targeted—attacks in this gigantic haystack. Sometimes the security companies are informed by their customers who found APT malware in their network more or less accidentally. But often creativity of the analysts is more important. For example, the malware Flame was discovered because Kaspersky analysts searched their databases for malware that was only observed in regions like Palestine or Lebanon. This was a first rough hint that it may be a targeted campaign, which turned out to be true later [22].

Another source for data are on-site investigations of compromised networks. In the case of the notorious APT1, Mandiant's incident handler-teams were requested by various customers worldwide to remediate IT-security incidents. More than 900 control servers and 140 affected companies were identified, and dozens of different malware families were found, including BISCUIT, MINIASP, and MANITSME.

Phase 2: Clustering Regardless of how the data about APT malware and attacks were found, the next step of attribution is to partition the data into intrusion sets. At first the attacks, malware, and control servers are just unconnected (or at least incompletely connected) data points stored in databases and customer reports. In our example, the Mandiant analysts analyzed some malware files that had been developed in diverse styles and had different functions, so they categorized them into different *families*. However, some of them communicated to the same control servers such as blackcake[.]net or satellitebbs[.]com. This was a first indication that the different malware families were used by the same culprits. So the incidents at the customer sites were most likely not isolated attacks, but part of several coordinated campaigns since 2006. Mandiant looked into which sectors and regions were targeted. It was striking that most victim organizations were English-speaking, namely companies in the USA, Canada, and Great Britain, as well as international organizations using English as working language. The affected sectors were wide-ranging, from IT to aviation, satellites, energy, law firms, and media. It was obvious to the analysts that such large-scale campaigns could only be carried out by a well-organized group with substantial financial and human resources.

In order to refine the intrusion sets, the analysts collected all malware *samples* that were discovered on the systems of affected customers. A sample is the concrete manifestation of malicious software in the form of a file. The samples of a malware family can differ because the attackers vary them routinely to make detection more difficult. Also, samples can be configured differently, e.g. in order to communicate with varying control servers. In contrast, samples from disparate families differ fundamentally in their code structure or functionality. Yet, by using and configuring them, the attackers often involuntarily link samples together Analysts use graph-like data structures that help to understand if and how samples are related to each other. For example, identical malware samples were found in multiple victim networks, or samples from different families were configured with the same control servers. Additional parallels were that multiple control servers were registered and rented with the same fake personal data. The culprits had used the email address uglygorilla@163[.]com over and over, which made finding additional pieces of the attack infrastructure much easier. These observations were very strong indications that the same attackers were behind these incidents, warranting the creation of a new intrusion set.

So apparently some types of technical similarities are strong indications that attacks were carried out by the same perpetrators, while other similarities are only weak indications. The difference is based on how easy it is for other attackers to mimic the TTPs or to use the same tools and infrastructure. Using the same control server, for example, is a strong indicator because attackers usually do not grant another group access to their operations. A weaker indication is the use of the same password to encrypt stolen data, because other actors may have analyzed the TTPs of the group and then used the same password in order to create a red herring.

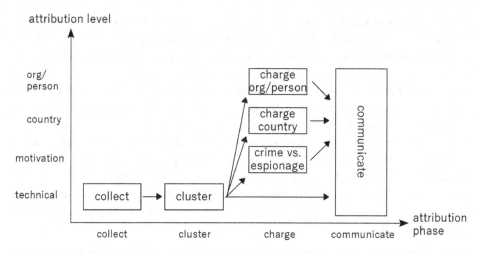

Fig. 2.2 Overview of the levels and phases of attribution in the 4 C model

All samples, control servers, and victims constitute a tangled network in which some areas form *clusters* that contain stronger connections than outside the clusters. These areas are candidates for intrusion sets. It is very rare that clearly isolated islands are discovered; instead, the experience and intuition of analysts is required to define the clusters and their boundaries, and to assess whether they specify useful intrusion sets that precisely define attacks from only one (potential) APT group.

Security companies usually track several hundreds of such clusters and continually redefine them to include or exclude newly observed attacks. Those clusters that are stable over time and contain enough information are finally used to define an APT group, in our case APT1. Back then it was one of the largest clusters that Mandiant investigated, with more than 40 malware families, over 1000 samples, and 2551 servers.

Up to this point, the attribution process remains on a purely technical level. The objects of analysis are technical artefacts and all hypotheses and conclusions refer to objective and reproducible technical data. The later phases of attribution usually require some form of inductive hypotheses and step out of the cyber domain into the real world. Figure 2.2 depicts these steps in attribution analysis in the *4C model* (collect, cluster, charge, communicate).

While meaningful clustering is crucial for the later attribution phases, it is the step that is least formalized and described in APT reports. An exception is FireEye who have published about their ATOMIC framework, a machine learning system that supports analysts in defining clusters of malware, infrastructure, and attack activity [23]. Each data point is represented by a set of technical features, so that the similarity between data points can be calculated by counting the number of matching features. Using standard algorithms ATOMIC identifies sets of data points that are promising candidates for intrusion sets. An analyst then decides whether the machine-deduced clustering is adopted as a named group.

Phase 3: State-sponsored versus criminal activity With the intrusion set and group defined, the next question was whether the motivation behind the campaigns was criminal or state-sponsored espionage. The nature of the stolen data was clearly in favor of the latter, as it was not easily monetizable information such as credit card data or online banking credentials. Instead, blueprints, configurations of manufacturing processes, minutes of meetings, contracts, and business plans were exfiltrated. According to Mandiant's report, the stolen data was of a kind that would clearly be useful for state-owned enterprises in China.

The enormous scale of this hacking activity was also a strong indication that a government was supporting the attackers with vast resources. The culprits were simultaneously active in dozens of corporate networks, administrating a three- to four-digit number of control servers, while still having time to reconnoiter and attack new targets. An operation of this dimension requires several dozen or even several hundred people—which is very atypical for cyber criminals.

Phase 4: attribution to a country of origin State-sponsored activity calls for the identification of the country the attackers work from—thereby linking the attacks to a specific government. The culprits do not connect their own computers directly to the victim networks, but instead use hacked servers of uninvolved third parties or rented anonymous servers as jump servers. Often they traverse from one of these servers to the next before connecting to their control servers. The order in which the servers are connected to is usually not random, because the servers are organized into layers, usually three or more. After connecting through these layers, the attackers log into their control servers to send commands to their backdoors. Mandiant was able to do what normally only government agencies can do: they watched the activity of the perpetrators on the control servers in real-time. This was possible because the security company had identified control servers in the previous analysis phases, and then had contacted the legitimate owners of the hacked servers. They asked for logs and network protocols, which allowed them to identify one layer after the other. Additionally, with the owners' consent they installed software that recorded network traffic to and from these servers. The attackers used the Remote Desktop Protocol (RDP) to log into to the graphical user interface of the machines, which allowed them to operate the servers as if they were sitting directly in front of them. But since Mandiant recorded the RDP traffic, the security analysts could metaphorically look over the perpetrators' shoulders as they hacked their victims. And with the traffic recorded and stored in the company's databases, the analysts later were able to fast-forward or rewind the hacking activities like a video clip.

The captured network traffic also contained two types of information that were relevant for attribution to a country. One was the IP addresses from which the RDP connections were established—before traversing through the various layers of jump servers. In almost all cases, these IPs belonged to four network areas registered on a fiber optic network of the telecommunications company China Unicom in the Pudong district of Shanghai. The other type was the keyboard settings that the RDP software transmitted to the remotely-controlled machines. In all cases, these were configured to display Chinese characters. These obervations made Mandiant generate the working hypothesis that the perpetrators were likely operating on Windows computers with Chinese language settings from Shanghai.

This hypotheses was corroborated by the evaluation of the information that the attackers were interested in. The hacked companies belonged to four of the seven industry sectors that had been announced as being fostered in the Five-Year Plan of the Chinese government.

Phase 5: attribution to organizations and persons The most specific step—which often does not succeed and is then omitted—is the identification of organizations or persons. As Fig. 2.2 illustrates, this phase may occur in parallel to the country-attribution.

Even if Mandiant's results formally are not legally binding, they do illustrate the data and techniques used for this most specific level of attribution. Strictly speaking, the APT1 report does not contain evidence that definitely proves the involvement of the PLA in the cyber-espionage campaigns. Instead, Mandiant presents a wealth of circumstantial evidence and parallels between the (technically defined) group APT1 and the military unit (existing in the physical world). For example, the already mentioned fiber optic networks in the Pudong district of Shanghai used by the APT1 hackers are mentioned in a memo of the telecommunication company China Unicom. It states that these networks were to be built for the PLA unit with the Military Unit Cover Designator 61398, which according to the same document is Bureau 2 of the Third Department of the General Staff Department. This department is also called 3PLA and has roughly the same tasks as the American NSA, namely interception of electronic signals (SIGINT) and computer espionage [24]. Bureau 2 is responsible for the target regions USA, Canada, and Great Britain. Public job advertisements of this unit list very good English-language skills and experience with network security and operating system internals as requirements.

Based on the parallels between APT1 and unit 61398 regarding tasks, regional responsibilities, staff requirements, and location in Pudong Mandiant concludes that it is very likely the same organization.

The report even names several individuals. Clues about the identity of involved persons were based on the lack of OpSec of the perpetrators. To a large extent the crucial mistakes are from the early days of the group and led to the (apparent) identification of a certain Wang Dong. Many of the control servers, including the oldest discovered domain hugesoft[.]org from October 2004, were registered with the email address uglygorilla@163[.]com. The same address was also used to create a profile in a Chinese hacker forum that listed its real name as Wang Dong. The person behind it used his pseudonym "UglyGorilla" for years in source code comments of malware like MANITSME. The associated control servers often contained the acronym "ug"—likely a reference to "UglyGorilla". However, a relationship to the PLA could not be proven by Mandiant.

Another hacker nicknamed 'Dota' was responsible for registering email addresses that were used to send spearphishing emails laden with malware. When creating an account at Gmail, a mobile number must be provided so that a confirmation code can be sent. Dota used the number 159-2193-7229. In China the digits '159' are used for the mobile network operator China Mobile and the area code '2193' references the Shanghai region—again. Unfortunately, it was not possible to come up with more information about the person behind it.

One of the perpetrators used the attack infrastructure to log into the hacker forum 'rootkit' as 'SuperHard_M'—remember that Mandiant recorded the network traffic of the control servers. The corresponding email address suggested a man named "Mei Qiang", who was apparently born in 1982 and had indicated his place of residence as Pudong in Shanghai—the same area that already several other traces had led to. "SuperHard" left its abbreviations in the APT1 malware Auriga and Bangat.

It was the FBI that finally established the exact identities of Wang Dong (UglyGorilla) and four other members of APT1, and could prove their affiliation to unit 61398 in 2014 [7]. How difficult the investigations were even for government authorities is probably evident by the fact that Wang Dong was not accused of being involved in the whole APT1 activities, but only of one concrete attack against an American steel company in 2010. While respecting *in dubio pro reo* which of course also applies to attribution, it is possible that Wang Dong was behind several more attacks in the APT1 campaigns, but his involvement could be proven only for the incident at the steel company.

Unfortunately, the FBI's investigation methods are not publicly documented.

Phase 6: assessing confidence and communicating hypotheses The last step of attribution is the presentation and communication of the results. Hypotheses are generated that have to be consistent with and supported by the evidence resulting from the analysis. Analysts check them for plausibility and consistency. Is the evidence backed from multiple sources? Are the hypotheses compatible with the data? How much effort would it have been for the culprits to plant false flags? These considerations are necessary to assess the strength of possible alternative hypotheses. Intelligence agencies use *estimative language*, standardized phrases that define the likelihood of events and the certainty of the results [25]. The scale ranges from 'nearly impossible', which stands for a likelihood of 0–10%, to 'improbable' (30–40%), 'probable' (60–70%), and 'nearly certain' (90–100%). The level of confidence in a hypothesis is assessed to be 'low', 'medium' or 'high'. For the APT1 report, Mandiant chose a less formal approach for the public audience. In their words, they were 'convinced' that the group was acting out of China and was at least tolerated by the Chinese government. For the affiliation of APT1 to the PLA they used the approach to formulate alternative hypotheses, which is also common among analysts in intelligence agencies. The conclusion in the report pitted two hypotheses against each other: Either APT1 is identical with unit 61398, or a large, well-organized organization employs a large number of Chinese-speaking employees, has been engaged in computer espionage in industry sectors relevant to China for years, has access to a fibre optic network in Shanghai, and is located in the immediate vicinity of Unit 61398 in Pudong.

The wording is almost ironic in its detailed formality and strongly suggests that Mandiant definitely tends towards the hypothesis that Bureau 2 of the 3PLA is the actor behind the computer espionage cases reported as APT1.

The 4 C model depicted in Fig. 2.2 covers the whole analysis process that needs to be followed if the attribution starts from scratch. Yet, there already exists a plethora of APT reports and other findings. Thus, analysts can use existing research, skip several process steps and start at the point they are most interested in. For instance, often the results from collection and clustering of other researchers are used as starting point to focus on the charge-phase. This does not prevent analysts to loop back to collect additional samples or maybe even adjust the definition of intrusion sets, though.

2.5 Premises Used for Attribution

Attribution is an instance of *abductive reasoning*. This is a form of logical inference that attempts to find the most likely explanation for a set of observations. This is very different from deductive reasoning, where conclusions strictly follow from facts.

The human mind is doing abductive reasoning all the time. If you hear your door bell ring (the observation), you assume that a person stands in front of your house and pushed the bell (explanation). You unconsciously disregard the alternative explanation that some switch or other component malfunctioned. And more importantly, you make use of a set of premises or assumptions that you are probably not even aware of. One premise is that only humans press the door bell, but not animals. Another is that this was done intentionally and not by accident. These premises have a substantial impact on the explanation that you come up with: Some person wants to talk to you.

Note that without premises it usually would not be possible to find any likely explanation at all. Premises are essential for abductive reasoning, so they better be true!

Analogously, premises are crucial also for attribution. Some were already mentioned, like the assumption that non-monetizable information is only useful for government agencies involved in espionage, or that hackers using Chinese keyboard settings are Chinese. There are many more premises—all of them at least plausible, but hard to check and prove. And many of them are not stated explicitly, but are tacitly accepted throughout the community.

It seems useful to explicitly formulate some of the fundamental premises in attribution that often determine the analysis results. Note that there is a vast, maybe infinite, number of premises, most of them true, including trivial ones like "Countries exist", "Countries have governments", or "Computers do not act on their own". So we focus on some selected premises, subjectively assessed as essential.

Some of these assumptions are even known to be incorrect or at least simplifications, but they proved to be useful and are thus often used as sort of working hypotheses at the beginning of an investigation. It is important to be aware of these tacitly accepted premises so that they can be discarded if enough evidence falsifies them later on.

Some of the following assumptions may not be self-explanatory for now, but they will be clearer after later chapters. Here they are listed for reference.

Premises about resources and relation to governments: A fundamental assumption for attribution is that attacks that were done by the same actor will be similar in certain ways. This is reasonable, since inventing new techniques and developing new malware for each attack would be costly in terms of time, skills, and money. Since even government agencies have to manage their limited resources (another assumption), it is likely that the same exploit or the same malware will be used against more than one target. This is a crucial requisite for the clustering phase. Empiric evidence (like the APT1 report) supports this assumption. However, it is important to keep in mind that hackers may decide to develop completely new tools and experiment with new TTPs. As we will see later, in these cases assigning a new incident to existing intrusion sets cannot be definite.

A few more words about the premise that groups may have vast, but limited resources are in order. Often in the infosec community the involvement of intelligence agencies is referenced to suggest that APT groups will have as much money, skills, and personnel at their disposal as they need. This needs to be assessed in a nuanced way. First of all, the intelligence agencies of countries differ in the budget that the government affords them. Secondly, in the cyber-domain human skills are arguably at least as important as money, and the availability of experienced operators is limited. This is crucial as the assessment that some evidence may be too much effort to be faked depends on this premise—as we will see in Chap. 10.

As already mentioned a central premise is that criminals do not engage in espionage—or if they do, they do it at the behest of a government. This assumption is generally reasonable, at least for political espionage. However, for industrial espionage there are cases where attacker groups are believed to work for rival companies. Since in international law, governments are responsible for crimes and attacks that originate from their territory, there is at least always a motivation for attribution to identify the country that may have sanctioned the cyber-activities or may be unaware of them for lack of competence or willingness (cf. [26]).

According to commonly accepted belief, most APT groups work for exactly one government, not for several. This is in line with classical espionage where each country keeps their own spying efforts to themselves. Yet, there are exceptions. The Five Eyes are an alliance between Australia, Canada, New Zealand, the United Kingdom, and the United States for exchanging information from intercepted electronic signals (SIGINT). It is plausible that such cooperations also exist for cyber-activities. For example, Regin is a malware that was reported of having been used against the telecommunication provider Belgacom, likely by the UK according to documents leaked by Edward Snowden. But public reports suggest that the malware is shared between the Five Eyes members [27]. Another caveat to the premise is that according to research reports an increasing number of contractors offer their services to several governments [28]. Analysts and researchers are aware of these caveats. Still, at the beginning of a geopolitical assessment about which country's interests are in line with the observed attacks the one-government assumption is sometimes used for simplification. After all, abductive reasoning searches for the simplest explanation consistent with the observations. And often enough this premise turns out to be true, as most APT groups still work for only one government.

Premises about the setup of teams: Especially in early APT reports, groups were implicitly characterized as if they were monolithic teams. The underlying assumption was that a group consists of a fixed set of members that work together in close proximity and over a long period of time. These group members cover all required skills and operate all phases of the killchain. An example for this assumption shaping an APT report is about an exploit framework called Elderwood [29]. This framework contained a large number of zero-day-exploits and methods to distribute them to targets. The analysts assumed that Elderwood was developed and used exclusively by one group of hackers, and assigned all attacks that used these exploits to the same intrusion set. However, later research suggested that Elderwood was in fact a shared platform that was used by several different APT groups. Nowadays, most researchers are aware that in some countries very complex cyber-ecosystems exist, in which universities, contractors, and government agencies fluidly cooperate and share tools and malware. Still, in public discourse and also in some research reports, the simplified idea of monolithic teams survives and might influence hypothesis generation. This is also reflected by reports that state that a group 'reappeared' after a few years of inactivity. Considering the dynamics of the cyber-domain, it is hard to believe that an APT group remains stable and constant over a period of several years—especially if it had to go dark because of public reports about their activities. Note, though, that the analysis of the exact internal setup of a group is already a very advanced level of attribution. As long as the group works for only one government, the attribution to a country is not hindered by wrong assumptions about monolithic teams. Yet, as we have discussed above, the one-group-one-government assumption needs to be verified regularly, too.

Cyber-espionage is generally assumed a full-time job. Basically all analysis methods about patterns-of-life and timestamp statistics rely on the premise that the attackers work regular office hours—roughly from 8 or 9 am to 5 pm. Empirical data corroborates that many groups show work intervals of roughly 8 h—and if the country attribution from other evidence is correct, many appear to indeed follow the 8–5 office hour pattern. Yet, some other groups (especially freelancers) may chose to work at different times of the day—or even at the weekends. In fact, such patterns are sometimes used to distinguish between government-employed groups and contractors—again based on the assumptions that members of the military or civil servants do not work at the weekends.

Another premise is that malware source code is owned by the APT group or its sponsor, and not by individual developers. This is an important requirement for clustering attacks into intrusion sets by the malware that was used. Clustering is of course complicated by the availability of open-source malware and by sharing of tools between several groups. The research community is aware of these caveats. Still, sharing of tools is usually framed to happen on the level of groups. It is rarely suggested that an individual developer might have left a group and taken his source code with him.

Thus, when dealing with the names and definitions of APT groups like Snake or Deep-Panda, it should be kept in mind that they are simplified idealizations of the complex internal setup of cyber-operations. Figure 2.3 is an analogy, illustrating that traces found on computers

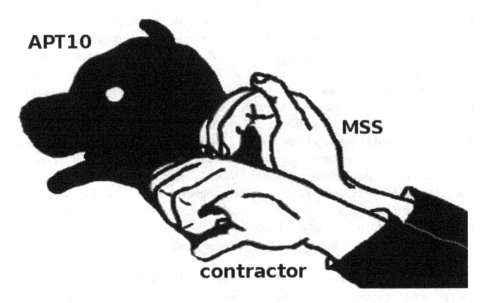

APT10

MSS

contractor

Fig. 2.3 The technical traces used for attribution are to the real-world actors what shadows are to physical objects (Shadow play based on a design by [30])

are only sparse manifestations from the complex intricacies of the physical world, just like shadows formed by tangible objects.

Premises About Data: Malware does not come with a name attached. In this book we will often use names to categorize malicious files, but it needs to be stated clearly that identifying malware is not trivial and not a clear-cut process. Just like intrusion sets are made up of similar attacks, malware families consist of malicious files whose code are similar. An important premise is that code similarity does not happen by chance, but is more likely due to the same developer having written it. This assumption is certainly reasonable. But analysts have to verify that shared code is not based on examples from developer forums or other sources. In its generality, it is impossible to exclude the possibility that code came from private or niche developer forums. But the more extensive the shared code parts are and the more specific their functionality, the more likely it is that the same developer was involved.

Some premises for abductive reasoning may also be framed as cognitive fallacies— systematic errors in human thinking. One such example is the assumption that the data of an analysis is representative of the attack landscape. This is also known as the *collection bias*. As we will discuss in Chap. 7, security companies have better visibility into some regions and phenomena than into others. If, for example, their products are popular in the finance sector, but not in government organizations, for them an APT group may appear to be limited to financial services (since attacks against governments are not observable for their products). So it is important to treat data only for—in logic terminology—existence statements, not for universal statements.

Table 2.3 Aspects of an attack in the MICTIC framework

	Aspect	Example evidence	Chapters
M	Malware	e.g. language settings, timestamps, strings	3
I	Infrastructure	e.g. WHOIS data, links to private websites	4
C	Control server	e.g. source code or logs on seized hard drives	5
T	Telemetry	e.g. working hours, source IPs, malware generation	7
I	Intelligence	e.g. intercepted communication	8
C	Cui bono	Geopolitical analysis of strategic motivation	6

An often used observation is the co-occurrence of malware. If a malware that has been attributed to an APT group is found on a computer, for simplicity it is usually assumed that other malware on the same device was also installed by the same actors. If the malware was unknown or unattributed until then, it will be assigned to the same group. Analysts of course know in principle that several groups may have compromised the same machine. Yet, if no evidence suggests otherwise, the default assumption is that only one group is active in the same network. Most of the time this assumption is valid and it helps to define intrusion sets. But once a malware has been assigned to a group, its attribution may become independent of the observed co-occurrence, so that years later—if need be—it is hard to retrace why it was attributed to that group. That is why some reports explicitly state that one malware downloaded files of another malware family or that they used the same control server. In such situations it is rather clear that only one group was involved.

If you ask infosec experts about these premises, most will be able to explain under which circumstances they hold. However, these assumptions can bias an analysis subconsciously or as part of abductive reasoning to find the simplest (if not to say simplified) explanation. So it is useful to state these tacit premises explicitly from time to time.

2.6   The MICTIC Framework

Although attribution is undertaken by several security companies, non-government organizations, and government agencies, there is no public framework yet that defines the technical process of attribution. Companies and agencies may have their own established internal processes, but they have not published them. There is the Q model by Thomas Rid and Ben Buchanan [31], which focuses strongly on political considerations whether an attribution result should be made public, and only roughly covers the technical process of reaching these results.

We do not aim to present a universally valid framework for technical attribution. But for the purpose of this book a framework helps to define a common thread that keeps the following chapters consistent and coherent. To this end the *MICTIC* framework is introduced. Its general idea is that cyber-espionage and -sabotage consist of several aspects. These aspects are not phases like in the cyber killchain, but are artefacts, resources, and activities of an APT group. The acronym MICTIC is made up of the aspects' names: Malware, Infrastructure, Control servers, Telemetry, Intelligence, and Cui bono (cf. Table 2.3). In a way it is a more fine-grained version of the Diamond model, tuned to correspond to the typical areas of expertise of infosec analysts while also following the assumed separation of work within APT groups. Each MICTIC aspect defines a source or type of information useful for attribution. This is often mirrored by tasks that may be delegated to individual members or subteams of an APT group.

The aspect *malware* covers the development and configuration of backdoors, trojans, and exploits. On the attacker side, this lies in the responsibility of developers, while on the infosec side reverse engineers and malware analysts are involved. The process of renting and operating servers used to download malicious code and exfiltrate data to is covered by the *infrastructure* aspect. Many APT groups are believed to have dedicated group members that manage the infrastructure. On the analysis side this is mirrored by researchers that track and monitor C&Cs via publicly accessible services. Individual servers and the artefacts that can be found on them make up the *control server* aspect. They are the main resources used by operators who execute the actual cyber-espionage operations. Getting hold of a control server is usually a task of law enforcement. *Telemetry* is data about the (largely manual) activities of the operators inside a victim network, which security companies can analyze. Government agencies have additional sources that are part of the *intelligence* aspect. Finally, the aspect *cui bono* corresponds to the tasking that the group's state sponsor—usually a non-technical department—requests. In the infosec community this aspect is covered by geopolitical analysis which country's strategic motivations are in line with the observed attacker activity.

The next six chapters flesh out these aspects (though not necessarily in that order) and describe which evidence can be found in each of them.

Note that all attribution phases mentioned above make use of these aspects. While the phases structure the attribution process regarding the sequence of analysis steps, the MICTIC framework can be used to make sure that all aspects of a cyber-activity are covered, and is also useful for defining work packages for a team of analysts. For example, for collecting data in phase 1, reverse engineers can focus on the malware aspect, while liaison officers can reach out to law enforcement to seize control servers, and political analysts may focus on the cui bono aspect.

The attribution process should cover as many MICTIC aspects as possible, and the more aspects the evidence comes from, the more confidence they provide for the attribution hypothesis.

Aspects have no temporal or causal order but are operated in parallel. They require different skills and different resources. Therefore, they may even be operated by different subteams of an APT group. In this regard the framework is a useful tool to define the monolithicness or self-containedness of an intrusion set or (technically defined) APT group. As we will see later, some cyber-attacks may be linked to several actors of varying relationships. Some attacks may involve malware that was acquired by a government agency from a freelancer and then handed to another contractor, so that the contractor can use it to target a specific set of organizations. Such a scenario is plausible for the use of the malware Winnti. An indictment of the US Department of Justice claims that the Chinese Ministry of State Security (MSS) hired hackers to use Winnti against companies to steal intellectual property about turbines [32]. If cyber-attacks were clustered only by the use of this malware, the intrusion set would also include attacks against online-gaming platforms with a financial motivation [33]. This would be an intrusion set based on only one aspect (malware). In the terminology of the framework this is called a MICTIC-1 intrusion set. Now, if the difference in motivation—industrial espionage versus crime—is used to partition the attacks, two different intrusion sets are defined, each of them MICTIC-2 (using malware and cui bono). The analysis can be refined further, for example by investigating differences in the manual activity—as covered by the telemetry aspect. This will lead to a rather well-defined intrusion set or APT group of at least MICTIC-3 like APT41, as reported by FireEye [34].

At least for the purpose of this book, the number of aspects covered in an intrusion set are thus a rough indicator of how well-defined a group is. The MICTIC-level also hints at the confidence that the internal set-up, i.e. the separation of work, of the group has been understood. E.g. defining a group just by the use of Winnti does not state much about the inner set-up. Additionally differentiating the motivation leads to the assumption of parallel activities or even parallel actors. By also defining the manual TTPs, the analysts suggest that they have even understood and characterized the day-to-day operations of the group.

In Chap. 10 we will use MICTIC to assess the likelihood of a hypothesis being based on false flags. The general idea is that a hypothesis is more robust against red herrings, the more aspects are used in the analysis. This is based on the assumption that consistently leaving false flags in different aspects is more effort than in only one aspect and possibly requires coordination between several sub-teams.

In the same vein, when communicating the attribution results, the number of covered MICTIC aspects is part of the confidence assessment.

So, in the remainder of this book the framework will be used in the phases of collecting data, clustering (defining intrusion sets), the different granularity levels of attribution (country, organization, and persons), and the communication of the results.

References

1. CrowdStrike: Hat-tribution to PLA Unit 61486. In: CrowdStrike Blog (2014). S. 14. https://cdn0.vox-cdn.com/assets/4589853/crowdstrike-intelligence-report-putter-panda.original.pdf. Accessed 8th Oct 2017

2. ThreatConnect: Camerashy—Closing the aperture on China's Unit 78020. In: Threat Connect Blog (2015). http://cdn2.hubspot.net/hubfs/454298/Project_CAMERASHY_ThreatConnect_Copyright_2015.pdf. Accessed 9th Oct 2017

3. Symantec: Iran-based attackers use back door threats to spy on Middle Eastern targets. In: Symantec Connect (2015). http://web.archive.org/web/20170726133140/https://www.symantec.com/connect/blogs/iran-based-attackers-use-back-door-threats-spy-middle-eastern-targets. Accessed 26th July 2017

4. Drozhzhin, A.: Russian-speaking cyber spies exploit satellites. In: Kaspersky Lab Daily (2015). http://web.archive.org/web/20170727075548/https://www.kaspersky.com/blog/turla-apt-exploiting-satellites/9771/. Accessed 27th July 2017

5. Nickels, K.: Cyber indictments and threat intel: why you should care. In: Katies Five Cents (2019). https://medium.com/katies-five-cents/cyber-indictments-and-threat-intel-why-you-should-care-6336a14bb527. Accessed 25th Oct 2019

6. Timberg, C., Nakashima, E.: Chinese hackers suspected in attack on The Post's computers. In: The Washington Post (2013). http://web.archive.org/web/20170722105458/https://www.washingtonpost.com/business/technology/chinese-hackers-suspected-in-attack-on-the-posts-computers/2013/02/01/d5a44fde-6cb1-11e2-bd36-c0fe61a205f6_story.html. Accessed 21st July 2017

7. United States Department of Justice: U.S. Charges Five Chinese Military Hackers For Cyber Espionage Against U.S. Corporations And A Labor Organization For Commercial Advantage (2014). https://www.fbi.gov/contact-us/field-offices/pittsburgh/news/press-releases/u.s.-charges-five-chinese-military-hackers-with-cyber-espionage-against-u.s.-corporations-and-a-labor-organization-for-commercial-advantage. Accessed 18th July 2017

8. Kopan, T.: White House readies cyber sanctions against China ahead of state visit. In: CNN Politics (2015). http://web.archive.org/web/20170718181028/http://edition.cnn.com/2015/08/31/politics/china-sanctions-cybersecurity-president-obama/. Accessed 18th July 2017

9. FireEye iSIGHT Intelligence: red line drawn: China recalculates its use of cyber espionage. In: FireEye blog (2016). http://web.archive.org/web/20170718181214/https://www.fireeye.com/blog/threat-research/2016/06/red-line-drawn-china-espionage.html. Accessed 18th July 2017

10. United States District Court Southern District of New York: Unites States of America versus Zhu Hua, Zhang Shilong (2018)

11. The White House: FACT SHEET: Actions in response to Russian Malicious cyber activity and harassment. In: White House Briefing Room (2016). https://obamawhitehouse.archives.gov/the-press-office/2016/12/29/fact-sheet-actions-response-russian-malicious-cyber-activity-and. Accessed 18th July 2017

12. Heider, F.: The Psychology of Interpersonal Relations. Psychology Press (1958)

13. Baird, S., Carter, E., Galinkin, E., Marczewski, C., Marshall, J.: Attack on critical infrastructure leverages template injection. In: Talos Intelligence Blog (2017). http://web.archive.org/web/20170718181549/http://blog.talosintelligence.com/2017/07/template-injection.html. Accessed 18th July 2017

14. MITRE: ATT&CK. (2015) https://attack.mitre.org/. Accessed 27th Oct 2019

15. Roth, F.: The Best Possible Monitoring with Sigma Rules (2017). https://www.bsk-consulting.de/2017/07/06/the-best-possible-monitoring-with-sigma-rules/. Accessed 27th Oct 2019

16. Carr, N.: Cyber espionage is alive and well—APT32 and the Threat to Global Corporations. In: FireEye Blog (2017). https://www.fireeye.com/blog/threat-research/2017/05/cyber-espionage-apt32.html. Accessed 28th Oct 2019

17. GReAT: Cloud Atlas: RedOctober APT is back in style. In: Securelist (2014). http://web.archive.org/web/20170718181955/https://securelist.com/cloud-atlas-redoctober-apt-is-back-in-style/68083/. Accessed 18th July 2017

18. Berke, J.: 'Winnti' spioniert deutsche Wirtschaft aus. In: Wirtschaftswoche (2017). http://web.archive.org/web/20170718182311/http://www.wiwo.de/technologie/digitale-welt/hackerangriff-auf-thyssenkrupp-winnti-spioniert-deutsche-wirtschaft-aus/14984480.html. Accessed 18th July 2017

19. Caltagirone, S., Pendergast, A., Betz, C.: The diamond model of intrusion analysis. In: Defense Technical Information Center (2013). http://www.dtic.mil/docs/citations/ADA586960. Accessed 18th July 2017

20. United States District Court for the District of Columbia: United States of America V. Viktor Borisovich Netyksho et al. (2018). https://www.justice.gov/file/1080281/download. Accessed 5th Nov 2019

21. Mandiant: APT1—Exposing One of China's Cyber Espionage Units (2013). https://www.fireeye.com/content/dam/fireeye-www/services/pdfs/mandiant-apt1-report.pdf. Accessed 21st July 2017

22. Gostev, A.: The flame—questions and answers. In: Securelist (2012). https://securelist.com/the-flame-questions-and-answers/34344/. Accessed 1st Nov 2019

23. Berninger, M.: Going ATOMIC-Clustering and associating attacker activity at scale. In: FireEye Blog (2019). https://www.fireeye.com/blog/threat-research/2019/03/clustering-and-associating-attacker-activity-at-scale.html. Accessed on 25th Jan 2020

24. Stokes, M.A., Lin, J., Russell Hsiao, L.C.: The Chinese people's liberation army signals intelligence and cyber reconnaissance infrastructure. In: Project 2049 Institute (2011). https://project2049.net/documents/pla_third_department_sigint_cyber_stokes_lin_hsiao.pdf

25. Office of the Director of National Intelligence: Background to 'Assessing Russian Activities and Intentions in Recent US Elections': The Analytic Process and Cyber Incident Attribution (2017). https://www.dni.gov/files/documents/ICA_2017_01.pdf. Accessed 23rd July 2017

26. Maurer, T.: Cyber Mercenaries—The State, Hackers, and Power. Cambridge University Press (2018)

27. Bing, C., Stubbs, J., Menn, J.: Exclusive—Western intelligence hacked 'Russia's Google' Yandex to spy on accounts—sources. In: Reuters (2019). https://www.reuters.com/article/us-usa-cyber-yandex-exclusive/exclusive-western-intelligence-hacked-russias-google-yandex-to-spy-on-accounts-sources-idUSKCN1TS2SX. Accessed 2nd Nov 2019

28. Kirkpatrick, David, D., Frenkel, S.: In: New York Times (2017). https://www.nytimes.com/2017/06/08/world/middleeast/qatar-cyberattack-espionage-for-hire.html. Accessed 2nd Nov 2019

29. O'Gorman, G., McDonald, G.: The Elderwood project. Symantec (2012). https://www.symantec.com/content/en/us/enterprise/media/security_response/whitepapers/the-elderwood-project.pdf. Accessed 3rd Nov 2019

30. Barbulat, D.: Vector—Figures for a shadow play on white. In: 123RF. https://www.123rf.com/photo_10304199_figures-for-a-shadow-play-on-white.html. Accessed 6th Dec 2019
31. Rid, T., Buchanan, B.: Attributing cyber attacks. J. Strateg. Stud. **38**(1–2) (2015)
32. United States District Court Southern District of New York: Unites States of America versus Zhang Zhang-GUI, Zha Rong, Chai Meng et al. (2017). https://www.justice.gov/opa/press-release/file/1106491/download. Accessed 4th Nov 2019
33. Leveille, Marc-Etienne M.: Gaming industry still in the scope of attackers in Asia. In: We Live Security (2019). https://www.welivesecurity.com/2019/03/11/gaming-industry-scope-attackers-asia/. Accessed 4th Nov 2019
34. Fraser, N., Plan, F, OLeary, J., Cannon, V., Leong, R., Perez, D., Shen, C.: APT41—a dual espionage and cyber crime operation. In FireEye Blog (2019). https://www.fireeye.com/blog/threat-research/2019/08/apt41-dual-espionage-and-cyber-crime-operation.html. Accessed 4th Nov 2019

Part II

Attribution Methods

Analysis of Malware

A few years ago the term APT was used like a synonym for sophisticated malware. And even today the most famous APT groups are best known for their professionally developed malware. And sure enough, backdoors and trojans play a central role in attacks—they provide the functions that the attackers need to roam through internal networks, to gather data, and finally exfiltrate documents. However, malware also contains a wealth of information that is useful in most phases of attribution and forms the first aspect of the MICTIC framework. This chapter looks at how malware is developed and employed, and how analysts collect samples and find clues about the perpetrators.

3.1   Attacker Perspective: Development of Malware

Throughout this book we will discuss mistakes of the attackers and decisions that were suboptimal or even plainly silly. Considering that many APTs are likely linked to intelligence agencies, such blunders are surprising. Should they not professionally plan ahead for any possible situations, double-check every step, and counter-think at least two levels deep? To illustrate why mistakes and suboptimal decisions happen, we start each of the chapters about MICTIC aspects with a section explaining the attacker perspective. This will show that cyber-activity is operated differently than classic intelligence operations. Instead of solely focusing on one attack and planning and preparing it for months, hackers usually run several operations simultaneously—as their day-to-day work. We will not cover the domain-independent challenges like having a bad day because boss Badin did not approve a promotion or because colleague George called in sick (again!). Instead we will look at the many cyber-specific trade-offs that hackers have to make.

For an attacker malware is both a curse and a blessing. On the one hand, using them provides arbitrary and convenient control over the victim's systems. On the other hand, using them runs the risk of being detected by security products, thus alerting the victim. In

© Springer-Verlag GmbH Germany, part of Springer Nature 2020
T. Steffens, *Attribution of Advanced Persistent Threats*,
https://doi.org/10.1007/978-3-662-61313-9_3

addition, malware has the disadvantage that it necessarily runs on systems accessible to IT-security teams—who will be happy to get their hands on them for analysis. These flipsides of the coin have an effect on the development of malware. Malware is never finished, but is continuously refined and extended with new functions. The goal is to stay under the radar of security products but also to provide new functionality and efficiency for their users.

In many cases cyber-espionage has to deeply compromise a network over a long period of time. This requires several types of malware. *Exploits* are—strictly speaking— not malware, since they usually consist of only a few lines of code and can only be executed if they are passed as data to another vulnerable program. But they are often necessary to run the actual malware on a target system in the first place. A *dropper* is a stand-alone executable binary that either contains the actual malware and installs it during execution, or downloads it from the Internet first. Very similar is the concept of a *loader* that is used to execute dropped malware. The actual malware is often called *payload* because installing it is the whole purpose of droppers and exploits. In most cases the payload is a *backdoor*, which provides the attacker with mechanisms to connect to the infected system remotely—that is, from the Internet. A backdoor usually has the functionality to collect information about the system, download additional tools, and transmit documents to the perpetrators. They communicate with a *command-and-control server (C&C)* to receive commands from the attacker and to exfiltrate collected data. Many backdoors are *Remote Administration Tools (RATs)*, which give the offender full administrative control over the compromised computer—with a convenient graphical user interface (GUI). Some backdoors are *rootkits* that hide from the operating system and are almost undetectable.

Once the perpetrator has logged on to the target system via a backdoor, he or she must complete a multitude of tasks in order to move inside the network or to collect data. In principle these functions could all be bundled in one single RAT. However, this would inflate the malware files to unhandy and suspicious sizes. Instead, the functionality is usually distributed over a large number of smaller tools. This also has the advantage that detection of one tool may leave the others tools unaffected. Important examples are *password dumpers*, that read credentials from memory, and *pass-the-hash tools*, which are used to log into other computers in the network with stolen password hashes.

For all these types of malware and tools the perpetrators have the option of either using publicly available software, sharing non-public tools with other groups, developing them themselves, or having them programmed by contractors.

Obviously, not all members of an APT group are developers. Instead, most of them are concerned with employing the malware against targets. The job of these *operators* is to move unnoticed in the victim's network for weeks or months. No malware development skills are required for this. It is even assumed that some groups have no members at all who develop code themselves. Examples are groups that use the same arsenal of tools for years without any code updates and groups that completely rely on public tools.

As a rule of thumb, technically advanced groups prefer to develop malware themselves or to hire professional contractors, while technically less savvy perpetrators prefer to use publicly available resources. Snake uses a self-developed rootkit called Uroburos and APT1 had dozens of malware families that they did not share with anyone outside the group. In contrast, APTs in the Middle East often use standard RATs such as njRAT or XtremeRAT, which are available on the Internet (see Table 3.1). A RAT popular in East Asia is PoisonIvy. In recent years, PowershellEmpire has been popular with APT groups from almost all regions. These publicly available backdoors are by no means simple or amateurish. Especially PoisonIvy is a professionally developed tool, that offers many convenient functionalities and can bypass security software again and again with only minor adjustments.

Using publicly available malware and tools is not exclusively a feature of inexperienced groups or those with little development resources, though. Since at least 2016 a trend has been observed that even groups who develop their own malware expand their arsenal with standard tools. The penetration-test framework CobaltStrike provides a dropper, loader, and backdoor. Although it is a commercial product, there are free trial versions and an old version has been leaked on the Internet. There were cases when attackers switched to CobaltStrike after their own arsenal had been outed in public reports, while other groups may have migrated to it in order to make attribution more difficult.

However, APT groups are so diverse and work under so different conditions that no trend is universal in the cyber-domain. Therefore, many groups still develop their own tools. We can only speculate about the exact reasons, but obviously publicly available tools have the disadvantage that they can be readily analyzed by security teams. So the attackers never know if their target organization has configured detection methods for Poison Ivy, Cobalt Strike or njRAT. In contrast, as long as a self-developed malware can remain under the radar of security companies, it is ideally suited to carry out stealthy attacks.

Table 3.1 Examples of publicly available, privately shared, and group-specific malware families

Malware family	Used by	Type	Availability
MANITSME	APT1	Backdoor	Group-specific
SourFace	APT28	Dropper	Group-specific
MiniDuke	APT29	Backdoor	Group-specific
Uroburos	Snake	Rootkit	Group-specific
RemSec	ProjectSauron	Backdoor	Group-specific
PlugX	e.g.. APT3, AuroraPanda	Backdoor	Shared
Derusbi	e.g. APT17, DeepPanda	Backdoor	Shared
Mimikatz	e.g. APT1, APT28, Snake	Password-dumper	Public
PoisonIvy	e.g. Nitro, TropicTrooper	RAT	Public
njRAT	e.g. Sphinx, MoleRats	RAT	Public
XtremeRAT	e.g. DeadeyeJackal, MoleRats	RAT	Public
Empire	e.g. Snake, APT33, WIRTE	Post-exploitation	Public

For the developers of malware it is not just a hobby, it is their daily job. So many of them are well organized and efficient. Decisions in software development start even before writing the first line of code, for example by choosing a programming language. Must it be suited for a project that will be used and developed over many years? Will it be necessary to flexibly add modules to the malware depending on the application scenario? Should the software project be a framework so that various malware programs can be developed from it? Then languages such as C or C++ are suitable, even if they require comparatively large effort and experience. In comparison, if the project is rather a small tool that needs to be developed quickly and will be replaced soon afterward, a simpler language like Delphi or even a scripting language such as PowerShell is suitable for fast development. Also uncommon or new programming languages have advantages that need to be considered. The detection engines of anti-virus programs are usually less optimized for code that is compiled from unusual languages such as Golang [15]. And also the tools of malware analysts are typically tailored to reverse engineer malware written in established languages like C or C++.

The source code is written in *development environments* that provide a convenient editor, *linker*, and *compiler*. The latter is responsible for translating the source code into binary object files. The linker inserts standard code into these binary object files for general-purpose functions that developers do not want to program themselves, and finally generates the executable file.

For most programming languages development environments are available in different variants. Some are commercial and must therefore be purchased, others are offered free of charge.

Malware gets extensively tested regarding its functionality. Otherwise, crashes or error messages on the target machine could alarm the user and lead to detection. Similarly, errors in the communication with the control server could result in the attackers losing control of the deployed malware, resulting in being no longer able to access compromised computers— with no chance to clean up logs and evidence. For testing their malicious software extensive *debug* information and output is integrated into the source code. In the test environment, messages about the success or failure of each function can be logged. For instance, in APT1 malware lines like 'File no exist' or 'Fail To Execute The Command' were found. Outputting such lines should actually not only be deactivated but removed from the code before using them against targets.

Developers do not always start from scratch with their different projects. Many tools and malware require the same basic functionality like encryption and contacting the control server. Therefore, parts of the code are often reused in new malware families years after they were initially written. Depending on the professionalism of the developer, this can either be well organized by designing these functions as a reusable *library* from the beginning. Or the code parts are simply copied and—if necessary—slightly adapted for the new project.

Most of these malware development projects are constantly in flux as small adjustments are made for functionality or to evade security products. Interestingly, these changes do not always occur one after another in one continuous branch, but sometimes several variants are discovered, looking like different strains of the same family. This may be due to several developers working on their own copies of the source code, or groups sharing an initial version whose development commences in several different places. So the concept of a family of malware is an idealization that security analysts use to structure the haystack of millions of samples. This means that assigning a discovered sample to a malware family is not as clear-cut as it might look. Similarly to assigning incidents to their idiosyncratic APT group definitions, security companies may disagree whether a sample is just another variant of a known malware or an instance of a new family.

As already mentioned, for attackers there is a trade-off between using malware or avoiding it. If they do not need specific functionality, it is reasonable for them to work only with the tools that are already installed on the compromised computer. A task that is repeated inside each victim network and that is performed similarly each time is lateral movement. Modern Windows operating systems provide legitimate administration tools that are completely sufficient for the attackers in this killchain phase. With PowerShell they can script command sequences, such as searching memory for credentials, sending them to remote servers, and using them to spread in the internal network. For security products it is hard to distinguish such lines of code from legitimate tasks of the IT-administrators. Therefore, nowadays lateral movement is rarely done using functionality from backdoors.

Yet, if the attackers cannot avoid using a malware for whatever reasons, a growing trend can be observed to execute backdoors only in memory without writing any files to the hard disk. This is a challenge for many security products that rely on scanning files when they are read by the operating system.

The publications of WikiLeaks about Vault 7 offer a very detailed insight into the day-to-day work of state-sponsored malware developers [1]. The leak contained internal manuals and guidelines for users and developers at the CIA. Their professionalism regarding the standardization of development processes might be exceptionally high even for APT groups. Several manuals contain instructions how to avoid repeating patterns that would facilitate clustering or even attribution. For example, an explicit instruction is to remove all debug information, user names, and file path information after testing. The executable programs must also not contain any information about the developer's time zone. In addition, the guidelines specify that each program must have an uninstall function that deletes all traces after use. The list of instructions is very extensive and reflects the many mistakes developers can make that would play into the hands of security teams.

Another remarkable fact documented by Vault 7 is the scrupulous documentation of source code—a stern discipline that not even developers of legitimate software exhibit often. Also, the CIA tools follow a common usability design making it easier for the operators—i.e. users of the malware—to employ it in their operations. This is likely an efficient requirement for groups that have a high number of operators. Uniform usability and the availability of documentation reduce the need for training and the risk of blunders.

3.2   Sources for Analysts

In order to analyze a malware, security companies and intelligence services of course first
need samples. These can be obtained in several ways.

Sample-Databases For analysts working at companies that sell security software, the online
service VirusTotal is an important source of malware that is not yet detected by their own
products. On the VirusTotal website, users can upload files and have them scanned by more
than 40 different virus scanners. The business model of this service is that the files are made
available to the vendors of these virus scanners. These vendors are particularly interested
in files that are not flagged as malicious by their own product but by several others. These
samples have to be analyzed so that the detection signatures can be improved. In addition,
analysts continuously comb through the database to look for interesting samples. The criteria
for these searches can be much less precise than virus signatures because false alarms—also
called false positives—are less critical for the analysts than if AV scanners block benign
files on computers of customers. This way analysts can turn up new variants of malware that
the security products do not detect yet.

Since files are uploaded to VirusTotal mainly by non-experts, many of them are mail
attachments with exploits or droppers. This is because many employees in companies are
aware that documents in mails may be malicious, but they are unsure how to tell them apart
from benign files—so they check them on VirusTotal. In contrast, if a backdoor or RAT
has been stealthily installed on a system, it is unlikely that its owner will find and upload
it to VirusTotal. Therefore, in the database there are enormous numbers of documents with
exploits and droppers from the first phases of the killchain, but fewer backdoors and rootkits.
They may end up there, though, not least because some unexperienced APT groups use
VirusTotal to test their new malware against the anti-virus scanners. Obviously these actors
are not aware that they make their samples accessible to analysts this way.

For companies and organizations VirusTotal can be a data privacy challenge. Again and
again unwitting users upload legitimate documents with sensitive information to VirusTotal
to make sure that they are benign. Another issue is that malware used in targeted attacks
may contain configurations such as proxy addresses that can be traced back to the attacked
organization. In order to avoid that the uploaded files can be viewed by thousands of analysts,
many companies and organizations block the upload from their networks. This is particularly
the case in Europe and North America. VirusTotal therefore over-represents files from other
regions, especially Asia and Eastern Europe.

Security Software Other sources for samples are regionally inhomogeneous, too. Security
software is inherently unevenly distributed depending on market share in different regions
of the world. ESET's virus scanners, for example, are hardly known in Western Europe,
while they are widely used in Eastern Europe. Qihoo 360 is installed on many computers in
China, TrendMicro is strongly represented in Japan and also in Germany.

Most security products transmit information about detected attacks to the vendor. For instance, if a malicious program is blocked by a security software, its detection name, file name, size, hash, and the geolocation of the computer are sent to the vendor's database. This functionality can be deactivated by the user. Although this opt-out provides data privacy, it introduces another bias in the data about malware prevalence in different regions. The data privacy awareness differs from country to country with Germany being a notorious case where most installations of security software are configured to not send detection data to the vendor. Consequently, reports about the *prevalence*, i.e. frequency and regional distribution, of malware families in Germany are often not statistically representative.

A security feature that inherently requires data to be sent from users are reputation services. The idea behind this category of products is that a file that is present on thousands of machines is more likely to be benign than a file that is seen on very few systems. The inverse likelihood of a file to be malicious is called reputation. It is calculated by transmitting a hash—which is a unique fingerprint—of a file to the reputation database. There it is looked up and checked how often the same hash has been seen in different regions of the world and how long it has been around. Legitimate software, run-of-the-mill malware, and targeted attack tools can be differentiated this way—to a certain degree. The transmitted data remains stored in this database. If weeks later an analyst analyzes a new malware and identifies a hash, he or she can query the reputation database to assess how often it has already been seen and where it first appeared.

Security software can be a source for samples from all killchain phases. Exploits and droppers may be collected from anti-virus scanners on mail-servers, loaders, backdoors, rootkits, and auxiliary tools are detected by products on the endpoint.

On-Site Incident Handling The business model of companies like Mandiant is not based on selling security software, but on offering incident handler teams that help the customer to investigate and clean up a compromised network. Often these investigations involve forensic analyses of entire hard disks of compromised systems. This can turn up many details that are inaccessible to standard security software. Incident handling is an important source for malware and tools from later phases of the killchain. But since typically the attack has been going on for months until the incident handling starts, samples from the first phases are only rarely found.

Sharing Between Analysts Not to be underestimated is the worth of sharing of samples between analysts from different security companies. Depending on the philosophy and competitive behavior of the employer, some security researchers are free to share information with others. Because of the different types of data each company collects giving and taking information often leads to considerable insights. Such sharing is almost always based on personal relationships of trust, which are formed, among other things, at conferences and through recommendations from colleagues. A concept called Traffic Light Protocol, or short TLP, has been introduced that governs how the shared information may be used. This ranges from TLP-WHITE (free to publish), over TLP-GREEN (shareable with anyone except public venues), and TLP-AMBER (free to use in a given organization), to TLP-RED (for personal use only).

3.3   Evidence from the Development Environment

By default, the compiler and linker used by the malware developers leave a considerable amount of useful information in the generated binaries. Some of these tell-tale traces can be avoided, as documented in the afore-mentioned CIA guidelines. However, many APT groups are less professionally organized than their American counterparts, so blunders and systematic patterns occur time and again.

Timestamps Some traces from the development environment cannot be avoided in the first place, but have to be removed with additional effort after compilation. This is due to the structure of executable files. Binaries do not simply start with a sequence of machine commands. Instead, they are divided into different sections for meta information, command sequences, and data. Under Microsoft Windows, any executable program needs to be in the format of Portable Executable (PE) [2], which specifies the file structure. The PE header is mandatory and specifies the size of the individual sections and also defines the start of the command sequences. For attribution purposes only a few fields in this structure are relevant. This includes the timestamp that the linker sets when the file is created—in the form of number of seconds that have passed since 31.12.1969 at 16:00. (This is a slightly different starting time than the usual 1.1.1970 at 0:00 in the Unix world).

That does not sound very helpful at first glance. And indeed, if only a few individual samples of a malware family are available for analysis, there is not much to be gleaned from the creation times. But this changes if a few dozen or even hundreds of samples from the same malware family can be collected. Simple statistical methods can be used to determine the *patterns of life* of the developers. On which days of the week have the samples been generated? And at what times of the day do the developers work?

In many cases, the timestamps fall into intervals of 8–10 hours, which is typical for office hours in most countries. Assuming that work starts at 8 or 9 am local time, likely time zones can be identified that define possible countries that the developers work in.

For example, the group APT10 compiled most of its malware on weekdays between 8am and 6pm—if the time zone UTC+8 [4] is assumed. This time zone is used in Russia, China, Australia, and Mongolia—among others. This set of potential countries of origin can be refined further. Between 12 and 14 o'clock there was often a lull in activity, which is consistent with the typical extended lunch break in China (see Fig. 3.1). Of course this does not give rise to a definite attribution. Taken alone these timestamps only amount to MICTIC-1, as they only come from the aspect malware. So these findings were only one first piece of evidence that the analysts needed to corroborate with more information.

Throughout the world, the days of the week on which work is carried out can vary. This is illustrated by the fact that malware of the group Cadelle [3] was compiled between

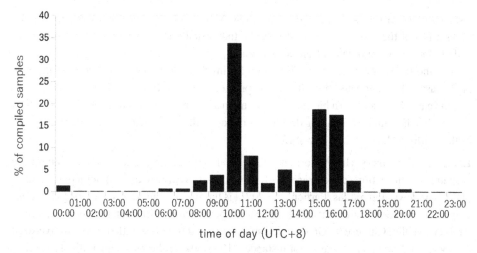

Fig. 3.1 Plot of the compilation timestamps of APT10 malware adjusted to time zone UTC+8 (figure based on [4])

Saturday and Thursday. In relation to the Western world the working week of the developers is shifted, which is a weak indication of which country they may be based in. In Iran Saturday to Wednesday are full working days, with Thursday being a shortened day of usually six work hours.

Even despite all the effort that the CIA had taken to define guidelines for non-attributable development, it seems that the developers also showed cultural peculiarities in the way they defined weekdays. In samples of the group Longhorn, which the security company Symantec attributes to the CIA on the basis of the leaked Vault 7 documents, there were tell-tale configurations that specified on which days the malware should report to the control server. The developers used the character string MTWRFSU for this purpose, which stands for 'Monday Tuesday Wednesday thuRsday Friday Saturday sUnday' (note the capital letters), which is a idiosyncrasy used in North America [12].

If the sample data provides a dense distribution of timestamps, it is worthwhile to check if some untypical days are missing from the data. These can be compared with holiday lists of different countries. Missing activity on a country-specific holiday can support attribution hypotheses. Longer breaks of activity during the protracted celebrations of the Chinese New Year can, for example, be first indications regarding the attribution. Yet, of course such patterns can also be simulated by non-Chinese actors in order to plant false flags. Either they cease their activity like Chinese citizens, or they manipulate the timestamps.

Therefore, an analyst must take into account that timestamps can be manipulated. There are different ways the culprits can do this. The developers can run their development computers with a wrong system time, or they can modify the timestamps in the binaries after compilation. So the findings must always be compared with other evidence. In most known cases it turned out at the end of the attribution process that the Patterns of Life were consistent with other traces. Apparently, only a few APT groups systematically manipulate the timestamps of their malware. And if they do, they usually overwrite the dates with zeroes and do not try to simulate a different time zone.

Yet, the timestamps related to the group Spring Dragon make for an unusual mystery [13]. Kaspersky's analysis showed that compilation times were spread over two intervals of 8 hours each. Such a pattern has not been found in any other group. The security researchers figured that the Chinese-speaking developers either work at two locations in different regions of the world or they work in two shifts.

Language Resources The PE format often contains further references to the origin of the perpetrators. In sections called *resources*, programs store information about icons, images, dialog windows, and menus. Particularly useful is the structure used to store strings for these graphic user-interface elements. To be able to display them in different alphabets like Latin, Arabic, Cyrillic, Chinese or Greek, each string is stored together with a three- to five-digit number specifying its codepage. For instance, 819 stands for the codepage Latin-1, which is common in Western Europe, 720 for the Arabic alphabet, and 1251 for the Cyrillic alphabet. Of course malware contains menus and buttons only in rare cases. But the developers use resources to store and hide configurations and other data. And even when PE resources are used in this atypical way, a data field in the structure must be generated for the codepage. And luckily for attribution, by default the development environment sets this field to the codepage used on the developer machine. So if the programmer is using a Russian Windows version with a Cyrillic keyboard layout, the codepage in the PE resources of his malware files will also be set to 1251—unless the developer intentionally overrides this.

As an example, some samples of the backdoor Turla used by Snake contained language resources with codepage 1251 (Cyrillic). This is consistent with strings that were found in other parts of the malware, such as 'Zagruzchik', which is the Russian word for bootloader [5].

Also the exploit-laced documents in spearphishing attacks can provide useful clues. The exploit framework Lady Boyle [6] for instance used a Chinese codepage for the lure documents, although the documents contained English content. With the caveat that the codepage could have been configured as a red herring, it can be an indication of the language setting of the computer on which the exploit document was created. As always in attribution, this finding needs to be corroborated with additional evidence (preferably from other MICTIC aspects).

Debug Information As mentioned earlier, developers test their malware before using it. Finding and fixing bugs is also called *debugging*. Modern compilers provide the functionality to generate additional information for debugging during development and testing. 'Microsoft Visual Studio' is a popular development environment which is also widely used by APT groups. If the developer activates the debug functionality for compilation, it stores the debug information in a *program database (PDB)*. This is a file that is created in a directory of the development environment. When the final release version is used, the PDB is not bundled with it because it is not needed for the actual functionality of the software. Still, the linker writes the path to this file into the PE header so that the debug information can be found during execution for test purposes. This provides opportunities for attribution. Sometimes the developers forget to deactivate the debugging switch when compiling the final version. Then the path to the PDB remains in the binary that is planted on the victim system where it can be found by security teams. Again, there are example cases by Snake for this phenomenon. In some variants of their backdoor, for example, this PDB path was found:

\Workshop\Projects\cobra\carbon_system\x64\Release\carbon_system.pdb

This path indicates that the developer apparently named the malware 'Carbon'. Although this is somewhat interesting, it does not allow conclusions to be drawn about the identity of the perpetrators. More telling was the path found in malware of the HangOver campaign [7] of another group:

C:\Users\neeru rana\Desktop\Klogger-30 may\Klogger-30 may\Release \Klogger.pdb

Windows creates a directory for each user account. On German systems they are located under *C:\Benutzer*, on English systems under *C:\Users*. 'neeru rana' is apparently the Windows account used to develop this keylogger project. In another PDB path the user name 'ita nagar' was found:

R:\payloads\ita nagar\Uploader\HangOver 1.5.7 (Startup) \HangOver 1.5.7 (Startup) \Release\Http_t.pdb

These account names are weak indications for Indian-speaking developers.

Dates like '30 may' are not uncommon in PDB paths, as some (usually unexperienced) developers use them to label different versions. If the date format is uncommon, it might hint at a cultural background. The European format uses the order day, month, year. In the USA, in contrast, the sequence month, day, year is standard. Very particular dates were found in the malware CadelSpy of the group Cadelle [3]. The PDB paths contained '94-01' and '94-06', which denote March and August 2015 in the Iranian solar calendar. Remember that also the shifted working week had indicated Iran as possible origin of this group.

So far, the findings have been used for country attribution. However, PDB paths can also provide information about the likely organization that developed the malware. In other debug paths of the already mentioned HangOver campaign several strings were found which resemble the name of an Indian software company called Appin Security Group, e.g.:

D:\Projects\Elance\AppInSecurityGroup\FtpBackup\Release\Backup.pdb

According to its website this company buys zero-day exploits [7]. Despite additional evidence, in the corresponding report the analysts left it at the statement that the perpetrators most likely operated from India. That Appin may have been involved as a contractor was merely listed as a weak hypothesis [7]. This illustrates that attribution statements based only on data from a single MICTIC aspect (here malware) are not definite. If no information from other attribution methods supports the statement, it should only be reported as a hypothesis with weak certainty.

PDB paths are even used in another attribution phase, namely clustering. Once analysts have found such a path in a sample, they search through their databases for binaries that exhibit a similar pattern. For files belonging to the same malware family, there is a chance that they will contain the exact same PDB path. But it is also worthwhile to check for substrings. From the above examples, 'AppInSecurityGroup' or 'Elance' are promising search terms that could even turn up unknown malware families from the same developer. Even more general, looking for PDBs with potential Iranian solar calendar dates could be part of a systematic investigation.

Rich Header A feature that has been identified as useful for clustering only quite recently is the Rich header. It has already been introduced in Microsoft Visual Studio 6.0 (1998) and is embedded in all PE files that were linked with this development environment [14]. Yet, this structure was never officially documented so it was often overlooked—both by analysts and attackers. It can be viewed as a fingerprint of the development environment and the code base, making it an informative indicator for clustering samples from the same developer or the same malware family. The Rich header lists the compiler, linker, and imports that were used to build a sample. Most importantly, this also includes the number of times the import were used in the development project, and even their order. Taken together the entries are rather specific for each malware project. There now exist analysis tools that search sample databases for specific Rich headers, so that more samples can be assigned to the same malware family.

But there is also a use-case on higher levels of attribution. Since the configurations of development environments may differ between two computers, analysts can catalog the different Rich header settings in order to estimate how many developers compiled samples of a given malware family [16]. This can be useful to generate hypotheses about whether only one group has access to the source code or whether it is shared between several of them.

3.4   Analysis of Functionality

The traces considered in the previous section are purely technical details that are irrespective of the actual functionality of the malware. They are usually not analyzed en masse, that is, not automatically for every sample that the security company collects. Only if a sample looks interesting or belongs to a relevant group, analysts will focus on it with that level of detail. In contrast, in the day-to-day business of IT-security companies, where tens of thousands of samples are processed each day, the actual binary code plays a more important role. It determines which functionality a malware has, which changes it makes to the victim system, and how it attempts to evade detection.

For attribution, the code almost always provides opportunities for clustering samples, i.e. it allows the grouping of similar attacks. It is also indispensable to distinguish between targeted and criminal activities. But only rarely does it provide information for the later phases of attribution, the attribution to a country or to specific organizations.

Malware Families An important level of attribution which often looks like granted or self-evident in analysis reports, but is by no means trivial, is the assignment of a malware sample to a family. As mentioned earlier, malicious programs are continuously adapted and sometimes their development is split into different strains at some point. Therefore, a family is not defined by exact descriptions. Instead, a sample is compared to other samples and the respective code similarity determines which malware it is assigned to. If there are no samples that are sufficiently similar, a new family is created. The threshold of 'sufficient' similarity is somewhat arbitrary, though. There are rules of thumb stating that samples whose code is 80 percent identical should belong to the same family. However, some security companies may have different thresholds—at least, empiric evidence shows that many samples are assigned to different families depending on the security company. With approximately 60,000 new samples to be analyzed every day, assigning them to families is done by algorithms. The approaches of security companies range from statistical vector models to Machine Learning. Details are seldom known, as these are the essential intellectual property of companies such as Symantec, Kaspersky, TrendMicro, or F-Secure. However, the internal similarity clusters have nothing to do with the detection names that customers see when they are alerted by their anti-virus programs. Virus definitions are optimized for performance, therefore it is advantageous to cover several families by generic patterns. These patterns often have detection names that include words like 'Heuristic' and 'Generic', as in 'Trojan.Generic.KD.382581' or 'Heuristic.ADH'. In contrast, when clustering samples for their own internal analyses the vendors can use more computationally intensive algorithms and signatures. This way samples are assigned to families and—if applicable—also to an intrusion set or a group.

Control Servers The addresses of control servers which the sample connects to are automatically extracted. Often one or more IP addresses or hostnames are configured in the malware. In the simplest case these are contained in plain text, so that a simple search for strings can reveal these addresses. In more advanced families, however, they are obfuscated or decrypted in memory at runtime. Therefore, security companies use *sandboxes* on a large scale. These are (often virtualized) analysis environments in which samples are executed in a controlled manner and all activities and system changes are logged. If, for example, the malware writes files to the hard disk, adds itself to autostart, or establishes connections to the Internet, all this is logged and made available for analysis.

Just like the malware family name, C&C servers are important features to find some order in the vast haystack of samples. Samples from different attacks can be grouped together if they use the same C&C (see Fig. 3.2). Assuming that control servers are used by only one group, these addresses are useful indicators to define intrusion sets.

Reverse-Engineering Some advanced malware applies some tricks to protect itself against analysis in sandboxes. Most of these tricks are basically about detecting if the binary is running in a virtualized analysis environment and then aborting execution before any malicious (and thus suspicious) functions are performed. This can be done in a variety of ways. Simple tricks are to check the user name of the active Windows account for keywords such as 'analysis' or 'lab'. There are many variations of measuring the time of certain actions that

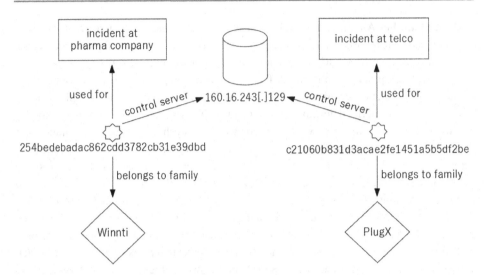

Fig. 3.2 Example of two attacks with samples belonging to different malware families but using the same control server

will be different on real computers than on virtual analysis machines. Other methods are to wait for user interactions such as mouse movements that do not happen in an automated environment. Or technical data is read from network cards or hard disks that often reveal sandbox installations. It is also difficult to analyze malware that sleeps several hours before performing suspicious functions. So if the goal is to extract the command and control server addresses, but the sample does not run in sandboxes, a *reverse engineer* is required to convert the binary format of the sample into readable source code and to understand the malware's mode of operation.

Certain functionalities and characteristics of a sample cannot be analyzed automatically or in sandboxes at all. A typical function which is often analyzed by reverse engineers in detail is the encryption of communication with the control server. In many difficult cases of assigning samples to a family the specific implementation details of encryption algorithms provided crucial clues.

Encryption One of the most complex and professional malware frameworks was developed by the Equation Group. According to media reports and leaked confidential documents this group is likely part of the NSA [8, 9]. In several of their malware families, the group's developers use an unusual constant in the implementation of the well-known RC5 encryption algorithm. This detail was so rare in the available sample collections that it was used as a strong TTP to combine the different families into one intrusion set.

But analysts do not blindly rely on such single TTPs, but take the whole code and functionality of malware into account. As a case in point, the same constant was also found in the RC5 implementation of the backdoor Regin, which was used to spy in the Belgian telecommunications company Belgacom [10]. But the rest of the code showed substantial differences between Equation Group malware and Regin. Therefore, the analysts of Kaspersky Lab assigned them to two different intrusion sets [11].

According to the Vault 7 documents published by WikiLeaks the developers of the CIA learned from the mistakes of the Equation group. Their manuals contain instructions not to use self-developed crypto-algorithms in more than one malware family [9]. Instead, using standard libraries is encouraged. This shows that professional actors even view the clustering of different malware families into the same intrusion set as a risk to their operations.

3.5 Overview of Relevant Information Types

Figure 3.3 lists typical types of information that can be analyzed in the aspect malware.

Malware		
type of information	check for	attribution phase
code similarity	crypto implementation	clustering
	C&C protocol	clustering
	obfuscation	clustering
	generally code reuse	clustering
control servers	Domains / IPs	clustering
	URL patterns	clustering
rich header	setup of environment	clustering
	diversity of environments	clustering
linker timestamp	time zone	country
	working week	country
	unusual holidays	country
PDB path	naming patterns	clustering
	project names	clustering
	OS language	country
	person or org names	org and person
language resources	codepage IDs	country
strings	keywords	clustering
	language, grammatical characteristics	country

Fig. 3.3 Overview of information types in the aspect malware

References

1. WikiLeaks: Development Tradecraft DOs and DON'Ts. In: Vault 7: CIA Hacking Tools Revealed. http://web.archive.org/web/20170725092909/https://wikileaks.org/ciav7p1/cms/page_14587109.html (2017). Accessed 25 July 2017
2. Pietrek, M.: Peering inside the PE: a tour of the Win32 portable executable file format. In: Microsoft Developer Network. https://msdn.microsoft.com/en-us/library/ms809762.aspx. Accessed 26 July 2017
3. Symantec: Iran-based attackers use back door threats to spy on Middle Eastern targets. In: Symantec Connect. http://web.archive.org/web/20170726133140/https://www.symantec.com/connect/blogs/iran-based-attackers-use-back-door-threats-spy-middle-eastern-targets (2015). Accessed 26 July 2017
4. Pricewaterhouse Coopers: Operation Cloud Hopper. In: PwC UK Cyber security and data privacy. https://www.pwc.co.uk/cyber-security/pdf/cloud-hopper-report-final-v4.pdf (2017). Accessed 26 July 2017
5. Drozhzhin, A.: Russian-speaking cyber spies exploit satellites. In: Kaspersky Lab Daily. http://web.archive.org/web/20170727075548/https://www.kaspersky.com/blog/turla-apt-exploiting-satellites/9771/ (2015). Accessed 27 July 2017
6. Haq, T., Gomez, J.: LadyBoyle Comes to Town with a New Exploit. In: Fire-Eye Blog. http://web.archive.org/web/20170727080716/https://www.fireeye.com/blog/threat-research/2013/02/lady-boyle-comes-to-town-with-a-new-exploit.html (2013). Accessed 27 July
7. Fagerland, S., Kravik, M., Camp, J., Moran, S.: Operation Hangover-Unveiling an Indian Cyberattack Infrastructure. http://enterprise-manage.norman.c.bitbit.net/resources/files/Unveiling_an_Indian_Cyberattack_Infrastructure.pdf (2013). Accessed 27 July 2017
8. Schneier, B.: Major NSA/Equation Group Leak. In: Schneier on Security. http://web.archive.org/web/20170708101448/https://www.schneier.com/blog/archives/2016/08/major_nsaequati.html (2016). Accessed 28 July 2017
9. WikiLeaks: What did Equation do wrong, and how can we avoid doing the same? In: Vault 7. http://web.archive.org/web/20170720152522/https://wikileaks.org/ciav7p1/cms/page_14588809.html (2017). Accessed 28 July 2017
10. Marquis-Boire, M., Guarnieri, C., Gallagherm, R.: Secret Malware In European Union attack linked to U.S. and british intelligence. In: The Intercept. http://web.archive.org/web/20170719231033/https://theintercept.com/2014/11/24/secret-regin-malware-belgacom-nsa-gchq/ (2014). Accessed 28 July 2017
11. Kaspersky Labs: Equation Group-Questions and Answers. In: Securelist. https://securelist.com/files/2015/02/Equation_group_questions_and_answers.pdf (2015). Accessed 28 July 2017
12. Symantec security response: longhorn: tools used by cyberespionage group linked to vault 7. In: Symantec.Connect. http://web.archive.org/web/20170624183052/https://www.symantec.com/connect/blogs/longhorn-tools-used-cyberespionage-group-linked-vault-7 (2017). Accessed 4 Aug 2017
13. Shabab, N.: Spring dragon-updated activity. In: SecureList. http://web.archive.org/web/20170812085701/https://securelist.com/spring-dragon-updated-activity/79067/ (2017). Accessed 12 Aug 2017
14. Bytepointer: The Undocumented Microsoft 'Rich' Header. http://bytepointer.com/articles/the_microsoft_rich_header.htm (2017). Accessed 15 Nov 2019
15. Kremez, V.: Here we go-crimeware virus & APT journey from 'robbinhood' to APT28. In: SentinelOne Blog. https://www.sentinelone.com/blog/here-we-go-crimeware-apt-journey-from-robbinhood-to-apt28/ (2019). Accessed 10 Dec 2019

16. Webster, G., Kolosnjaji, B: Finding the needle: a study of the PE32 rich header and respective malware triage. In: Detection of Intrusions and Malware, and Vulnerability Assessment: 14th International Conference, DIMVA 2017, Bonn, Germany, July 6–7, 2017, Proceedings (pp. 119–138) https://www.researchgate.netpublication/318145388_Finding_the_Needle_A_Study_of_the_PE32_Rich_Header_and_Respective_Malware_Triage. Accessed 29 Jan 2020

Attack Infrastructure

If APT groups were invited for security conferences, they could just use the domain names of their control servers as name badges. Network defenders and analysts use C&C domains as shortcut for attributing incidents and samples to intrusion sets on a daily basis. Yet, rarely has an APT group become known for the architecture of its control server infrastructure. Nevertheless, the server infrastructure used by the perpetrators is at least as characteristic as their backdoors and RATs.

This chapter looks at how domains are registered, how servers are rented, how they are organized in layers, and what mistakes and patterns can be exploited for attribution.

4.1 Attacker Perspective: Managing the Control Server Infrastructure

Control servers have two contrary functions. On the one hand, they serve as a defensive wall against analysts and security companies by forming one or more anonymization layers between the victim networks and the attackers' computers. On the other hand, they are often the only means to keep access to compromised networks.

Therefore, maintenance and administration of C&C servers is an integral task in all APT groups. Looking at groups like APT1 [1] and APT28 [2] with more than 2.500 or even 9.000 domain names, respectively, it is safe to assume that there are dedicated group members who are responsible for managing the server infrastructure. A particularly clear-cut and detailed example is the Project Raven, that according to public reports was a cyber-operation team working for the UAE government [3]. Leaked documents show that their was a dedicated infrastructure team that even had its own dedicated office room. Since the MICTIC framework is designed to reflect possible division of labor in sub-teams, *infrastructure* is a distinct aspect.

© Springer-Verlag GmbH Germany, part of Springer Nature 2020
T. Steffens, *Attribution of Advanced Persistent Threats*,
https://doi.org/10.1007/978-3-662-61313-9_4

```
<!- Clicky Web Analytics (start) ->
<script type="text/javascript">// <![CDATA[
var clicky_site_ids = clicky_site_ids || [];
clicky_site_ids.push(100673048);
(function() {
  var s = document.createElement("script");
  var a = "http://www.mentalhealthcheck.net/";
  var b = "update/counter.js";
  s.type = "text/javascript"; s.async = true;
  s.src = "//static.getclicky.com/js"; s.src = a.concat(b);
  ( document.getElementsByTagName("head")[0] ||
    document.getElementsByTagName("body")[0]).appendChild(s);
})();
// ]]></script>
```

Fig. 4.1 HTML code inserted into a watering hole page by the group Snake to load an exploit from the server www.mentalhealthcheck[.]net (cf. [4])

Cyber-attacks require servers for a variety of functions. They can be used to serve exploits linked from watering hole sites (see Fig. 4.1). They can be used as mail servers to send phishing mails. Also scanning for vulnerable systems requires servers to run the reconnaissance software. Droppers download malware from them. They are used as *dropzones* to temporarily store stolen data. And finally, backdoors connect to them so that the attackers can issue commands.

For all these use-cases the attackers can either compromise legitimate servers or rent their own. The former approach generates less traces for attribution and is thus very convenient for staying anonymous. If the attack is detected, it can be traced back only to the server of the unwitting owners. In most cases these servers host the web sites of small companies, schools, or associations who have only small budgets for IT-security. This is why the attackers chose these servers in the first place, because vulnerabilities may stay unpatched very long. The perpetrators attack vulnerable servers usually via an anonymization service such as Tor or from other compromised servers. So if incident handlers or analysts examine the log files of compromised web sites, they often hit a dead end.

But using hacked servers also has disadvantages and entails risks for the perpetrators. The owner of the server might accidentally discover the compromise or might reinstall the entire system for a new software version. Such situations can lead to the attackers losing access to their C&C and thus to their backdoors. To mitigate this risk, the attackers sometimes configure several C&C addresses in their malware to make up for ones that become unusable. In any case, on compromised servers they must operate much more cautiously than on their own rented ones. They need to limit the volume of transferred data, hide exfiltrated documents or delete them quickly after downloading, and install tools very stealthily. Otherwise the owner of the hacked server might be alerted to their activities.

Therefore, APT groups often chose to use servers that they rent themselves. They have several options. The most flexibility and control is provided by a *dedicated root server*. This is a computer where they are granted full administrative privileges and which they have at their exclusive disposal. Very similar are Virtual Private Servers (VPS), which offer the customer a similar range of functions, but are significantly cheaper than root servers, since they may share hardware with other customers. As a downside, the hoster has access to the virtual machines and the network traffic, which is a risk from the attackers' OpSec perspective. On both types of servers the culprits can install arbitrary software, such as vulnerability scanners to search for vulnerable computers, or a mail server, in order to send phishing mails. For efficiency reasons, some groups use pre-configured virtual machines that they copy to newly rented servers.

A different setup than root servers is *shared hosting*. Here the domains of several customers are served from the same physical machine. This means that the attackers share resources and the IP address with other customers, and usually have less flexibility to install software.

Another decision that needs to be made is whether the C&C should be addresses only via its IP address or whether a domain name should be used. This decision also depends on the hosting setup, since for shared hosting registration and administration of a domain name is mandatory. Otherwise there would be no way to serve the websites of different customers from the same server and IP.

In contrast, when renting a root server, at first the attackers can only use its IP address for connecting to it. From a technical perspective, this is sufficient and in fact many malware samples contact their C&C via IPs. Yet, if network defenders monitor their traffic or look through proxy logfiles, connections such as—say—http://10.10.1.1/module/ldr.php are more suspicious and eye-catching than if the address contains a seemingly legitimate domain name, such as http://www.steffens-advertising.de/module/ldr.php. What is more, domain names offer more flexibility. If the attackers need to move their root server to another hosting company, the IP address will inevitably change. Without domain names, this would require changing all deployed backdoors. But if the backdoors are configured to use domain name, moving the server only requires assigning the domain to the new IP address on the *DNS* server. DNS, or Domain Name System, acts like a phone book to assign IP addresses—which are inconvenient for humans—to domain names.

In order to use a domain name, the culprits need to register a domain name via a registrar. For a small fee (usually a few Euros per year), the registrar enters the domain name together with the IP address of the server into the database of the registry of the relevant top-level domain. For registering a domain name, several types of information have to be entered. Before the GDPR (General Data Protection Regulation) came into effect, this information was accessible in public databases via the Whois protocol. Nowadays, only law enforcement agencies and selected organizations like national IT-security teams can look up this data. The attackers have to enter the name of a contact person, a post address, telephone number, organization, country, and email address. Most of this information can be fake because many registrars do not check its veracity. Many do not even carry out the simplest plausibility checks, so that for instance address data can be entered which does not even conform to the address patterns of the alleged country. The only field that serves a functional purpose is the customer's email address, as many registrars send a confirmation email that must be confirmed. APT groups usually pay the registration fees using stolen credit card data. As an alternative, since the widespread adoption of digital currencies such as Bitcoins, these anonymous means of payment have also been used by several groups. For example, APT28 selects its registrars and hosters based on whether they accept digital currencies.

Also popular are those registrars that anonymize the registration data for a small extra charge. For this they cooperate with service providers such as WhoisGuard, PrivacyProtect or DomainsByProxy. When the registrar's database is queried, most fields are anonymized and the mail address of the customer (i.e. the attacker) is provided in a pseudonymized[1] form. So the anonymization service provider can forward messages to the customers without making him or her identifiable. Anonymization is offered even free of charge if the perpetrators rent a domain with the top-level domain .tk (for Tokelau, a small country in the South Pacific). The responsible registrar replaces the customer's data in the publicly accessible Whois data with his own contact data.

An often used alternative to individual domains are dynamic DNS services. These are providers who administer several second-level domains, such as dyndns.com, servebeer.com or no-ip.org. Customers can rent a subdomain, for example mydomain.dyndns.com, and specify an IP address that will be stored in the provider's DNS database. The advantage for the culprits is that IP addresses can be changed quickly and easily. From an OpSec perspective, Whois databases do not provide contact data for subdomains at dynamic DNS services. When DNS was introduced, the assumption was that the contact person for the second-level domain would be responsible also for all subdomains—which is in fact usually the case. So for APT groups dynamic DNS services work like a cover under which they can hide the registration data of their subdomains.

Nevertheless, dynamic DNS services are no silver bullet for attackers. Subdomains of these services are much more suspicious than self-registered second-level domains. For instance, in a spearphishing mail from APT1 a link to www.satellitebbs[.]com appeared more legitimate than www.satellitebbs.dyndns[.]com would have. In addition, some security-affine companies and organizations rigorously block access to dynamic DNS domains because business-relevant content is usually hosted on more professional hosting infrastructures.

Irrespective of the setup the perpetrators choose for their servers, during the actual attacks they usually conceal their location by routing connections through multiple layers of servers. The backdoor on an infected machine reports to a control server. Often this server is only a simple relay—forwarding traffic to the next layer of servers using proxy software such

---

[1] The difference between anonymization and pseudonymization is that the latter can be mapped to an identity given additional information that someone (here: the service provider) has.

as Nginx. All incoming network traffic is forwarded to another server, which is usually located in a different country and may be hosted by a *bulletproof-hoster*. These are hosters that guarantee their customers that they do not respond to requests from law enforcement or security companies. In addition, they do not store any log data, so even if the server is seized, no connection data exists. Some APT groups use up to four layers before the data arrives on a server to which the perpetrators connect via Tor or several layers of VPNs (Virtual Private Networks). Some groups like Snake and the developers of Winnti implement proxy functionalities directly into their malware so that they do not need additional tools like Nginx. They install their backdoors Uroburos or Winnti, respectively, directly on the control server. In this sense, the malware acts like a peer-to-peer network in which it does not matter whether the server runs in the internal network of a victim or on the Internet—traffic is just forwarded to the next layer.

Using so many layers means that APT groups need an enormous number of control servers. There are even reports about attack campaigns whose sole purpose was to take over new C&C servers by compromising legitimate websites. For instance, the security company RSA discovered a campaign that compromised more than two thousand servers worldwide, apparently with the aim of using them as control servers in later attacks [5]. Schools were among the most affected, which is not surprising, as they rarely have enough staff or budget to implement all necessary IT-security measures.

Considering the large number of servers at the disposal of APT groups, it is surprising that they often use the same C&C for several victims. The attackers have even developed methods to organize data of different victims on the same server. They use *campaign codes*, short strings denoting a target organization. These codes are configured in malware samples and are transmitted each time a backdoor reports to the control server. Often one directory per victim is created on the server, named after the corresponding campaign code. In this way, the perpetrators can deposit targeted commands for individual targets or manage stolen data. Analysts can sometimes use the campaign code to infer hypotheses about the identity of the attacked organization, as in the case of "1108navyeast" suggesting a military organization [6]. Since these campaign codes are configured in samples, this is another reason why many companies block the upload to VirusTotal for their employees. Otherwise it can happen that external analysts or journalists may find out that the company was compromised or at least targeted (e.g. [7]).

As we will see in the remainder of this chapter, many groups invest substantial effort into OpSec for their infrastructure. However, often their focus is on minimizing the risk of attribution to a country or organization—while being unaware that their servers can still be tracked for clustering purposes and attribution to intrusion sets (e.g. [8]). OpSec against attribution is just a small subset of more general OpSec that also prevents tracking. Many groups do not appear to apply *OpSec-by-design* but rather follow a reactive approach. They do not pro-actively scrutinize their TTPs with regards to potential analysis methods of security companies. Instead, they seem to learn about their own weaknesses only after analysts describe in reports how they tracked them.

4.2   Public Information and Tools

Since its beginnings in the late 60s the Internet is very transparent in terms of its architecture and infrastructure. Originating from the academic wish to exchange ideas and establish contact with other researchers, there have always been tools that provide information about the operators of networks and servers. Although the character of the Internet has become more commercial and less open, analysts today can still take advantage of some of the original design decisions to investigate attack infrastructures.

Often a single control server extracted from a malware sample is enough to serve as a starting point to find additional servers which can then provide relevant information about the perpetrators.

Registration data A first starting point is the aforementioned registration data that the perpetrators must provide when registering a domain. Many registrars need a working email address for confirmation mails. So APT groups often use freemail providers such as Google Mail, Mail.Ru, Hotmail, Yahoo or 163.com. For efficiency some of them use the same email address for many control server domains—sometimes over a period of several years.

Prior to the introduction of the GDPR, the contact details of a domain holder could be requested from the registrars by anyone. These queries were made via the *Whois* protocol, which provides the data in a standardized structure. For some use-cases of analysts the traditional Whois is not sufficient, though. Commercial services like DomainTools or RiskIQ have specialized in collecting all Whois data from the registrars and providing additional search functionalities. Now analysts can also search in the reverse direction, that is identifying all domains that have been registered with a given email address. This is relevant for the collection and clustering phases of attribution.

For example, an APT28 phishing email contained a link to the domain worldpostjournal[.]com [9], which pretended to contain a news article but in fact served an exploit. The domain had been registered usind the email address shawanda.kirlin37@mail[.]com. The Whois reverse search lists three more domains with this email address (see Table 4.1). Since the domain owners had to reply to the conformation email, they must have had access to that email account—justifying the assumption that all domains were registered by the same group.

Security companies can match the identified C&C domains against their sample databases and identify malware that connects to these addresses. If there are samples that are configured to use several C&Cs, additional domains will be found, which can be fed into a Whois and Reverse Whois search again. This way, intrusion sets can be extended step by step with IoCs covering the activities of a group.

Table 4.1 Example for registration data that was used for several domains

Domain	Registrant	Registrar
worldpostjournal[.]com	shawanda.kirlin37@mail[.]com	PDR LTD. D/B/A
trasitionmail[.]com	shawanda.kirlin37@mail[.]com	PDR LTD. D/B/A
swsupporttools[.]com	shawanda.kirlin37@mail[.]com	PDR LTD. D/B/A
wmepadtech[.]com	shawanda.kirlin37@mail[.]com	PDR LTD. D/B/A

Sometimes Whois data can also be used in later attribution phases. For instance, several C&C domains from the aforementioned HangOver campaign were originally registered via WhoisGuard, so that the registration data was anonymized. However, domains are only paid for a certain period of time, which also applies to the anonymization. If the domain registration is not renewed, the WhoisGuard service will also be deactivated. Thus the Whois data of some control server domains from the HangOver campaign became visible when the culprits chose or forgot to renew the registration. The domains bluecreams[.]com, nitrorac3[.]com, and others were registered with the contact details of a certain Prakash Jain from Delhi, with the phone number +011.9873456756 [10]. The exact same data was used as contact data for the domain hackerscouncil.com, which did not serve a malicious purpose and was not used in the attack campaign. This website was originally registered a month earlier by the company Appin, which—as mentioned earlier—had also appeared in the PDB paths of the malware (see Chap. 3). It is conceivable that the company wanted to disguise the ownership of the domain and therefore subsequently changed the contact data and activated WhoisGuard. Another C&C domain of the campaign was piegauz[.]net. This was also registered in the name of 'Appin Technologies' and with the email address rakesh.gupta@appinonline[.]com [10]. Attributing cyber-activity to a company purely on the basis of the Whois data would not be very convincing, as it would be a MICTIC-1 statement in our framework. But in combination with the strings in the PDB paths, the attribution becomes as strong as MICTIC-2, covering also the aspect malware. This means, that if in the future both types of evidence should turn out to be false flags, the attackers have gone to great lengths and paid attention to consistency—likely even across two subteams responsible for development and infrastructure, respectively.

DNS resolution and PassiveDNS Another fundamental mechanism of the Internet can be used to enrich intrusion sets, namely DNS resolution. APT groups run more than one domain on the same server surprisingly often. This facilitates enumerating their C&C domains, so it can be considered poor OpSec. Still, even some of the most sophisticated groups host domains on the same IP. There are several reasons for this. The most important one is purely pragmatic: Running large campaigns requires more domains than IP addresses, because the former are often only suitable for certain types of targets. For example, APT28 used the domain globaldefencetalk[.]com as a link in a mail to lure members of military organizations to exploit pages [9]. For targets in other sectors such as media, this domain was less suitable.

Similarly, in attacks on journalists and politicians in Turkey posta-hurriyet[.]com was used, because it resembles the name of a Turkish newspaper. The domain webmail-cdu[.]de was used in spearphishing mails against members of the German party CDU, likely in an attempt to lure recipients into entering their webmail credentials [11]. The purpose of the already mentioned domain trasitionmail[.]com, on the other hand, is unclear. It could be a generic address or an allusion to the transition phase of administrations between two presidencies. In principle, all these domains can lead to the same IP. The address trasitionmail[.]com, for example, resolved to 87.236.215[.]143. Using the DNS for queries in the other direction, it turns out that the IP also hosts the domain mailtransition[.]com. Strictly speaking this does not necessarily prove that this domain belongs to the same intrusion set, unless it is a root server. If it is shared hosting or the setup of the server cannot be determined, additional information must be found to assess the domain. In this case, mailtransition[.]com was registered at a registrar who accepts Bitcoins, which is a typical payment method for APT28, thus strengthening the hypothesis that the domain was used by that group.

Why do APT28 and other groups not use individual IPs for each domain? Because to get an IP a server must be rented, installed, configured, and maintained. Provisioning IPs is more costly and requires more effort than provisioning domains. A particularly obvious case is Snake, who use cheap subdomains at Dynamic DNS services and host them on hijacked satellite provider networks. As these IPs are hard to acquire, even this sophisticated group hosted several subdomains on the same IP. Even worse, when they changed IPs, they sometimes distributed the domains from one IP to diverging servers. Analysts who had cataloged the domains were then able to easily track their reassignment to all new IP addresses.

Analysis is even more clear-cut if root servers are used. If C&C domains are hosted on a root server at the same point in time, this is a very strong indication that they belong to the same group. In contrast, in the case of shared hosting servers that store websites of dozens of different customers, two domains may be co-located by pure coincidence. In such cases, the co-located domains should be assigned to the intrusion set with low confidence. If they lead to new data such as associated malware, the newly found information needs to be assessed whether it is consistent with the intrusion set.

In the same vein, analysts must exercise caution if domains resolved to the same IP, but at different times. Such cases are very common. The analyst needs to assess the time between the resolution of the two domains and whether other domains were hosted on the IP in between. Historical IP resolutions (that is, resolutions from the past) cannot be analyzed using the DNS infrastructure. Instead, analysts use a method called *passive DNS* (or short pDNS). Sensors are placed in the networks of central DNS servers to monitor the Internet traffic. Each time the DNS server responds to a DNS request, the pDNS stores the assignment of an IP to a domain along with a timestamp in a large database. Even years later, when the domain no longer exists or has moved to another IP address, the record can be retrieved from this pDNS database.

Nameservers All the aforementioned analysis methods are only applicable after the attack has happened and has been detected. That is, either a malware must have been employed against a target, or a spearphishing mail must have been sent, or a C&C domain must have been assigned to an IP address. In certain cases, however, it is possible to detect attacker infrastructure before it was even used. APT28 is a good example again. The group uses relatively uncommon registrars and hosters, which operate only a few domains. Domains4Bitcoins is one such provider [12]. Hosters usually have their own *nameservers*, which resolve the domain names of their customers to IP addresses. All domains of a name server can be queried via the same (usually commercial) databases that also enable reverse search in Whois data. Although the websites of legitimate customers are often included in these lists, they can be filtered out manually by checking their Whois data for plausibility or assessing the content provided on the websites. The remaining domains do not necessarily belong to APT28, but they are candidates that should be further investigated. On the name servers of Domains4Bitcoins, for example, four new domains were found that were suspected of having been registered by the group. And indeed, analysts were then able to discover APT28 malware samples that used these domains as control server, or exhibited the same registration data as known APT28 domains [12].

The clou is that the workflow of the culprits gives analysts and network defenders time windows for preparing IT-security measures. Usually, APT groups first register a handful of domains, often some days prior to the actual attack campaign. Only later they set up servers and assign the domains to the IP addresses. In the time period between domain registration and IP assignment, the hosters park the domains on default IP addresses that deliver a standard website. This default IP is stored on the nameserver and can be queried. This way, network defenders can identify suspicious domains and block them in their firewalls. Even more effective was a takedown operation by Microsoft. The company seized several thousand domains belonging to APT28 from the registrars before the C&Cs were even used [2]. Seizing domains that are not linked to malicious behavior cannot be taken away from their owners under normal circumstances. But for these domains Microsoft was able to assert their trademark rights, as the culprits had used terms such as 'Windows', 'Microsoft' or 'Azure' in the domain names in order to give them an appearance of legitimacy. For domain names that do not infringe trademark rights, deactivation is not always successful before the actual attacks can be referenced to prove malicious intent.

Surprisingly, although the methods how analysts identify APT28 domains have been publicly described [12, 13], the group did not change their course of action immediately, or at least not fundamentally. This is because attack methods can be successful even if they are publicly outed, since not all targeted organizations have the resources to stay on top of analysis results and take appropriate actions.

4.3   Active Scanning

The methods described so far can be applied without the culprits noticing. This has the advantage that the attackers are less likely to change their TTPs, since they are unaware that they can be tracked. But if analysts are willing to accept the risk of alarming the perpetrators under certain circumstances, they can collect valuable additional information through active scanning on the Internet. To do this, it is necessary to scan entire address ranges, i.e. systematically send data packets to a large number of servers. This approach takes advantage of the fact that control servers of certain malware families respond differently to network requests than legitimate or non-compromised servers.

Two types of scans can be differentiated. One is generic and does not search for specific malware control servers, but collects information from each server about the software version used or encryption configurations. These scans do not alert the culprits as they are indistinguishable from normal Internet traffic. The other type, however, is specific to certain malware families and requires uncommon data packets. For instance, one of these methods is to check whether certain characteristic directory paths or files exist on the server. Attackers with high OpSec can detect such network connections and recognize them as a targeted search for their C&C infrastructure. Nevertheless, some security researchers perform such scans because they expect to gain information that will outweigh the risk of alarming the attackers.

Public reports rarely describe specific scans for control servers in detail because the attackers might learn about their own OpSec failures. In this book we try to strike a similar balance, by describing general methods and approaches while avoiding to give away specific details. Luckily, it was already reported in open source that the PoisonIvy RAT (used among other things by APT1) had a very unique characteristic. The corresponding C&Cs responded to certain very small network packets with a constant response. Security researchers therefore scanned several network ranges and listed those servers that responded with the byte sequence $0x000015D0$ [14]. While the purpose of these scans is primarily to collect data for the clustering phase of attribution, also some weak indications about the country of origin of the attackers were found. The identified control servers were distributed over six different network ranges, but they were all used during working hours that indicated the time zone UTC+7 or UTC+8 [14]. These time zones include Australia, Russia, and China. This was consistent with prior findings documenting that PoisonIvy is popular among Chinese groups.

Using a similar approach, the Shodan search engine regularly scans for control servers of a number of malware families whose source code is publicly available [15]. This prerequisite is necessary in order to find characteristic patterns in the network responses that the servers exhibit. The data that is collected during the scans can be queried free of charge via the service known as 'MalwareHunter'. Unfortunately, the number of malware families covered is limited and does not contain group-specific families as their source code is usually not publicly available. For most scans for specific malware analysts must therefore develop their own tools and perform the scans themselves.

In contrast to MalwareHunter, projects like PassiveSSL from the Luxembourg CIRCL [16], Censys [17] or FoFa [18] perform generic scans. These do not search for control servers of specific malware, but collect general data, including from benign hosts. The actual purpose of these projects is to provide information about devices and computers that are accessible via the Internet, independent of malware. For example, Censys can be used to determine how many installations of a manufacturer's software or hardware are connected to the Internet. Version numbers can also be determined for many products so that the number of vulnerable systems can be estimated for newly discovered vulnerabilities. PassiveSSL collects information about encryption certificates, which are essential for online banking, social networks, or any other websites that need to verify their own authenticity, request login credentials, or serve sensitive content. Similar data is stored by CRT.sh [19] (pronounced 'search') which does not scan the Internet but receives information from the certificate transparency logs, that are provided by the Certificate Authorities generating the certificates.

Also malware uses such certificates to encrypt the communication with the control server. Certificates for TLS (Transport Layer Security) and its predecessor SSL (Secure Sockets Layer) consist of a private and a public part. The first part is stored on the C&C and is known only to the attackers. The latter is delivered by the server to anyone who establishes a network connection to it. This makes it possible for PassiveSSL to set up databases that store the public certificates for every IP address it has scanned. For analysts it is essential that the attackers sometimes use the same certificate on several servers. This may be due to laziness (in the case of less sophisticated APT groups), or—suprisingly—due to a high level of professionalization: Groups that have automated setting up their servers for efficiency may copy the same software packages and certificates to each of their control servers. This circumstance is useful for attribution, since domains sharing the same certificate can be assigned to the same intrusion set with high confidence.

It may be counter-intuitive why it is technically possible that the same certificate is reused on several servers. After all, the purpose of the SSL and TLS technology is not only to encrypt data, but also to prevent web pages from being faked. This is—among others—important for online banking, where users want to make sure that they are indeed entering their login credentials on the genuine website of their bank. Because the private key of a certificate for, say, mybank.com is stored only on the web server of the bank, it can authenticate itself as the legitimate website. Web sites that use SSL or TLS certificates are indicated in almost all browsers by an encryption symbol in the navigation bar. For this it is necessary that the domain name of the server is listed as *Common Name* in the certificate. This prevents using the same certificate on different domains—at least for connections via a browser. Yet, malware behaves differently and ignores the mismatch between the Common Name in the certificate and the domain name of the control server. Encrypting the C&C traffic works irrespective of the mismatch.

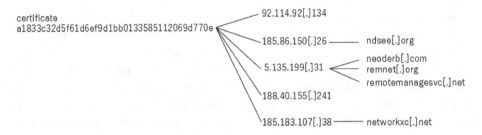

Fig. 4.2 Part of the infrastructure of APT28 that uses the same SSL certificate (based on [13])

All certificates can be uniquely identified by a hash. This is intended for the cryptographic check whether the certificate matches the website. For example, the certificate with the hash *a1833c32d5f61d6ef9d1bb0133585112069d770e* was used both in the attack on the Democratic National Committee (DNC) and the German Bundestag [13]. This is a very strong indication that the same group was behind both attacks, in this case APT28. Via PassiveSSL, crt.sh or other commercial services it is possible to search for even more servers that use this certificate. Even two years after the network of the German Bundestag was compromised, analysts of the security company ThreatConnect identified four additional IP addresses via this hash [13] (see Fig. 4.2). Subsequently, they used PassiveDNS to identify eleven domains that shared the same IPs, were resolved by the same nameservers, and showed similar Whois data, making them strong candidates for the APT28 intrusion set.

APT28 is not the only group that can be tracked this way. Also Snake reuses the same SSL certificates again and again [20]. This is all the more surprising as they go to a lot of technical trouble to disguise their control servers. The group hijacks IPs of telecommunication providers that offer satellite connections and uses their own antennas to receive the data transmitted from the satellites back to Earth [21]. This finding of the security company Kaspersky is also corroborated by documents leaked by the former NSA employee Edward Snowden [22]. According to these documents, the Canadian intelligence agency suspected that different teams were responsible for the interception of the satellite data and managing the servers. They apparently differ in their skills and OpSec.

For the methods presented so far, it is necessary to have a concrete technical feature pointing to a unique resource, e.g. an IP address, domain or a certificate hash. In contrast, the Censys search engine allows to run more generic searches based on patterns. In order for these to turn up relevant results, it is necessary to identify some TTPs of a group first. Once such a characteristic habit of a group has been found and turned into a query, it can be used for months and sometimes years to track the infrastructure. Analysts value such tracking opportunities highly.

When ThreatConnect decided to publish a blog article about how a certain TTP of APT28 can be used to find their C&Cs [23], they were criticized heavily by members of the infosec community. Many analysts worried that the group would become aware of their OpSec failure and change their behavior. And indeed, some time after the blog article appeared, the following TTP was not observed anymore. This was disadvantageous for analysts, but makes it a justifiable example to be discussed in this book, as it illustrates the analysis method but does not give away new information to the culprits.

APT28 had the habit of generating SSL certificates on their own, using the OpenSSL toolkit. When used for benign and legitimate purposes, certificates are means to prove the identity of the website owner. Therefore, they contain several fields to systematically and consistently specify information about the organization that owns the certificate. Each field is named and abbreviated for efficiency: country (C), state (ST), location (L), organization (O), organizational unit (OU), and common name (CN). For example, the certificate for the website of the German BSI contains the following information:

C=DE, ST=Nordrhein-Westfalen, L=Bonn, O=Bundesamt fuer Sicherheit in der Infor-mationstechnik, OU=Referat B23, CN=www.bsi.bund.de

Obviously, APT28 will need to fill these fields with some fake information. Analysts of several organizations had discovered that the group's certificates always contained the same values, probably because APT28 used a script or some form of automation for generating them via OpenSSL:

C=GB, ST=London, L=London, O=Security, OU=IT, CN=(varying)

ThreatConnect documented this peculiarity in their blog article and explained that this pattern can be used in Censys to find servers using such certificates [23]. They found 47 certificates for 46 domains, which were candidates for the APT28 intrusion set. Since also unrelated websites could—by coincidence—exhibit the same pattern, they corroborated their findings with additional information. At that time, the group was known to host their domains on small hosters like Domains4Bitcoins, ITitch, and Njalla. For registration they often used email addresses at sapo[.]pt, mail[.]com, centrum[.]cz, and cock[.]li (information which at that time was available via Whois). ThreatConnect was confident that all domains they had found via the certificate pattern were used by APT28.

Another tracking approach is to look for unusual patterns in the HTTP responses of control servers. Also called *banners*, they contain information about the installed software and configurations of servers and are part of the HTTP standard. For example, a webserver may respond to a scan with the header field $Server : Apache/2.4.1(Unix)$, specifying the server software, its version, and the operating system of the server. If additional webserver modules are installed, they may also be listed in the banner. Why is this relevant for collecting data for attribution? There are at least two scenarios in which server banners can be used to track certain attacker infrastructure. One is that some APT groups use uncommon combinations of server modules and operating system versions. There are strong indications that some attackers use pre-configured virtual machines and put the exactly same image on each of their control servers. With Censys scanning large parts of the IP address space and storing the banners in its database, it is easy to find candidates for C&Cs of these groups.

Another scenario is that control servers do not run standard webserver software such as Apache and Microsoft IIS, but proprietary programs. An example that has been publicly described is the pentesting tool Empire and the banner that it generated [24]. It falsely identified itself in the HTTP header as "Microsoft-IIS/7.5", a very common webserver. However, in the HTTP status code, it specified "HTTP/1.0", a very old version, while real installations of IIS 7.5 use "HTTP/1.1".

Empire is a tool that is publicly available and thus used by many different persons and groups. So searching for Empire C&Cs does not automatically lead to clear-cut intrusion sets. Yet, often these servers will show additional evidence like registration data or hosting characteristics. Often the same server is even used for several malware families (on different ports), which can help to attribute the server to a group.

While Empire is an example where identified control servers need additional analysis and information before they can be assigned to an intrusion set, several group-specific malware families have similar characteristics that make their C&Cs trackable. Assuming a family is used by only one group, searching for these banners can enrich intrusion sets easily.

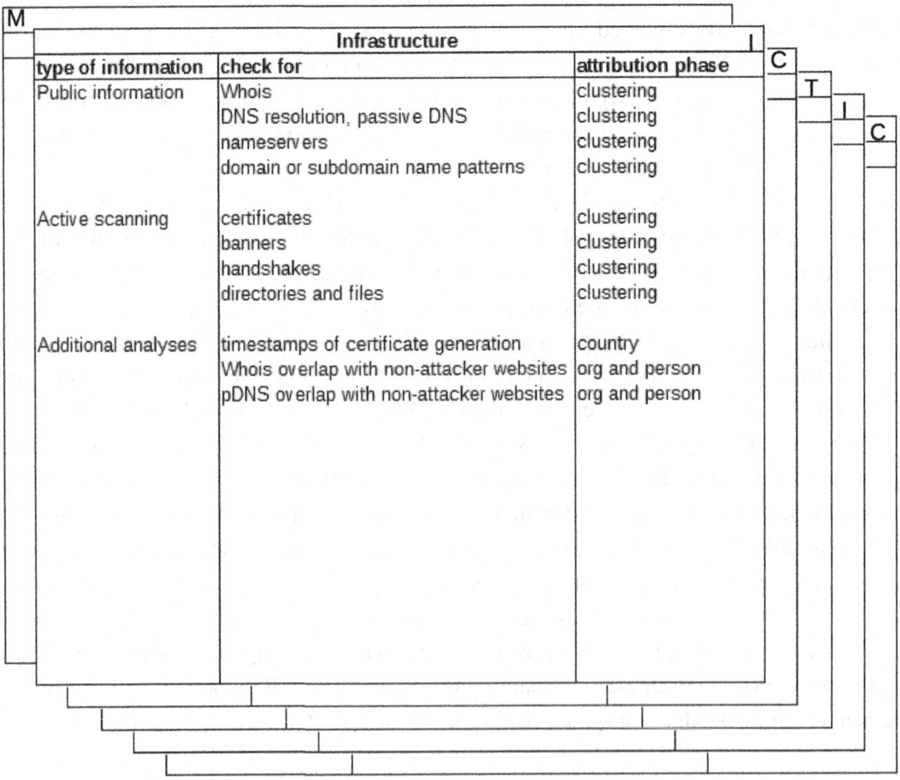

Infrastructure		
type of information	check for	attribution phase
Public information	Whois	clustering
	DNS resolution, passive DNS	clustering
	nameservers	clustering
	domain or subdomain name patterns	clustering
Active scanning	certificates	clustering
	banners	clustering
	handshakes	clustering
	directories and files	clustering
Additional analyses	timestamps of certificate generation	country
	Whois overlap with non-attacker websites	org and person
	pDNS overlap with non-attacker websites	org and person

Fig. 4.3 Overview of information types in the aspect infrastructure

The fascinating thing is that this way new control servers may be found even before they are used in attacks—provided the scan results are updated regularly enough.

It goes without saying that the perpetrators change their SSL certificates over time, migrate to newer software, and develop new TTPs. Therefore, the methods presented here should be regarded as a toolbox for analysts to refine and adapt as needed.

4.4 Overview of Relevant Information Types

Figure 4.3 lists typical types of information that can be analyzed in the aspect infrastructure.

References

1. Mandiant: APT1—Exposing One of China's Cyber Espionage Units (2013). https://www. fireeye.com/content/dam/fireeye-www/services/pdfs/mandiant-apt1-report.pdf. Accessed 21st July 2017
2. Poulsen, K.: Putin's Hackers now under attack—from microsoft. In: The Daily Beast (2017). http://web.archive.org/web/20170726100833/http://www.thedailybeast.com/microsoft-pushes-to-take-over-russian-spies-network. Accessed 29th July 2017
3. Bing, C., Schectman, J.: Inside the UAES Secret Hacking Team of American Mercenaries. In: Reuters (2019). https://www.reuters.com/investigates/special-report/usa-spying-raven/. Accessed 8th Dec 2019
4. Boutin, J.-I.: Turlas watering Hole Kampagne: Firefox-Erweiterung missbraucht Instagram. In: Welivesecurity Blog (2017). http://web.archive.org/web/20170617181752/https://www. welivesecurity.com/deutsch/2017/06/07/turla-watering-hole-firefox-erweiterung-missbraucht-instagram/. Accessed 29th July 2017
5. Backman, K., Stear, K.: Schoolbell: class is in session. In: RSA Blog (2017). http://web.archive. org/web/20170429075107/https://blogs.rsa.com/schoolbell-class-is-in-session/. Accessed 30th July 2017
6. Forward-Looking Threat Research Team: Luckycat Redux—Inside an APT Campaign with multiple targets in India and Japan. In: Trend Micro Research Paper (2012). https://www. trendmicro.co.kr/cloud-content/us/pdfs/security-intelligence/white-papers/wp_luckycat_redux.pdf. Accessed 30th July 2017
7. Tanriverdi, H., Eckert, S., Strozyk, J., Zierer, M., Ciesielski, R.: Attacking the heart of the German industry. In: Bayerischer Rundfunk (2019). https://web.br.de/interaktiv/winnti/english/. Accessed 18th Nov 2019
8. Hacquebord, F., Pernet, C., Lu, K.: More than a Dozen Obfuscated APT33 Botnets used for Extreme Narrow Targeting. In: TrendMicro Blog (2019). https://blog.trendmicro.com/trendlabs-security-intelligence/more-than-a-dozen-obfuscated-apt33-botnets-used-for-extreme-narrow-targeting/. Accessed 18th Nov 2019
9. Hacquebord, F., Hilt, S.: Pawn Storm intensiviert Spear-Phishing bevor Zero-Days gepatcht werden. In: TrendMicro Blog (2016). http://web.archive.org/web/20170225184537/http://blog. trendmicro.de/pawn-storm-intensiviert-spear-phishing-bevor-zero-days-gepatcht-werden/. Accessed 2nd Aug 2017

10. Fagerland, S., Kravik, M., Camp, J., Moran, S. : Operation Hangover—Unveiling an Indian Cyberattack Infrastructure (2013). http://enterprise-manage.norman.c.bitbit.net/resources/files/Unveiling_an_Indian_Cyberattack_Infrastructure.pdf. Accessed 27th July 2017
11. Cabrera, E.: Pawn Storm: the power of social engineering. In TrendMicro Blog (2017). http://web.archive.org/web/20170724130037/http://blog.trendmicro.com/pawn-storm-power-social-engineering/. Accessed 3rd Aug 2017
12. ThreatConnect Research Team: What's in a Name... Server? In: ThreatConnect Blog (2016). http://web.archive.org/web/20170405141634/https://www.threatconnect.com/blog/whats-in-a-name-server/. Accessed 4th Aug 2017
13. ThreatConnect Research Team: How to identify potential malicious infrastructure using Threat-Connect, DomainTools, and more. In: ThreatConnect Blog (2017). https://www.threatconnect.com/blog/finding-nemohost-fancy-bear-infrastructure/. Accessed 5th Aug 2017
14. Rascagneres, P.: APT1—technical backstage malware (2013). https://malware.lu/assets/files/articles/RAP002_APT1_Technical_backstage.1.0.pdf. Accessed 5th Aug 2017
15. Shodan: Malware Hunter. https://malware-hunter.shodan.io. Accessed 5th Aug 2017
16. CIRCL.LU: Passive SSL (2017). https://www.circl.lu/services/passive-ssl/. Accessed 5th Aug 2017
17. Durumeric, Z., Adrian, D., Mirian, A., Bailey, M., Halderman, J. A.: A search engine backed by internet-wide scanning. In: Proceedings of the 22nd ACM Conference on Computer and Communications Security (2015)
18. FoFa. (Chinese device search engine). https://fofa.so/. Accessed 29th Nov 2019
19. Comodo: crt.sh Certificate Search (2017). https://crt.sh. Accessed 5th Aug 2017
20. PassiveTotal: Snakes in the Satellites—On-going Turla infrastructure. In: PassiveTotal Blog (2016). http://web.archive.org/web/20170606162033/http://blog.passivetotal.org/snakes-in-the-satellites-on-going-turla-infrastructure/. Accessed 5th Aug 2017
21. Tanase, S.: Satellite Turla—APT command and control in the sky. In: SecureList (2015). http://web.archive.org/web/20170720061322/https://securelist.com/satellite-turla-apt-command-and-control-in-the-sky/72081/. Accessed 5th Aug 2017
22. Biddle, S.: White House Says Russia's Hackers are Too Good to be Caught but NSA Partner Called them 'Morons'. In: The Intercept (2017). https://theintercept.com/2017/08/02/white-house-says-russias-hackers-are-too-good-to-be-caught-but-nsa-partner-called-them-morons/. Accessed 5th Aug 2017
23. ThreatConenct Research Team: A Song of Intel and Fancy. In: ThreatConnect Blog (2018). https://threatconnect.com/blog/using-fancy-bear-ssl-certificate-information-to-identify-their-infrastructure/. Accessed 23rd Nov 2019
24. Felix Aime: Unveil the devils. In: Security Analysts Summit (2019). https://twitter.com/felixaime/status/1182549497538318337/photo/4. Accessed 24th Nov 2019

Analysis of Control Servers

For some members of an APT group, control servers are the center of their daily work. They use them to distribute exploits, control backdoors, and temporarily store stolen data. This is fundamentally different from the tasks of registering domains and setting up servers. In some groups setting up the infrastructure and employing the servers in actual operations are responsibilities of different team members or even sub-teams—giving rise to the *control server* aspect in the MICTIC framework. This chapter covers the types of evidence that can be gleaned if analysts get hold of a control server—very different from the typically public sources used for the infrastructure aspect.

5.1 Attacker Perspective: Using Control Servers

The group members who use control servers for their daily work are called *operators*, because they carry out the operational attacks. For these activities usually little technical know-how is needed. Among analysts there is the (not easily provable or refutable) prejudice that operators are technically less gifted than their team members who develop exploits or malware. The operators of some groups are believed to follow so-called playbooks, step-by-step instructions about what to do in a compromised network. For instance, an indictment of the FBI expounds that an operator got detailed—if not patronizing—instructions which commands to use, how to package stolen data, how to avoid detection by avoiding traffic peaks, and when to use backdoors [1]. Illustrating the bad reputation of operators even more crassly, Canadian secret service employees called the operators of the Snake group "morons"—while calling the group members who setup the infrastructure "geniuses", according to leaked documents [2].

From the outside it is not possible to determine who picks the actual C&C from the available control servers for an attack against a particular target. Often the C&C addresses are already specified at compile time in the malware samples. Although this is done by the

© Springer-Verlag GmbH Germany, part of Springer Nature 2020
T. Steffens, *Attribution of Advanced Persistent Threats*,
https://doi.org/10.1007/978-3-662-61313-9_5

developers, it is unclear whether they select the C&Cs based on instructions from someone else or by their own choice. If the domain names are tailored to the target, it is likely that the developers have received specific instructions for a particular campaign.

Some groups systematically decide in which country they operate C&C servers for an attack. There are essentially two different strategies. Either the control server is hosted in the same country as the target. This makes the C&C traffic to this server less suspicious as it will not be flagged by geo-IP analysis. Or the attackers deliberately select a different country than the one the target is located in. This makes it more difficult for law enforcement to gain access to the control server once the compromise is detected. The perpetrators behind the aforementioned Regin malware, for example, used compromised servers of organizations that had relations to the target [3], the presidential palace in a Middle Eastern state. The control servers of the first layer were hosted in the same country in networks of a research institution, a bank, and a university. Only the C&C servers of the second layer were operated in a different country. This combines the benefits of both strategies. For the victim, the C&C traffic to the first layer is hard to detect among the daily legitimate network traffic, and the servers in the second layer are out of reach of the local law enforcement.

Such a well-orchestrated setup is the exception and is usually only applied by very well organized groups. The impression analysts get from most groups is that the selection of control servers for targets is more or less random. Since IP addresses need to be changed frequently to make detection and tracking more difficult, it would be much effort for operators to maintain a consistent strategy each time the C&C is moved.

The purpose of the first-tier C&C servers is to receive and process the network connections of the backdoors. Thus, a server counterpart of the malware on the client is necessary, just like in the normal client-server architecture in software development. The server-side logic is often programmed in a scripting language such as PHP or Python. Typical functionalities are decrypting C&C connections, receiving exfiltrated data, logging successful infections, and providing a graphical user-interface with an overview of active backdoors. A particularly well-camouflaged implementation of server-side logic was found during investigations into the Flame backdoor. This malware was mainly used in the Middle East and had many similarities to the infamous Stuxnet trojan, which had sabotaged Iranian nuclear facilities. On the Flame control servers, the developers disguised their PHP scripts as a news portal [4]. The functionality was comparatively limited. To send new commands to their malware, the operators had to upload files to directories on the server via a web interface. Via the same logic, they could download stolen data. All these scripts were disguised by naming them as if they were part of a framework for news articles or advertising banners. The main directory was called "newsforyou" and contained scripts with names like *NewsQueue.php*. The directories for commands and stolen data were called *news* and *ads*.

Even though the camouflage of the C&C scripts for Flame was unusual, there were also features typical for APT groups, like a graphical user interface (GUI) for the operators. In principle, all functionalities could have been provided by command line interfaces. However, because APT groups usually manage many victim systems, GUIs provide the needed efficiency and convenience. So instead of sending commands via uploading files like the Flame operators, most *C&C panels* offer a graphical user interface to control backdoors via mouse clicks. The active implants are typically displayed in a sortable and filterable list, showing the IP addresses, uptimes, victim countries, and campaign codes. The operator selects the backdoor on the victim's computer that he wants to remotely control and can display directory contents, search for keywords or file extensions, download documents, or put the malware into sleep mode.

Another way to use control servers is as a simple proxy for accessing victim computers via RDP. This way, the operators connect to the graphical user interface of the compromised computer via the C&C as an intermediate server. They can control the infected system as if they were sitting directly in front of it. Such connections require control servers that have a good Internet connection, since the RDP protocol requires significantly more bandwidth and lower latency than the proprietary C&C traffic of backdoors. This is generally regarded as the reason why APT groups often select control servers at American and Western European hosters. In these regions, the Internet infrastructure is well developed.

Unlike the operators who control backdoors, the group members who manage the servers often use command-line tools such as SSH. These provide the functionality to log on to the server over an encrypted network connection and execute commands on the command-line. SSH access to a C&C is usually available if the server was rented by the attackers themselves. In contrast, on compromised servers the perpetrators typically install a webshell, a small program that is accessed via a browser and executed by the webserver software, and that provides almost the same command set as SSH access.

Since operators work with control servers on a daily basis, they might develop the false impression that they are almost a part of their own network and not an outpost in networks under external control. For instance, for attackers from non-democratic countries C&Cs are also useful beyond their work. Some APT groups are located in countries where Internet usage is severely restricted by censorship measures. Social networks or foreign news portals are rigorously blocked if they are regarded as promoting opposition or dissident opinions. Connections to control servers, however, are designed to pass through censorship filters. It was reported again and again that operators connect to C&C servers and use them to access censored websites—generating large amounts of tell-tale evidence. Since the servers are part of an external network, law enforcement and security companies can sometimes cooperate with the hosters to access them, hoping to find such OpSec failures of the attackers.

5.2 Network Traffic

The fact that many control servers are operated in Western Europe or the USA makes it easier for authorities in these regions to gain access to them. Law enforcement agencies in many countries have the mandate to seize servers or wire-tap network traffic if there is substantial suspicion of malicious activity. Capturing network traffic is referred to as lawful interception.

But the mandate of law enforcement is usually limited to servers in their jurisdiction. For servers abroad, requests for Judicial Assistance need to be submitted to the foreign authorities responsible there, but this formal process is known to take some time. Often the culprits have moved the server before the formalities of Judicial Assistance have been sorted out. An alternative approach which can be taken if there is no cooperation agreement with the country concerned, is to involve the foreign intelligence service. Depending on their technical capabilities and legal mandate they can try to obtain information about the server. However, the findings from these methods are of course more limited than if direct access to the server and its hard disk is possible.

Also security companies have more options if C&C servers are located in Western countries. Although companies are not entitled to demand information from the hosters, some of them have established trusted contacts with relevant hosting companies over the years. In some cases, this lead to cooperation on a voluntary basis so that analysts get access to control servers or at least to a subset of selected data.

An example for this is the investigation of Mandiant into APT1 [5]. As mentioned in Chap. 2, the analysts were allowed to record RDP connections on several hundred control servers. This was only possible because the hosters had agreed to install Mandiant's sensors on their networks. After FireEye bought Mandiant, it continued this cooperative model with hosters of server farms. The recorded network traffic from control servers contains a wealth of information useful for attribution, such as the IPs of victims, the C&C protocol of the malware, the perpetrators' working hours, the backdoor commands they issued, the exfiltrated data, and under certain circumstances even the IPs or identities of the attackers. For instance, recorded RDP traffic was the source for evidence about the Chinese keyboard settings mentioned in Chap. 2.

As outlined earlier, control servers are usually organized in several layers, which means that data is forwarded from one server to the next. If security researchers can record network traffic on a first-tier server, they gain visibility into connections from infected victim systems to the C&C server configured in the malware. The source IP addresses can be used to identify victim organizations. For static addresses, i.e. those directly assigned to a company, this can be done by a simple Whois query. Even under GDPR the registrant organization is included in the publicly accessible data, as it is not regarded as personal data. In contrast, for dynamic addresses—such as those assigned to DSL customers—a Whois query only provides the name of the telecommunications provider. The identity of the end customer may only be disclosed by the telco after official inquiries by law enforcement authorities. Luckily for analysts, many if not most targets of APT attacks are companies or organizations, and these predominantly use static IP addresses.

Identification of victims is relevant for three reasons. First and foremost, it enables security companies to notify affected organizations. Secondly, even without more details about what the attackers tried to achieve, the identity of the target, its sector and region helps the analysts to understand the cui bono of the campaign. (Chap. 6 looks at the geopolitical analysis, i.e. the question which states or groups are interested in certain targets.) And thirdly, if the victims cooperate with the analysts, information useful for attribution may be found in log data and samples from the compromised network.

An essential philosophy in attribution is to use data that the perpetrators cannot forge or can only forge with great effort. Timestamps in malware (see Chap. 3) can be systematically modified by the culprits. In contrast, this is not possible with recorded network traffic, as this data is generated in real time and on systems that are not under the full control of the attackers. In principle, it is conceivable that the operators deliberately do not work during normal office hours, but at night, on weekends, and on public holidays. However, it has to be considered that most APT groups are not made up of anarchistic or individual criminals, but are organized teams, for whom cyber-attacks are their daily bread-and-butter job and who lead a normal life with families and friends. As a rare exception, North Korean hackers are rumored to have worked from the Chilbosan hotel in Shanyang, China [6], which is in a timezone one hour after the North Korean one. Still, working abroad or shifted work times over periods of years are a rather unattractive working condition for qualified experts. So, camouflaging the patterns of life does require a lot of effort to maintain. This makes captured network traffic a source for comparatively reliable timestamps.

The malware used in the CloudHopper campaign contained, as mentioned earlier, com-pilation timestamps pointing to the time zone UTC+8. The working hours documented by C&C connections also suggest a location in this time zone [7]. This finding from the MICTIC aspect of control servers corroborates the hypothesis about the origin of the perpetrators that was based on the malware aspect, and is an indication that the time stamps in the malware were not forged. The more clues from different analysis methods are consistent with an attribution hypothesis, the stronger it becomes.

What analysts always hope for are connections to the control server that originate from the perpetrators' own network. Yet, on most C&Cs only a proxy is installed that forwards traffic to the next layer. But if analysts get access to the C&C, they can at least determine the IP address that connections are forwarded to. Then they can try to approach the hoster to get information or even data about the server in the next layer. In principle, this can be repeated step by step. However, often the last layer consists of servers that do not initiate or forward connections themselves, but that are accessed by the perpetrators directly. This is usually done via an anonymization service like TOR or other VPN services. Only a small number of groups relies completely on the multi-layer setup of their infrastructure and connect to the last layer directly from their own network (see Fig. 5.1). In the case that anonymization services are used, the traces get lost in the service's network. In the other case, however, the source IP addresses reveal the location of the perpetrators. Sometimes the investigators still hit a dead end because an Internet cafe or a public WLAN was used. But there are also examples in which the perpetrators apparently logged on from their regular workstations. In Chap. 2 it has already been shown that Mandiant was able to trace RDP connections to IP addresses of a fiber optic network in Shanghai when investigating APT1. The report suggested that these networks were used by the PLA. Another example was reported by the security company Group-IB. The group Lazarus is believed to have been behind the sabotage attacks on the

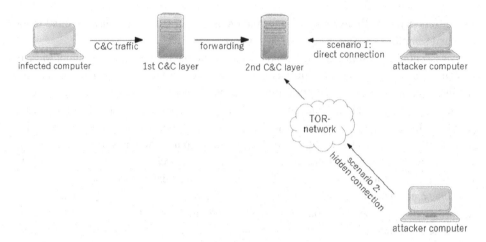

Fig. 5.1 Control servers are often organized in multiple layers. The attackers can either completely rely on these layers to conceal their location or they can additionally use an anonymization service

entertainment company Sony and the cyber heists transfering millions of dollars from several banks [8]. The perpetrators used three layers of control servers. Nevertheless, step by step their connections could be traced back to the third layer. On those servers logins from IP addresses belonging to a hotel in Pyongyang were found. The hotel was located in the immediate vicinity of the North Korean Ministry of Defense.

But how can analysts be sure that these IP addresses are really part of the perpetrators' network and not just another layer of compromised servers? In fact this is seldom a clear-cut assessment and often requires plausibility checks and cross-checking with other evidence. For instance, a typical characteristic for attacker networks is that source IPs are clustered in the same network ranges. Compromised servers, in contrast, are usually widely distributed. Furthermore, compromising a system in a cyber-related agency and using it as a jump server (and false flag) runs a high risk of being discovered and monitored by that agency. Still, in the end the IP addresses have to be consistent with other findings—as always in attribution.

In most cases, the source IP addresses get lost in anonymization networks or the layers of the control server infrastructure anyway. But even then the perpetrators occasionally make mistakes that identify them. If they use a wire-tapped C&C to circumvent censorship filters and log into social networks or their personal webmail accounts, this traffic is recorded and can be analyzed by law enforcement or security companies. Publicly documented cases of wire-tapped C&Cs are rare. An example was given in Mandiant's APT1 report. A group member with the nickname DOTA accessed a Gmail mailbox via a monitored control server. Since he used RDP to control the graphical user interface, Mandiant's analysts were able to watch him read his mail. Unfortunately, in this case the mailbox did not contain any additional evidence regarding DOTA's real identity.

Even members of very professional groups like Snake are not immune to such OpSec failures [2]. They used the satellite connections that they had hijacked for their attack operations to read private emails and to access their profiles in the Russian Facebook pendant VKontakte.

Such profiles are usually not connected to the cyber-espionage activities of the culprits. So they use them like any other social network user, posting pictures of holidays, family, and themselves doing their hobbies. If analysts get the opportunity to capture such account logins on a control server, they can make use of at least the login name. Usually it is trivial to view the social network profile once an account name is known. Then all data that the perpetrators reveal about themselves on their public profiles can be used for identification. A legal grey area is when analysts also extract passwords from the captured network traffic and use them to access the accounts. This can provide even more data such as billing addresses, recovery phone numbers, or alternative accounts. But strictly speaking such investigations are reserved for law enforcement with a legal mandate.

5.3   Hard Disks

If the hoster of a control server cooperates with the analysts, recording network traffic is not the only option. Also the hard disk of the server sometimes provides a trove of information for attribution.

The server-side components of malware are typically written in non-compiled scripting languages such as PHP or Python. This is because common web server software directly supports these languages. So if analysts get their hands on the hard disk of a server (or a copy of it), the source code for the server-side modules can be found there. This is very different from binary samples found on clients. Binaries need to be reverse engineered and large parts of the mnemonic characteristics of the developers get lost during compilation. But in source code the function and variable names are contained exactly as the developers wrote them. Also comments, i.e. non-technical documentation and notes, can be found in the source code. In some cases, these findings may indicate the native language of the developers.

Surprisingly many comment lines were found in the C&C modules of the Flame malware which were disguised as a news framework [4]. Four developers seemingly documented the changes they made in the source code and signed each entry with their nicknames. However, given the effort the perpetrators put into disguising the actual purpose of the scripts, it is unclear whether these comment lines were genuine or also part of the camouflage. For a group that developed a rather advanced malware like Flame such OpSec failures are very surprising. In principle, however, it is conceivable that the server-side scripts were developed by a less professional team. In fact some characteristics of Flame suggest that it was created by professional software developers who had no experience in developing malware. Some points in case are their usage of the unusual programming language Lua, the inefficient use of modules, and the enormous size of 20 MB of the binary [9]. Still, these features could be deliberately chosen in order to increase the likelihood that anti-virus programs regard the malware as benign software. Similarly, the verbatim comment lines could be a means of camouflage.

The high degree of camouflage in the server-side scripts of Flame are not typical for APT groups. In general, perpetrators seem to assume a much lower risk that control servers fall into the hands of analysts as compared to the client-side malware binaries. As conjectured earlier it sometimes seems as if the culprits regard C&C servers as an extension of their own work environment. This is supported by the fact that sometimes unsecured user interfaces and even rudimentary user manuals can be found on control servers. For example, during the investigation of the GhostNet campaign, which spied on the Dalai Lama's staff, a very comfortable graphical user interface was found on a C&C [10]. The server-side component of the Gh0st trojan was a Windows program with dialog boxes, menus, and labeled buttons. It listed all infected computers that had connected to the server, along with their IP address and the time of the last connection. The column captions and menus were labeled in Chinese.

Another source of information can be the configuration of the operating system, if the control server was rented by the perpetrators themselves. If a, say, Chinese language version of Windows is found on a C&C, this means that the perpetrators can work in that language [11], to say the least.

The campaign Advtravel, which targeted individuals and organizations in Egypt and Israel [12], showed a particularly obvious blending of control server and development environment. Trend Micro's analysts were able to show that the server had been used as both a development and testing environment. This was possible because the culprits had misconfigured the C&C server advtravel[.]info so that all directories were openly accessible. Some files seemed to belong to a Visual Studio configuration which suggests that the server was also used for writing code and compiling it into executables. The log data showed that an account on the server was called Dev_Hima, corroborating the hypothesis that a developer used the C&C. This string was also found in the PDB path of malware samples used in that campaign. Even more surprising than this usage of the server was that there were screenshots showing the development environment and the source code. As it turned out, the malware included the functionality to take screenshots on victim computers and transmit them to the control server. Dev_Hima apparently infected his developing computer (which also acted as a C&C server) with the malware for testing purposes, so that it captured and exfiltrated his own data. It even took screenshots of Dev_Hima surfing his Facebook profile. This disclosed his real name, occupation, contact information, and date of birth.

Such critical mistakes and substantial amounts of information are the exception in attribution analyses. Still, also in other cases the log data on a control server contained tell-tale hints about the origin of the perpetrators. Log data on a server can provide glimpses into the past and into the very first activities of the attackers. Each time the operators connect to the

C&C modules like the GUI showing an overview of the infected machines, the webserver generates an entry into the access log. By default, these entries include the source IPs from which connections (that is, HTTP requests) were made. Similarly, log entries for the server-side C&C modules that are accessed by infected computers are also relevant. In some cases, the first connections are logged immediately after the control server has been installed, followed by a longer period of inactivity. This can be an indication that these connections were done by the culprits who wanted to verify that the server-side scripts worked as intended. In these cases the source IPs of these connections very likely belong to the network of the attackers.

Another kind of evidence was found by researchers from the security company ESET. During the investigation of a control server of the group APT28 they stumbled across the source code of the Linux variant of X-Agent [13], a backdoor custom-developed by this group. Analysts almost never get the chance to see the source code of malware. But in this case, APT28 apparently had to compile an individual binary for each target system running Linux—and they did this on the control server. When the analysts read the source code, they discovered Russian-language comments and crude swear words. Back then, they concluded that APT28 was indeed Russian (which was later corroborated by the afore-mentioned indictment of the US Department of Justice [14]). The existence of the swear words in the source code was assessed as an indication that the developer was not part of a formal working environment, so the ESET analysts assumed that the developers were freelance contractors. However, this is at odds with the indictment which states that X-Agent was developed internally by GRU employees. If this is true, the culture of work environments must be assessed country- and even organization-specifically in order to distinguish between government employees and contractors.

Control servers are also a treasure trove of samples and tools, because the operators place them there so they can download them into victim networks when needed. When analysts find such files on a C&C, they will be used to extend the corresponding intrusion set.

Unfortunately, analyzing control servers forensically is very time-consuming both organizationally and technically. Unlike the analysis of malware samples, these tasks cannot be automated. Therefore, security companies and agencies carry out such investigations only for selected campaigns and groups.

5.4 Overview of Relevant Information Types

Figure 5.2 lists typical types of information that can be analyzed in the aspect control server.

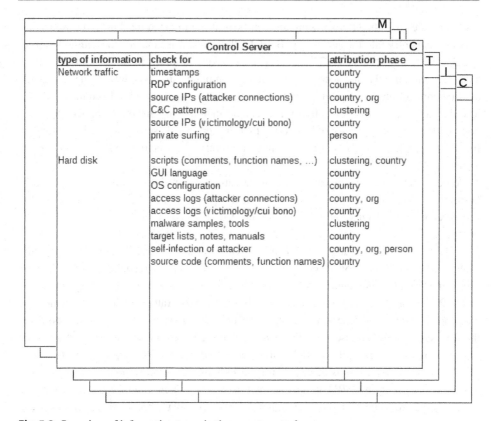

Fig. 5.2 Overview of information types in the aspect control server

References

1. Attorneys for the United States: United States of America, Plaintiff v. Yu Pingan, A.K.A. 'GoldSun', Defendant. In: Politico (2017). https://www.politico.com/f/?id=0000015e-161b-df04-a5df-963f36840001. Accessed 10th Dec 2019
2. Biddle, S.: White House Says Russia's Hackers are too good to be caught but NSA Partner called them 'Morons'. In: The Intercept (2017). https://theintercept.com/2017/08/02/white-house-says-russias-hackers-are-too-good-to-be-caught-but-nsa-partner-called-them-morons/. Accessed 5th Aug 2017
3. GReAT: Regin—nation-state ownage of GSM networks. In: SecureList (2014). http://web.archive.org/web/20170802165138/https://securelist.com/regin-nation-state-ownage-of-gsm-networks/67741/. Accessed 10th Aug 2017
4. GReAT: Full Analysis of Flame's Command & Control servers. In: SecureList (2012). http://web.archive.org/web/20170810172629/https://securelist.com/full-analysis-of-flames-command-control-servers-27/34216/. Accessed 10th Aug 2017

5. Mandiant: APT1—Exposing one of China's Cyber Espionage Units (2013). https://www.fireeye.com/content/dam/fireeye-www/services/pdfs/mandiant-apt1-report.pdf. Accessed 21st July 2017
6. Daly, M.: Inside the 'Surprisingly Great' North Korean Hacker Hotel. In: The Daily Beast (2017). https://www.thedailybeast.com/inside-the-surprisingly-great-north-korean-hacker-hotel. Accessed 10th Dec 2019
7. Pricewaterhouse Coopers: Operation Cloud Hopper. In: PwC UK Cyber security and data privacy (2017). https://www.pwc.co.uk/cyber-security/pdf/cloud-hopper-report-final-v4.pdf. Accessed 26th July 2017
8. Group-IB: Lazarus Arisen—Architecture, Techniques and Attribution (2017). http://web.archive.org/web/20170606050320/https://www.group-ib.com/lazarus.html. Accessed 12th Aug 2017
9. Heise: BSI: Flame keine 'Superwaffe im Cyberkrieg'. In: Heise Security (2012). http://web.archive.org/web/20120602141214/https://www.heise.de/security/meldung/BSI-Flame-keine-Superwaffe-im-Cyberkrieg-1587849.html. Accessed 15th Aug 2017
10. Villeneuve, N.: Tracking GhostNet—Investigating a Cyber Espionage Network (2009). www.nartv.org/mirror/ghostnet.pdf. Accessed 13th Aug 2017
11. Baumgartner, K., Raiu, C., Maslennikov, D.: Android Trojan found in targeted attack. In: SecureList (2013). http://web.archive.org/web/20170813125606/https://securelist.com/android-trojan-found-in-targeted-attack-58/35552/. Accessed 13th Aug 2017
12. Trend Micro Threat Research Team: Operation Arid Viper (2015). www.trendmicro.fr/media/wp/operation-arid-viper-whitepaper-en.pdf. Accessed 13th Aug 2017
13. Calvet, J., Campos, J., Dupuy, T.: Visiting The Bear Den. In: WeLiveSecurity Blog (2016). https://www.welivesecurity.com/wp-content/uploads/2016/06/visiting_the_bear_den_recon_2016_calvet_campos_dupuy-1.pdf. Accessed 13th Aug 2017
14. United States District Court for the District of Columbia: United States of America v. Viktor Borisovich Netyksho et al. (2018). https://www.justice.gov/file/1080281/download. Accessed 5th Nov 2019

Geopolitical Analysis

Cyber-operations have become an established tool to further the geopolitical and domestic strategies of some countries. Many leaders have grown accustomed to getting daily intelligence briefings about relevant events and topics, such as upcoming summits, negotiations, international disputes, or armed conflicts. They may or may not be aware that some of this intelligence comes from cyber-espionage. In any case, the government requirements for information lead to cyber-operations being strongly aligned with the strategic plans and activities of governments. With this in mind, the method that analysts apply first to get an intuition about the origin of an APT group is not a technical, but a geopolitical one. The *cui bono*, i.e. the question who benefits from the attacks, is often used as a first indication to drive the analysis. In which regions are the victims located? Which political conflicts are smoldering there? Which countries and organizations have interests in the region? To which industry sector or branch do the targets belong and who is interested in data from this branch? Are the attacks directed against ethnic minorities or opposition members? In order to assess these factors, many IT security companies and government agencies employ political scientists and region experts.

In terms of the MICTIC framework, the *cui bono* aspect covers the actors that define the tasking of APT groups, the "sponsors" as they are often referred to in reporting. Geopolitical analysts systematically assess the cui bono—usually applying open source intelligence (OSINT), in order to generate hypotheses about the state sponsor that an APT group works for.

6.1   Attacker Perspective: Tasking

In Chap. 1 APT groups were defined as groups that collect information that can be used strategically or politically. The generally accepted assumption is that these attackers do not select their targets indiscriminately, but receive orders—directly or indirectly—from

© Springer-Verlag GmbH Germany, part of Springer Nature 2020
T. Steffens, *Attribution of Advanced Persistent Threats*,
https://doi.org/10.1007/978-3-662-61313-9_6

government agencies. Depending on the country of origin, these can be intelligence services, law enforcement, military, ministries of foreign affairs, or even economic ministries. The group's tasking may be derived from either plans for economic growth, or may be motivated by current political situations, i.e. needed for short term decision-making, or it may be strategically motivated and meant to assist in long term planning.

It is not known how government-agencies or other organizations (usually called *sponsors* in the infosec community) translate their intelligence requirements into concrete tasks for APT groups. Economic espionage, for instance, is only productive if the government has a vision which sectors and technologies it wants to foster. The domestic industry's status quo needs to be assessed, technology deficiencies recognized, and foreign technology leaders identified. This requires a well-oiled bureaucracy and cooperation of technical and economic experts, agencies, and companies.

An US indictment charged a Deputy Division Director of the Ministry of State Security (MSS) in the Jiangsu Province with tasking Chinese citizens to collect information about aerospace technology. According to the indictment, the Defendant worked together with his colleagues to identify aviation technology "that was desired by the Chinese government and associated aviation entities and universities", sometimes as specific as "containment analysis of fan blade encasements" [1]. They also "selected and targeted companies that are leaders in the field of aviation technology" [1]. However, the method of data theft was not related to cyber-means, instead employees of the selected companies were recruited for espionage. It is also unclear how exactly the Jiangsu bureau of the MSS was tasked with acquiring information for the aerospace sector. This illustrates that tasking usually involves several hierarchical levels from ministries to specialist departments, to intelligence agencies and then to the actual APT groups.

Unfortunately, for the cyber-domain there are almost no publicly reported cases that illustrate the role of agencies in tasking, be it economic or political espionage.

Even in the few cases in which APT groups were reliably linked to an agency, it is not well-understood how the internal process of tasking works. One notable exception is the operation Olympic Games, which is said to have developed and deployed the famous Stuxnet trojan. For his book 'Confront and Conceal' the US journalist David E. Sanger interviewed active and former intelligence service employees [2] who unisonously reported that the operation was ordered by the US National Security Council. The NSC's intention was to prevent or delay the development of nuclear weapons in Iran—if possible without Israeli air strikes. Therefore a—in the beginning rather abstract and untechnical—plan was developed to disrupt the Iranian nuclear facilities via malware by destroying turbines. According to Sanger's sources long legal assessments were carried out to ensure that the cyber-attacks were compatible with international law. Also diplomatic consequences were considered— not just regarding Iran but all relevant players in geopolitics. President Obama himself emphasized the necessity to minimize the risk of counter-attacks and proliferation of the sabotage software. According to Sanger the US intelligence service NSA and the Israeli cyber-unit 8200 were tasked to develop and use the trojan later known as "Stuxnet".

It is unlikely that such complex legal and diplomatic considerations are carried out by all countries that order APT campaigns. The academic literature convincingly argues that democratic countries tend to be more sensitive about the consequences of their cyber-activities, as they are obliged to greater accountability [3]. Additionally, Stuxnet was an exception that required more considerations than other cyber-operations, as it was an act of sabotage that had physical effects. In the diplomatic world espionage operations are regarded as more acceptable than those that serve sabotage. In any case, such lengthy legal considerations need to be clarified only once. The assessments can then be used as a framework for future operations. Then, a decision on the highest government levels is only necessary if operations go beyond espionage and are likely to lead to diplomatic conflicts in case they get discovered. For example, according to a public statement, US intelligence services assume that the meddling in the US presidential election campaign from 2016 was directly approved by the head of the Russian government [4].

Some APT groups are made up of government employees working in an agency or for the military. Even though little is known about the details of tasking in such cyber-operation agencies, there seem to be two general ways these APT groups can be set up. There are units that serve as centralized service providers, i.e. they do not pursue their own strategic or geopolitical goals, but receive requests for intelligence from other departments. This approach concentrates the technical capabilities and thus avoids duplicating efforts in several departments. An example for this is the legendary department for Tailored Access Operations (TAO) at the NSA, which according to the Snowden leaks receives requests from the non-cyber departments of several intelligence services to collect information [5]. Consequently, the TAO department is astonishingly large—more than 1000 employees are believed to search for new vulnerabilities in software, develop malicious code, and conduct cyber-espionage operations.

The other organizational set-up in agencies is to equip specialist departments or regional offices with their own APT groups. This allows for a closer integration of the intelligence consumers with the cyber-operators, so that short-term requirements can be communicated easily and efficiently. The disadvantage, however, is that synergy effects for technical capabilities are lost—so not all groups will have access to zero-day-exploits or advanced malware if one unit develops them. An example for this decentralized set-up was APT1, which was part of the 2nd Bureau of the 3PLA. This bureau was responsible for conducting espionage against the USA, Canada, and Great Britain. Similarly, APT2 was reported to likely belong to the 12th Bureau of the 3PLA, and was thus responsible for collecting information about satellite and aviation technology [6].

The more centrally and service-orientedly a group is set up, the more latitude it will have for making decisions about the use of its resources. For example, it is unlikely that a customer (non-cyber) department will dictate whether to use a zero-day exploit or a malicious macro. This hypothesis is corroborated by documents that are believed to have been stolen from the NSA and published by a group called ShadowBrokers [7]. The leak contained tools and exploits, but also instructions that revealed that operators must obtain a formal permission for each exploit and malware that they want to use against a particular target. This approval is enforced not only organizationally, but also technically. For each tool a kind of license key is required, which can only be used for one operation at a time. And as a case in point, this permission is granted by a unit within the TAO, not by the department requesting the intelligence.

Unfortunately, there are no public examples that illustrate how groups that are embedded decentralized in specialist departments decide about using exploits and malware.

A different set-up are APT groups that do not work directly for the government, but as contractors. These are often called proxies, as one of their functions is to provide a layer of plausible deniability for the government. Additional reasons for using contractors can be lack of skills on the government side, temporary demand for additional personnel, or paying higher salaries than rigid government pay schemes allow. It is safe to assume that governments differ greatly in how they control these cyber-teams. Tim Maurer, a US scholar, differentiates between delegation, orchestration, and sanctioning [3]. *Delegation* is the most direct form of tasking, where a 'principal' (typically the government) assumes perfect alignment between its intelligence requirements and the proxy's activities. Maurer argues that the US Cyber Command applies this model with its contractors. In contrast, *orchestration* tasks the attackers indirectly, by providing them with general ideological or religious directions, so that they can pursue political goals. The Iranian government is an example for this approach, according to Maurer. And as a security researcher convincingly put it, Chinese APT groups may be tasked indirectly, too, by the government defining general areas of interests via publishing Five-Year Plans and similar strategies [8] which the groups translate into specific targets themselves. Finally, *sanctioning* is a model where APT groups are granted maximal liberties and the government tolerates their activities, as illustrated by DDoS attacks against Estonian websites by hacktivists in 2007 [3].

A cross between a contractor and a government organization are front companies. They are set up as a cover for activities that the government wants to be able to plausibly deny. The FBI states in an indictment, that the North Korean government created the company Chosun Expo as a front for Lab 110 of the Reconnaissance General Bureau (RGB). Chosun Expo's employees were allegedly involved in attacking Sony because of a movie ridiculing Kim Jong Un and in stealing millions of dollars from banks worldwide [9].

Despite the premises discussed in Chap. 2, not all APT groups receive their orders from the government. There are reports plausibly suggesting that some groups act independently and steal data at their own risk before trying to sell it (cf. [10, 11]). For cui bono-analysis the decisive factor is whether a group is tendering to only one government (usually their own) or whether they have several international customers. Only in the former case, cui bono analysis can result in a consistent hypothesis—assuming that the group has some understanding what their potential government customer is interested in.

Note that cui bono analysis is only undermined by international contractors if they conduct operations. Contractors that develop and sell espionage software or exploits without using them themselves are not relevant for cui bono analyses. Often no investigations are necessary anyway, because these companies usually do not hide their business model and offer their products on their websites or at specialized trade fairs. Examples are Cellebrite, Vupen, the HackingTeam, or NSO. Leaked email conversations and documents suggest that several governments are among the customers of these software vendors. In contrast, contractors that conduct cyber-attacks themselves cannot publicly promote this as their business model, as data theft and accessing third-party systems is illegal in most countries. Most contractors offer their services only to their own government. A case in point is the UAE firm DarkMatter that allegedly helped the government of the United Arab Emirates to spy on dissidents and journalists in an operation called Project Raven [12]. It is safe to assume that such contractors receive formal or at least practical immunity against prosecution (cf. [13, 14]). In turn the respective government expects loyalty and disapproves working for other countries.

Still, there are contractors that apparently work for international customers. An example is the Bahamut group : Security researchers regard the diversity of targets as an indication that Bahamut is likely a contractor working for several governments [15]. It is unclear whether Bahamut's domestic government is unaware of these international activities or whether it intentionally ignores them.

An example of how governments crack down cyber-activities of their units that were not mandated by them is the approach taken by the PLA in China. Chinese APT groups were traditionally located in the various regional command centers [16] until they were merged into a central department called Strategic Support Force [17]. Until before Xi Jinping's presidency, regional commanders were notorious for using their subordinated cyber-units for moonlighting. They apparently received requests from Chinese companies and provided them with commercially valuable data, according to [16]. However, when Xi Jinping came into office, he implemented extensive punitive measures against corruption and moonlighting, making unauthorized operations much riskier. Still, recent research suggests that some groups such as APT41, believed to work for China, do espionage during the day and financially motivated side-projects at night [18]. In contrast to moonlighting by groups that are directly embedded in the military, the government seems to tolerate these apparent criminal activities of contractors [14].

In North Korea, on the other hand, it is a deliberately applied policy that military units have to finance themselves to some degree. This policy is consistent with the hypothesis that North Korean units are behind the ransomware WannaCry and the cyber-heists by the Lazarus group against banks [19]. In this sense, North Korean groups are likely choosing targets for their finances themselves while receiving tasking for espionage from the government.

6.2   Domestic and International Conflicts

Geopolitical analysis is very different from the other aspects in attribution, that cover artifacts like samples or server images directly linked to the attackers. In contrast, the *cui bono* is assessed on rather indirect information, typically from open source (OSINT). Therefore, it is important to realize that geopolitical analysis taken alone can only provide the weakest evidence of all MICTIC aspects. Cui bono can only be used to check whether an attribution hypothesis is plausible, i.e. whether the alleged actor has indeed a motivation for the cyber-operations in question. Still, often enough at the end of an attribution analysis it turns out that the first intuition based on geopolitical analysis was in fact correct.

Among other sources, strategic analysts regularly monitor international news from their region of interest in order to be aware of any upcoming summits, government plans for economic growth, trade negotiations, domestic or international conflicts. This is because APT attacks do not happen by coincidence and are not evenly distributed across regions or industries. For instance, they are more frequent in regions with international conflicts and hit organizations involved in these conflicts. Examples are the cyber-espionage incidents at the International Permanent Court of Arbitration in The Hague, shortly after the Philippines had lodged a complaint against China's claim to large parts of the South China Sea [20]. Another example is the cyber-operation attributed to APT28 against the Dutch authority investigating the shooting down of the Malaysian plane MH-17 over Ukraine [21]. Ukraine is a hot spot for several APT groups since the annexation of Crimea [22–24].

Therefore, robust and convincing attribution also requires the assessment of current geopolitical situations. Intelligence agencies have been doing this since even before the cyber-domain grew relevant. Now also the portfolio of threat intelligence providers includes alerting their customers of potential cyber-activities in relevant regions if there are indications of escalating international conflicts.

A particularly large number of APT groups are currently active in India and Pakistan, the countries around the South China Sea, Ukraine, and the Middle East. The characteristic that all these (otherwise rather diverse) regions share is indeed territorial conflict.

India and Pakistan both claim Kashmir since 1947. In the aforementioned HangOver campaign Pakistani military personnel were targeted and samples contained references to individuals and companies from India (see Chap. 3). Also registration data of control servers pointed to India (see Chap. 4). Coming back to the MICTIC framework, evidence from the aspects malware, infrastructure, and cui bono are consistent, leading to a strong attribution hypothesis of MICTIC-3.

Not only international conflicts correlate with increased cyber-espionage activity. In non-democratic countries opposition politicians, journalists critical of the government, ethnic and religious minorities, and dissidents face high risks of being targeted with malware. In China the so-called Five Poisons are regarded as threats to the Communist Party [25]. The Poisons are Tibet, Taiwan (both parts of the sacred and inviolable Chinese territory according to the

Communist Party), the Uyghur minority, Falun Gong, and the democracy movement. It is certainly no coincidence that these communities are regularly targeted by APTs [26–29].

Individual attacks are only of limited value for attribution. After all, any intelligence service may be interested in information from conflict regions. Therefore, attribution is not performed for individual incidents, but for clusters of similar attacks. Only a substantial number of incidents can document a focus on certain regions or industries. Also lack of activity in a specific country can be a relevant finding. Additionally, cross-targeting can strengthen hypotheses. For example, while many countries may be interested in current events in the Syrian civil war, the number of suspects is clearly smaller if the same intrusion set targets organizations like the NATO, Eastern European governments, and the afore-mentioned Dutch investigation of the flight MH-17.

6.3   Economic Interests

When investigating espionage cases in companies, political conflicts are of little relevance. Instead, it is necessary to analyze who has an economic interest in the stolen information. First, industrial espionage by a single competitor company must be distinguished from coordinated economical espionage by a government. In the former case, campaigns are very focused and, in some cases, directed only against a single company. In the latter case, an intrusion set or a group is active in several industries. For the analysis of the cui bono the economic structures and plans for economic growth of countries need to be matched with the assumed objectives of an APT campaign. The development plans of socialist (and communist) countries such as China and North Korea are particularly well documented and transparent, as these economies are centrally orchestrated and often publish strategies like Five-Year Plans at fixed intervals. In the Chinese plan societal and economic goals are defined in which the Chinese government wants to achieve substantial progress. These goals can usually be related to specific sectors. In recent years, the targets of alleged Chinese APT groups correlated with the industries that were relevant in the Five-Year Plan. A case in point was the activity of APT1 (see Chap. 2).

In the current Thirteenth Five-Year Plan, the Chinese government defines the goal to implement universal health care for all citizens, increase the share of non-fossil fuel energy to 15% by 2020, substantially improve city air quality, and to reduce soil and water con-tamination [62]. These goals were not chosen by chance. In recent years there have been a number of scandals about contaminated food and air pollution. The Chinese middle class reached an improved standard of living which leads to increased expectations regarding a clean environment and ubiquitous health care.

Since then, increased investments from China in many countries have been observed in the mentioned areas. For example, since 2015 there have been numerous takeover bids for renewable energy companies [30], and Chinese investors are trying to acquire shares in nuclear and semiconductor technology companies [31]. But also investments in start-ups dealing with artificial intelligence increased [32]. This topic was explicitly mentioned in the current Five-Year Plan as important for all economic sectors.

In addition to the Five-Year Plan, China announced the initiative "Made in China 2025", which aims to make the domestic industry world leader in a number of key technologies like Artificial Intelligence and new materials. The German Ministry of the Interior suspects Chinese APT groups behind a number of cyber-espionage cases in these sectors [33].

Another observation that is documented in several current APT reports is the increased cyber-espionage activity around projects related to the Belt and Road Initiative (BRI) (e.g. [34]).

The economic interests of other countries are much more difficult to determine as they are generally less centrally controlled. In democratic countries there are large legal and political hurdles for governments conducting espionage for intellectual property outside of the defense sector. For democratic governments it would be difficult to favor certain companies over competitors by providing them stolen intellectual property. Publicly documented cases all relate to national champions, state-owned enterprises, or the defense sector (cf. [35]). This general rule of thumb can be used to generate first attribution hypotheses for APT groups that collect intellectual property.

As already mentioned, large-scale espionage campaigns against companies are an indication that the attacker group is state-sponsored—either working directly in a government organization or working as a contractor. For groups that are likely of Chinese origin, differentiating between contractors and 'hackers in uniform' can be approximated by looking at the missions and responsibilities of the different bureaus of the PLA (cf. Fig. 6.1). Analysts assume that the individual units have thematically or regionally defined areas of responsibility. APT1 focused on English-speaking countries, PutterPanda collected information in the satellite and aviation sectors, the 2nd TRB (Technical Reconnaissance Bureau) in Nanjing is responsible for Taiwan. Therefore, analysts in IT-security companies use the heuristic that groups that do not focus on one region or sector, but are very opportunistically active in different regions and industries, are likely contractors. One example is the group Hidden Lynx described by Symantec, which has attacked hundreds of organizations worldwide in various industries [36]. A further indication that perpetrators do not work directly in government institutions is if their infrastructure or malware is also used for criminal activities—like the aforementioned group APT41. Analysts assume that the Chinese Ministry of State Security (MSS) works with contractors in most instances [16]. This is corroborated by indictments of the US Justice Department against APT3 for hacking the companies Siemens and Trimble [63]. The investigators amassed evidence that the individuals likely worked for the Chinese firm Boyusec. Prior to that, the Pentagon had identified Boyusec as working for the MSS [37]. Similarly, another indictment charged the MSS for hiring hackers to steal intellectual property about aeroplane turbines [38].

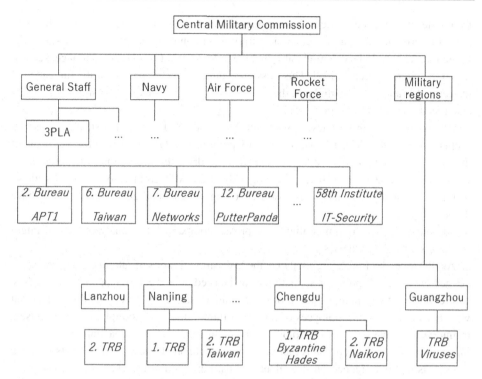

Fig. 6.1 Organizational chart of alleged cyber-units of the Chinese People's Liberation Army (PLA) prior to the formation of the SSF

6.4   Analysis of Organizations' Roles and Missions

The most successful cases of attribution are those that can present sufficient evidence to link an APT group to a specific organization. This also requires checking the mission and structure of this organization for consistency with the APT activity. Often the culprits are linked to intelligence services, and for most of these there is publicly available information that can be evaluated by strategic analysts and country experts. Some security companies employ such experts themselves, others rely on the published studies of think tanks and research institutions. And even government agencies that do attribution use public sources to supplement their assessments about foreign intelligence services.

The role and mission of intelligence agencies are usually defined abstractly in their respective laws on establishment. For example, the law for the German Federal Intelligence Service (BND) describes its tasks in §1 paragraph 2 as follows: "The Federal Intelligence Service collects information abroad that is necessary to evaluate intelligence with foreign and security policy relevance for the Federal Republic of Germany" [64] (author's translation). On first glance this may sound relatively generic. But two characteristics distinguish the BND from other intelligence services: It has no legal mandate to collect data domestically or to collect information for purely economic purposes. In contrast, the spectrum of tasks of the French secret service DGSE might also include industrial and economic espionage, according to the interpretation of [39]. This mission is phrased as "protection of the fundamental interests of France" [40]. Similarly, the Chinese MSS includes a department for "Scientific and Technological Information" [41].

Obviously, this can be relevant when attributing an APT group that steals intellectual property. If the other MICTIC aspects already point to a certain country, information about the missions of the country's different agencies can drive the generation of hypotheses on the level of organization attribution. Analogously, if the APT group also spies on dissidents or regime-critical journalists, it is worth checking which intelligence services also have domestic tasks.

Of course, if the group moonlights for private companies, this analysis method might generate screwed hypotheses.

As illustrated by the examples above, the tasks and missions of intelligence services are defined only vaguely publicly, so that they can be used only as a rough approximation. The nature of the actual implementation of the operative work must be explored in a different way. For journalists or employees of reputable think tanks, for example, it is not unusual to interview active or former employees of intelligence services as a source for general information. In the United States there is a more established tradition of contacts between journalists and intelligence services than in most other countries. The agencies use these contacts to clarify the context and background of operations if investigative reporters signal that they are going to cover them. In the past this has even sometimes led to journalists refraining from publication because they realized that it endangered lives of operatives or even national security. Such decisions may still turn out to be win-win situations, as journalists benefit from these meetings by having a better understanding of the greater picture which can be helpful for other or later stories. Over the years, some journalists have built up extensive networks of sources. This is how non-fiction books like David Sanger's 'Confront and Conceal' [2] are possible, which—among other things—covers the development of Stuxnet in great detail, or Tim Weiner's book on the history of the CIA which covers many covert and clandestine operations from the past [61].

Obviously, this proximity between the media and intelligence services does not exist in most countries. Still, also in Russia there are well-connected journalists who are regarded as experts for the secret services. Andrei Soldatov documents in 'The New Nobility' [42] the transition from the former KGB to the FSB and uncovers the enormous influence of intelligence officials on the country's politics and economy. In 'The Red Web' he lays open the Internet censorship and interception activities of the Russian state [43] based on information from informants and sources in the agencies. Such depictions provide relevant background information for attribution about the structure, the capabilities, and the operations of intelligence services.

On the basis of six sources from the nexus of Russian intelligence services Mark Galeotti documented the overlapping missions of these agencies in a study for the European Council on Foreign Relations (see Fig. 6.1). According to him, cyber-espionage in Russia is mostly the responsibility of the domestic intelligence service FSB and the military service GRU, and to a lesser degree of the foreign intelligence service SVR [13]. However, there is a strong rivalry between these agencies and the oversight is very weak. The overlapping missions complicate the attribution of APT campaigns to concrete agencies. They even lead to targets being compromised by more than one APT group. A famous example is the network of the Democratic National Committee (DNC) where the signature malware families of two groups were found [44], namely APT28 and APT29. The security company that investigated the incident discovered that some information was stolen by both groups, so that the analysts concluded that the groups acted independently of each other. The US government assessed that APT28 corresponds to a department of the GRU, while APT29 is generally believed to work for another Russian intelligence service (cf. [25]). The exact reason for this co-occurrence of the two groups in the same target network is unclear. Many analysts are convinced that APT29 collects information strategically and for long-term purposes, while APT28 is tasked with short-term tactical operations. But also the rivalry put forward in Galeotti's article is a plausible explanation, even though his sources also suggest that tasking from the political leadership is poorly organized and may lead to parallel assignments by accident. According to the same sources, the roles and tasks are more clearly defined when it comes to espionage on technologies. Here the publicly stated missions of the agencies become relevant. Both the SVR and the GRU are responsible for economic and technology espionage [13]. The former, however, has traditionally been active in classic espionage, that is, using human agents. In contrast, even before the attribution by the US government, the GRU was believed to have a cyber-program as it had been posting job offers for applicants with offensive computer skills for several years. Galeotti reasons that in the cyber-domain rivalry exists mostly between the GRU and the FSB, which has been trying to subsume all cyber-activities under its own roof for a long time [43]. Due to this self-proclaimed responsibility for cyber-espionage, Galeotti suggests that the FSB increasingly conducts operations abroad [13], which originally was not part of its mission.

If true, this would mean that the demarcation between responsibilities and missions of the Russian intelligence agencies is constantly changing and can only be roughly estimated on the basis of the objectives described in their Laws of Establishment. For counter-espionage units, it is further complicated by the fact that hackers inherently need to travel less abroad than traditional intelligence officers, and they are not stationed in embassies and do not take part in receptions or conferences as part of their jobs. As a result, cyber-espionage actors are harder to identify than classical intelligence personnel.

As already mentioned, attribution is made more difficult by moonlighting of APT groups. Galeotti's sources suggest that such side businesses exist in the Russian intelligence services [13].

In the attribution process, APT groups are usually assigned to organizations only after they have been assigned to a country of origin. A naive approach might be to map the groups one by one to the agency whose mission fits best. If this approach is attempted with the alleged Russian groups, it becomes apparent that there is a quantitative mismatch between three relevant intelligence agencies and a higher number of groups. Therefore, a simple one-to-one relationship is not feasible. Luckily, there are analytic methods to cope with this. Generally, the clustering into intrusion sets and groups may be too fine-grained, so that the activities of a (physical) team may correspond to several (technically defined) APT groups. Another possibility is that an agency does not conduct all cyber-operations via a central team, but via decentralized groups in the specialist departments (cf. Sect. 6.1). Some cyber-operations may have been conducted by contractors who—in the worst case for attribution—work for several agencies. Finally, it cannot be ruled out that the country-attribution of one or more groups was wrong in the first place.

The groups that are likely of Russian origin have some distinguishing characteristics (cf. Table 6.2).

APT28 APT28 has been active since at least 2009. In the early years it targeted mainly military organizations and defence contractors. Since about 2014 their activities have expanded significantly and now also include targets such as domestic government critics, journalists, and foreign parliaments. Among security researchers APT28 is considered risk-affine and comparatively easy to track because of its poor OpSec.

The initial focus of APT28 on military targets matches the main mission of the GRU (see Table 6.1). Also the lack of OpSec coincides with statements of Galeotti's sources that the GRU is willing to take risks [13]. These observations are in line with early public attribution by the German BfV of the group to the Russian military intelligence service. Surprisingly though, TrendMicro reported that APT28 also targeted Russian journalists and dissidents—among them the punk band Pussy Riot [45]. Obtaining information regarding domestic political security is not regarded as a mission of the GRU. Likely these activities of the group are due to parallel assignments by the political leadership or due to inter-agency rivalry. Nowadays, the attribution of APT28 to the GRU is considered reliable, not least because of an indictment of the US Department of Justice. The investigators even identified the military unit 26165 and several of their members as having developed APT28's signature malware X-Agent and having conducted the operation against the DNC [46].

The indictment also illustrates the division of labor in several sub-teams similar to the MICTIC aspects: According to the US investigators, there was a team responsible for developing malware, other members were operators setting up X-Agent C&Cs and monitoring the malware, and a completely different unit 74455 managed a vast server infrastructure.

Snake Snake stands out for its high OpSec. The group develops hard-to-detect root-kits and hijacks satellite connections to hide its control servers. Unlike APT28 Snake was never observed within Russia (the Trojan Agent.BTZ which infected Russian targets is also used

Table 6.1 Missions of selected Russian intelligence agenies (according to [13]). X: Main mission, O: Auxiliary mission

Mission	FSB	SVR	GRU
Political intelligence	O	X	O
Economic intelligence		X	O
Military intelligence		O	X
Active measures	O	X	X
Counter-intelligence	X	O	O
Political security	X	O	
Law enforcement	O		

Table 6.2 Groups that were reported by security companies as being likely of Russian origin

Name	Targets	Special feature
Red October	Embassies, research institutes	Now inactive
APT28	Military, defence contractors	Risk-affine
APT29	Diplomatic, government, drug trafficker	Steganography, web services for C&C
Snake	Diplomatic, government	High OpSec
Sandworm	Energy, industrial control systems (ICS))	Sabotage
Energetic Bear	Energy	Industrial control systems (ICS)
Gamaredon	Government, military	Focus on Ukraine

by other groups). This observation makes an attribution to the FSB unlikely, while Snake's focus on foreign government institutions matches the role of the SVR. This hypothesis is also corroborated by the secondary mission of the SVR to procure military intelligence: Snake compromised the network of the defence contractor RUAG [47].

APT29 APT29 focuses on embassies and ministries of foreign affairs, as well as other foreign government organizations. The group also collected information on Russian drug traffickers [48]. Both types of targets fit into the scope of tasks of the FSB. Of the Russian intelligence services which are said to have cyber-capabilities, the FSB is the only one responsible for criminal prosecution (see Table 6.1).

Yet, there is strong evidence linking APT29 to the SVR. Dutch journalists broke the story that the intelligence service AIVD had hacked the security cameras of a building in which APT29 conducted its operation against the DNC [65]. The Dutch were able to match the operators' faces to employees of the SVR.

Since then, the attribution of APT29 to the SVR is regarded as lore among some infosec analysts. Yet, there are some facts that demand caution. The domestic surveillance of drug traffickers by APT29 is much more in line with the FSB's responsibilities. Therefore, other analysts are convinced that APT29 are in fact contractors that either sell malware to or conduct operations for both the SVR and FSB. As already outlined, contractors screw up the cui bono analysis, and cui bono taken alone cannot be the basis for strong attribution. But if it turns out that SVR and FSB conducted their own operations and used malware by the same contractor, it shows that clustering operations into intrusion sets based on technical artifacts is inherently imperfect (as illustrated by Fig. 2.3)—at least for attribution on the organization level.

Sandworm and EnergeticBear Sandworm and EnergeticBear are particularly noteworthy as both use malware to obtain information about or from industrial control systems (ICS). These industrial networks differ fundamentally from office networks in terms of hardware, software, and network protocols. The malware and tools of most groups can only be used in Windows or Linux environments. Sandworm and EnergeticBear are among the few groups that have invested efforts to develop an arsenal for operations in networks with industrial control systems. An important difference between the two groups is that EnergeticBear only collects information. For instance, the group's trojan Havex was inserted into the installation files of legitimate software used in control systems. The IT administrators downloaded the software and manually installed it on systems in ICS networks. This was a brilliant attack vector to make sure that Havex even infected systems that were air-gapped from the Internet. It collected configuration data from ICS systems and processes. Manipulation of data or devices was not observed, so the motivation of the operation was not sabotage—at least for now. Also the operation targeting the energy sector in 2017 was limited to collecting credentials and other reconnaissance data.

The Havex and PalmettoFusion campaigns were very different from those involving Industroyer [22]—also called CrashOverride [49]—that was attributed to Sandworm. This malware was deployed against a Ukrainian substation to cause power outages. Prior to that incident, the backdoor BlackEnergy 3 had been used by the same perpetrators for sabotage in the Ukrainian power grid. Obviously, the difference between Sandworm and EnergeticBear is that the former is much more aggressive and conducts sabotage, while the latter restricts itself to information collection. Thus, the campaigns of Sandworm are consistent with analysts' assessment of the mission and operations of the GRU. In contrast, the reconnaissance activities of EnergeticBear have been attributed to the FSB by unnamed US intelligence officials [50].

Gamaredon This group is exclusively active against targets in the Ukraine, especially military and government organizations. Its malware and TTPs show a low level of sophistication, which is accompanied by poor OpSec. Infosec analysts amass indicators of compromise as the group is easy to track. There are no strong attribution hypotheses, but several analysts and the Ukrainian Security Service (SBU) believe the group might be part of a region-specific unit at the FSB, as the agency is responsible for the "near abroad" of Russia [51].

The above assessment of the Russian intelligence services serves as an example that can also be applied to other countries. For example, in China the People's Liberation Army (PLA), the Ministry of State Security (MSS), and the Ministry of Public Security (MPS) have cyber-capabilities [52]. Their missions differ more clearly from each other than those of the Russian intelligence services. The MSS is responsible for counterintelligence, non-military foreign espionage, and political security. The PLA (historically the 3PLA, now the Network Systems Department of the Strategic Support Force for military intelligence collection. Finally, the MPS is a law enforcement agency and responsible for domestic security. At present, however, it is expanding its counterespionage capabilities [52]. Thus, a method to generate first rough organization-attribution hypotheses for Chinese APT groups can be to check whether military targets, opposition members, or ethnic minorities like Uyghurs are targeted.

More complicated is the situation in Iran. Public reports suggest that the Intelligence Organization (IO) of the Islamic Revolutionary Guards Corps (IRGC) and the Ministry of Intelligence (MOIS) both control APT groups [53]. While the IRGC reports to the religious Supreme Leader, the MOIS is part of the presidential administration—two fiefdoms that continuously compete for influence and power. Similar to Russian agencies, the two intelligence organizations are regarded rivals for resources and reputation, leading to an overlap in targeting [54]. Even worse, Iranian APT groups are consistently in flux, so that even on a technical level security companies are more discordant about clustering of intrusion sets than usual.

6.5   Analysis of Organizational Structures

The internal organizational structures of intelligence services and military facilities are not transparent. Information about the interrelationships between departments, divisions, and units and their respective tasks are usually fragmented and have to be put together like a puzzle. Analysts identify and monitor public sources hoping that they contain not only agency names but also unit designators (e.g. [55]). These are numerical codes that organizations like the PLA use in public sources in order to cover the unit's real name and structure. But since these designators are reused consistently, they can be useful for deriving the tasks and capabilities of these units over time. An often referenced type of such sources are research publications. Although these organizations rarely publish themselves, in many countries the military is an important sponsor for projects and studies of research institutions. When the scientists publish their results in journals or conference proceedings, the sponsors are sometimes mentioned, because the paper usually benefits from the prestige of the military organization. So for example the 7th Bureau of the Third Department of the PLA (Unit 61580) was named in a study on network security and attacks, and an institution in Guangzhou (Unit 75779) conducted studies on Internet worms [56].

Other valuable public sources are job advertisements, as these sometimes explicitly list requirements like skills in malware development and network security. A famous example were the job postings of Unit 61398 that Mandiant linked to APT1 (see Chap. 2).

Also the awarding of medals is sometimes reported publicly and may contain unit names, locations, and (abstract) descriptions of the achievements that led to earning the commendation.

Many of these publicly available information types do not prove or even imply that the referenced units are engaged in espionage, nor does it result in a clear definition of tasks or attribution of APT groups. But they can serve as first hints about the type of tasks and the internal structure of units. If OpSec failures or traffic captures reveal geographical information about APT groups, it can be matched with the location of the (physical) units.

Figure 6.1 depicts the combined publicly available information about alleged cyber-units of the Chinese People's Liberation Army prior to the large reform that led to the implementation of the Strategic Support Force (SSF) at the end of 2015.

Little information is available about the cyber-capabilities of the Navy, Air Force, and Rocket Forces under the old structure. They seem to have had their own reconnaissance capabilities, but it is unclear whether these were exclusively based on electronic signals (SIGINT) or also included cyber-espionage. At least in slides leaked by Edward Snowden the NSA attributes the APT group Byzantine Viking to a reconnaissance office of the PLA Navy [57].

Several organizations engaged with cyber and IT-security topics were part of the Third Department (3PLA) of the General Staff Department. According to Mandiant's analysis, the 2nd Bureau is home to APT1. PutterPanda is part of Unit 61486 of the 12th Bureau according to the security company CrowdStrike [6]. Taiwanese secret services claimed that there is an APT-unit in the 6th Bureau which conducts computer espionage against Taiwan from the campus of the University of Wuhan [58]. The 7th Bureau works on network technology and the 58th Research Institute published about IT security [56].

The armed forces of the PLA are divided into 12 military regions. These maintain one or more Technical Reconnaissance Bureaus (TRB). The 1st TRB of the military region Chengdu was mentioned as home of the group "Byzantine Hades" in leaked cables of the US State Department [59]. The 2nd TRB is responsible for the APT group Naikon according to analyses of the IT security company ThreatConnect [60]. As mentioned above the TRB published studies about computer viruses in the military region Guangzhou. The 2nd TRB in Nanjing is suspected to conduct computer espionage against Taiwan [56].

The reform of the PLA may turn out to be an opportunity for the attribution on the organization level. Prior to that, the PLA's cyber-units were dispersed across regional command offices and Technical Reconnaissance Bureaus and were acting rather independent of each other [56]. Now they are to be merged or integrated into the newly established Strategic Support Force (SSF) [16], which will serve as a central service provider for the other departments of the PLA [17]. Such restructuring cannot be kept completely secret, but will be accompanied by announcements of politicians, who promise more efficiency due to the new organization form [16]. At the same time changes of appointments of high-ranking officers are reported in relevant military magazines and forums. For instance, Zheng Junjie was reported as Commander of the SSF Network Systems Department in 2018 [55]. Thus, reorganizations lead to many new puzzle pieces for country experts and researchers.

When the implementation of the SSF became publicly known, analysts expected substantial shifts in the activities of Chinese APT groups. It was predicted that some groups might disband, others might merge into larger units, others might change their tools and TTPs. Such changes would manifest in the observable technical data: The infrastructures and malware of disbanded groups should no longer be observed in attacks. Intrusion sets that had been disjoint so far should start to overlap. Some groups that had focused on very limited targets should become more active and expand their targeting. However, only some of these predictions became true. This may be due to a "bricks, not clay" approach in the reform, that is, units were just renamed and moved as a whole in the organizational chart [55]. Still, several groups that were believed to be PLA-related were indeed not observed anymore. Others seem to refrain from collecting economic and political intelligence now and limit themselves to military targets [55]. This lack of activity is apparently compensated by increased activity of groups that are likely contractors of the MSS, according to security companies and US indictments. Also, new intrusion sets emerged, but up to now it is not known whether they are made up of former 3PLA units. Attribution is a slow discipline and can provide insights only step by step.

6.6   Overview of Relevant Information Types

Figure 6.2 lists typical types of information that can be analyzed in the aspect cui bono.

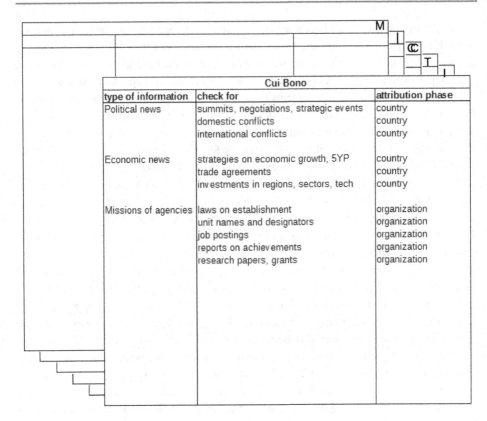

Fig. 6.2 Overview of information types in the aspect cui bono

---

References

1. United States District Court Southern District of Ohio Western Division: United States of America versus Yanjun Xu (2018). https://www.justice.gov/opa/press-release/file/1099876/download. Accessed 17th Dec 2019
2. Sanger, D.E.: Confront and Conceal. Crown Publishers, New York (2012)
3. Maurer, T.: Cyber Mercenaries—The State, Hackers, and Power. Cambridge University Press (2018)
4. Office of the Director of National Intelligence: Background to 'Assessing Russian Activities and Intentions in Recent US Elections'—The Analytic Process and Cyber Incident Attribution (2017). https://www.dni.gov/files/documents/ICA_2017_01.pdf. Accessed 17th Aug 2017
5. EFF: Computer Network Operations Genie (2015). https://www.eff.org/files/2015/02/03/20150117-spiegel-excerpt_from_the_secret_nsa_budget_on_computer_network_operations_-_code_word_genie.pdf. Accessed 17th Aug 2017

6. CrowdStrike: Hat-tribution to PLA unit 61486. In: CrowdStrike Blog (2014). http://web.archive. org/web/20170207031606/https://www.crowdstrike.com/blog/hat-tribution-pla-unit-61486/. Accessed 17th Aug 2017

7. Solon, O.: Hacking group auctions 'cyber weapons' stolen from NSA. In: The Guardian (2016). http://web.archive.org/web/20160817003759/https://www.theguardian.com/technology/2016/ aug/16/shadow-brokers-hack-auction-nsa-malware-equation-group. Accessed 17th Aug 2017

8. TheGrugq: enterprise security lessons from terrorists. In: Troopers Conference (2017). https:// grugq.github.io/presentations/how%20very%20apt.pdf. Accessed 12th Dec 2019

9. United States district court for the central district of California: United States of America v. PARK JIN HYOK (2018). https://www.justice.gov/opa/press-release/file/1092091/download. Accessed 10th Dec 2019

10. Symantec Security Response: Butterfly: Profiting from high-level corporate attacks. In: Symantec Connect (2015). https://www.symantec.com/connect/blogs/butterfly-profiting-high-level-corporate-attacks. Accessed 8th Dec 2019

11. The United States Department of Justice: Chinese National Pleads Guilty to Conspiring to Hack into U.S. Defense Contractors' Systems to Steal Sensitive Military Information (2016). https://www.justice.gov/opa/pr/chinese-national-pleads-guilty-conspiring-hack-us-defense-contractors-systems-steal-sensitive. Accessed 14th Dec 2019

12. Bing, C., Schectman, J.: Inside the uaes secret hacking team of American mercenaries. In: Reuters (2019). https://www.reuters.com/investigates/special-report/usa-spying-raven/. Accessed 8th Dec 2019

13. Galeotti, M.: Putin's Hydra—Inside Russia's intelligence services. In: European Council on Foreign Relations Publications (2016). http://ecfr.eu/page/-/ECFR_169_-_PUTINS_HYDRA_INSIDE_THE_RUSSIAN_INTELLIGENCE_SERVICES_1513.pdf. Accessed 18th Aug 2017

14. Merrigan, E.: Blurred lines between state and non-state actors. In: Council on Foreign Relations Blog (2019). https://www.cfr.org/blog/blurred-lines-between-state-and-non-state-actors. Accessed 10th Dec 2019

15. Anderson, C.: Bahamut revisited, more cyber espionage in the middle East and South Asia. In: Bellingcat (2017). http://web.archive.org/web/20171028201729/https://www.bellingcat.com/ resources/case-studies/2017/10/27/bahamut-revisited-cyber-espionage-middle-east-south-asia/. Accessed 29th Oct 2017

16. Mattis, P.: Three scenarios for understanding changing PLA activity in cyberspace. In: China Brief, vol. 15 Issue 23 (2015). https://jamestown.org/program/three-scenarios-for-understanding-changing-pla-activity-in-cyberspace/. Accessed on 17th Aug 2017

17. Costello, J.: The strategic support force: update and overview. In: China Brief, vol. 16 Issue 19 (2016). https://jamestown.org/program/strategic-support-force-update-overview/. Accessed 17th Aug 2017

18. Fraser, N., Plan, F, OLeary, J., Cannon, V., Leong, R., Perez, D., Shen, C.: APT41—A dual espionage and cyber crime operation. In FireEye Blog (2019). https://www.fireeye.com/blog/ threat-research/2019/08/apt41-dual-espionage-and-cyber-crime-operation.html. Accessed 4th Nov 2019

19. Recorded Future: North Korea Is Not Crazy. In: The Recorded Future Blog (2017). http:// web.archive.org/web/20170817185506/https://www.recordedfuture.com/north-korea-cyber-activity. Accessed 17th Aug 2017

20. South China Morning Post: 'Chinese cyberspies' hack international court's website to fish for enemies in South China Sea dispute (2015). http://web.archive.org/web/20151017050922/ http://www.scmp.com/news/china/policies-politics/article/1868395/chinese-cyberspies-hack-international-courts-website. Accessed 20th Aug 2017

21. The Guardian: Russia accused of series of international cyber-attacks (2016). http://web. archive.org/web/20160513174121/https://www.theguardian.com/technology/2016/may/13/ russia-accused-international-cyber-attacks-apt-28-sofacy-sandworm. Accessed 20th Aug 2017

22. Cherepanov, A., Lipovsky, R.: Industroyer—Biggest threat to industrial control systems since Stuxnet. In: WeLiveSecurity Blog (2017). https://www.welivesecurity.com/2017/06/12/ industroyer-biggest-threat-industrial-control-systems-since-stuxnet/. Accessed 19th Aug 2017

23. ESET: BlackEnergy and the Ukrainian power outage—What we really know. In: welivesecurity Blog. http://web.archive.org/web/20160114015324/https://www.welivesecurity.com/2016/01/ 11/blackenergy-and-the-ukrainian-power-outage-what-we-really-know/. Accessed 20th Aug 2017

24. Meyers, A.: Danger Close—Fancy bear tracking of Ukrainian field artillery units. In: CrowdStrike Blog (2016). http://web.archive.org/web/20170820103928/https://www.crowdstrike.com/blog/ danger-close-fancy-bear-tracking-ukrainian-field-artillery-units/. Accessed 20th Aug 2017

25. Bundesamt für Verfassungsschutz: Verfassungsschutzbericht (2016). https://www. verfassungsschutz.de/download/vsbericht-2016.pdfZitiertam. Accessed 19th July 2017

26. Villeneuve, N.: Tracking GhostNet—Investigating a Cyber Espionage Network (2009). www. nartv.org/mirror/ghostnet.pdf. Accessed 13th Aug 2017

27. Baumgartner, K., Raiu, C., Maslennikov, D.: Android trojan found in targeted attack. In: SecureList (2013). http://web.archive.org/web/20170813125606/https://securelist.com/ android-trojan-found-in-targeted-attack-58/35552/. Accessed 13th Aug 2017

28. Kozy, A.: Occupy Central—The Umbrella revolution and Chinese intelligence. In: CrowdStrike Blog (2014). http://web.archive.org/web/20160419233041/https://www.crowdstrike.com/blog/ occupy-central-the-umbrella-revolution-and-chinese-intelligence/. Accessed 20th Aug 2017

29. Van Horenbeeck, M.: JavaScript/HTML droppers as a targeted attack vector. In: Internet Storm Center Diary (2007). http://web.archive.org/web/20170820111504/https://isc.sans.edu/diary/ JavaScriptHTML+droppers+as+a+targeted+attack+vector/3400. Accessed 20th Aug 2017

30. Huotari, M., Hanemann, T.: Chinese investment in Europe—record flows and grow- ing imbalances. In: Mercator Insitute for China Studies (2017). http://web.archive.org/ web/20170823182222/https://www.merics.org/en/merics-analysis/papers-on-china/cofdi/ cofdi2017/. Accessed 23rd Aug 2017

31. Mohsin, S.: Mnuchin seeks greater scrutiny of Chinese investments in U.S.. In: Bloomberg (2017). https://www.bloomberg.com/news/articles/2017-06-14/mnuchin-seeks- greater-scrutiny-of-chinese-investments-in-u-s. Accessed 23rd Aug 2017

32. Kania, E.: Beyond CFIUS—The strategic challenge of China's rise in artificial intelligence. In: Lawfare Blog (2017). http://web.archive.org/web/20170823182426/https://lawfareblog.com/ beyond-cfius-strategic-challenge-chinas-rise-artificial-intelligence. Accessed 23rd Aug 2017

33. Heide, D., Kerkmann, C.: Berlin verdächtigt Chinas Regierung der Industriespionage im großen Stil. In: Handelsblatt (2019). https://www.handelsblatt.com/politik/deutschland/cyberattacken- berlin-verdaechtigt-chinas-regierung-der-industriespionage-im-grossen-stil/24911728.html. Accessed 14th Dec 2019

34. Chen, L.: 'Chinese' cyber spy ring accused of targeting key players in Belt and Road Initiative. In: South China Morning Post (2019). https://www.scmp.com/news/china/society/article/3014421/ chinese-cyber-spy-ring-accused-targeting-key-players-belt-and. Accessed 14th Dec 2019

35. Gertz, B.: U.S. hits back against Chinese cyberattacks. In: Washington Times (2019). https:// www.washingtontimes.com/news/2019/mar/6/us-counters-china-cyberattacks/. Accessed 14th Dec 2019

36. Doherty, S., Gegeny, J., Spasojevic, B., Baltazar, J.: Hidden Lynx—Professional hackers for hire. In: Symantec Security Response Blog (2013). www.symantec.com/content/en/us/enterprise/ media/security_response/whitepapers/hidden_lynx.pdf. Accessed 23rd Aug 2017

37. Gertz, B.: Pentagon Links Chinese Cyber Security Firm to Beijing Spy Service (2016). https://freebeacon.com/national-security/pentagon-links-chinese-cyber-security-firm-beijing-spy-service/. Accessed 13th Dec 2019
38. United States District Court Southern District of New York: Unites States of America versus Zhang Zhang-GUI, Zha Rong, Chai Meng et al. (2017). https://www.justice.gov/opa/press-release/file/1106491/download. Accessed 4th Nov 2019
39. Karacs, I.: France spied on commercial rivals. In: Independent (1996). http://web.archive.org/web/20170904162158/http://www.independent.co.uk/news/world/france-spied-on-commercial-rivals-1323422.html. Accessed 4th Sept 2017
40. DGSE: Controles. http://www.defense.gouv.fr/english/dgse/tout-le-site/controlesZitiertam. Accessed on 18th Aug 2017
41. Federation of American Scientists (FAS): Tenth Bureau Scientific and Technological Information Bureau. In: Intelligence Resource Program. http://web.archive.org/web/20140719034600/https://fas.org/irp/world/china/mss/org_10.htm. Accessed 18th Aug 2017
42. Soldatov, A., Borogan, I.: The New Nobility. Public Affairs (2010)
43. Soldatov, A., Borogan, I.: The Red Web. Public Affairs (2015)
44. Alperovitch, D.: Bears in the midst: Intrusion into the democratic national committee. In: CrowdStrike Blog (2016). http://web.archive.org/web/20160615025759/https://www.crowdstrike.com/blog/bears-midst-intrusion-democratic-national-committee/. Accessed 19th Aug 2017
45. Hacquebord, F.: Pawn Storm's domestic spying campaign revealed; Ukraine and US top global targets. In: TrendMicro Blog (2015). http://web.archive.org/web/20150822082002/http://blog.trendmicro.com:80/trendlabs-security-intelligence/pawn-storms-domestic-spying-campaign-revealed-ukraine-and-us-top-global-targets/. Accessed 15th Aug 2017
46. United States district court for the district of Columbia: United States of America v. Viktor Borisovich Netyksho et al. (2018). https://www.justice.gov/file/1080281/download. Accessed 5th Nov 2019
47. GovCERT.ch: APT Case RUAG—Technical Report (2016). http://web.archive.org/web/20170718174931/https://www.melani.admin.ch/dam/melani/de/dokumente/2016/technicalreportruag.pdf.download.pdf/Report_Ruag-Espionage-Case.pdf. Accessed 19th Aug 2017
48. F-Secure Labs: The Dukes—7 Years of Espionage (2015). https://www.f-secure.com/documents/996508/1030745/dukes_whitepaper.pdf. Accessed 19th July 2017
49. Dragos Inc.: CRASHOVERRIDE—Analysis of the Threat to Electric Grid Operations (2017). https://dragos.com/blog/crashoverride/CrashOverride-01.pdf. Accessed 19th Aug 2017
50. Nakashima, E.: U.S. officials say Russian government hackers have penetrated energy and nuclear company business networks. In: The Washington Post (2017). https://www.washingtonpost.com/world/national-security/us-officials-say-russian-government-hackers-have-penetrated-energy-and-nuclear-company-business-networks/2017/07/08/bbfde9a2-638b-11e7-8adc-fea80e32bf47_story.html. Accessed 19th Aug 2017
51. Paganini, P.: The Gamaredon Group is back with new weapons in its arsenal. In: Security Affairs (2017). https://securityaffairs.co/wordpress/56756/intelligence/gamaredon-group-backdoor.html. Accessed 15th Dec 2019
52. U.S.-China Economic and Security Review Commission. China's Espionage and Intelligence Operations (2016). https://www.uscc.gov/sites/default/files/transcripts/June%2009%2C%202016%20Hearing%20Transcript.pdf. Accessed 20th Aug 2017
53. Anderson, C., Sadjapour, K.: Iran's Cyber Threat—Espionage, Sabotage, and Revenge. In: Carnegie Endowment for International Peace (2018). https://carnegieendowment.org/2018/01/04/iran-s-cyber-threat-espionage-sabotage-and-revenge-pub-75134. Accessed 15th Dec 2019

54. Tomaj, A.: Restructuring in IRGC intelligence. In: Asharq Al-Awsat (2019). https://aawsat.com/english/home/article/1818656/restructuring-irgc-intelligence. Accessed 15th Dec 2019
55. Costello, J., McReynolds, J.: China's strategic support force—a force for a new Era. In: China Strategic Perspectives (2018). https://ndupress.ndu.edu/Portals/68/Documents/stratperspective/china/china-perspectives_13.pdf. Accessed 20th Dec 2019
56. Stokes, M.A., Lin, J., Russell Hsiao, L.C.: The Chinese people's liberation army signals intelligence and cyber reconnaissance infrastructure. In: Project 2049 Institute (2011). https://project2049.net/documents/pla_third_department_sigint_cyber_stokes_lin_hsiao.pdf. Accessed 23rd July 2017
57. NSA: BYZANTINE HADES—An evolution of collection. In: Spiegel Online (2015). http://web.archive.org/web/20150117190714/http://www.spiegel.de/media/media-35686.pdf.   Accessed 14th Sept 2017
58. Tien-pin, L., Pan, J.: PLA cyberunit targeting Taiwan named. In: Taipei Times (2015). http://web.archive.org/web/20150311141017/http://www.taipeitimes.com/News/taiwan/archives/2015/03/10/2003613206. Accessed 22nd Aug 2017
59. Grow, B., Hosenball, M.: Special report—in cyberspy versus cyberspy, China has the edge. In: Reuters (2011). http://web.archive.org/web/20160421125947/http://www.reuters.com/article/us-china-usa-cyberespionage-idUSTRE73D24220110414. Accessed 22nd Aug 2017
60. Mimoso, M.: Naikon APT group tied to China's PLA unit 78020. In: ThreatConnect Blog (2015). https://www.threatconnect.com/in-the-news/naikon-apt-group-tied-to-chinas-pla-unit-78020/. Accessed 22nd Aug 2017
61. Weiner, T.: Legacy of Ashes—The History of the CIA, Kindle edn. Penguin (2008)
62. Central Committee of the Communist Party of China: The 13th five-year plan for economic and social development of the people's republic of China. In: National Development and Reform Commission (NDRC) (2015). http://en.ndrc.gov.cn/newsrelease/201612/P020161207645765233498.pdf. Accessed 23rd Aug 2017
63. The US Department of Justice: United States of America V. Wu Yingzhuo, Dong Hao, Xia Lei (2017). https://www.justice.gov/opa/press-release/file/1013866/download. Accessed 13th Dec 2019
64. Bundesnachrichtendienst: Gesetzlicher Auftrag. https://www.bnd.bund.de/DE/Die_Themen/hidden_content1/Auftragsprofil/staaten_node.html. Accessed 14th Dec 2019
65. Modderkolk, H.: Dutch agencies provide crucial intel about Russia's interference in US-elections. In: Volkskrant (2018). https://www.volkskrant.nl/wetenschap/dutch-agencies-provide-crucial-intel-about-russia-s-interference-in-us-elections~b4f8111b/. Accessed 15th Dec 2019

Telemetry—Data from Security Products

Millions of computers worldwide run security software that is deeply interfaced with the operating system and has almost unlimited visibility on the system running it. Many IT-security companies collect data from the installed instances of their products: *telemetry*. While the main motivation is to enhance the detection quality of the security software, the same data can be used to gain insights into the operations of attackers and sometimes even about their origin. This chapter explains what types of data can be obtained and how they support attribution.

In the MICTIC framework the aspect *telemetry* does not translate to a clear-cut attacker sub-team. It is linked to the manual activities of operators, such as sending spear-phishing mails, installing malware, or even doing lateral movement. In this regard the aspect overlaps with operators working with control servers. But the type of data is very different from that obtained from C&Cs, resulting in different tools and workflows for analysts.

7.1 Attacker Perspective: Awareness of Telemetry

There is little evidence that APT groups are fully aware of the existence and potential of telemetry. While there is malware that disables security products on an infected computer, it is safe to assume that the attackers do this to prevent the anti-virus program from alerting the user or admins. While this technique also hamstrings the transmission of telemetry data, it is very likely not intended deliberately. Similarly, deleting log data and tools at the end of an incident does not help against telemetry, since at that point the data has already been sent to the vendors.

Even if they tried, perpetrators can avoid telemetry collection only to a very limited extent. Even before the malware executes and can deactivate an anti-virus scanner or delete log data, tell-tale information about the sample is already collected and transmitted to security companies. So attackers cannot completely avoid creating telemetry events.

© Springer-Verlag GmbH Germany, part of Springer Nature 2020
T. Steffens, *Attribution of Advanced Persistent Threats*,
https://doi.org/10.1007/978-3-662-61313-9_7

Still, telemetry is not a silver bullet. While security companies developed many automatic processes that use the data for generating new anti-virus definitions or malware statistics, these typically focus on run-of-the-mill malware. APT attacks are often overlooked in the vast amount of telemetry events that every-day criminal activities generate. For supporting attribution the telemetry data needs to be analyzed by a researcher with a specific intention. This means that analysts start to look into APT-related data only after parts of an attack campaign have been detected and selected for more detailed investigation. Since the culprits optimize their techniques to remain undetected for as long as possible, a lot of valuable information lies unused in the databases of security companies.

7.2   Types of Telemetry Data

So far in this book we have used the term "anti-virus programs" to cover different categories of security products. While this term works in most contexts, it is too imprecise for discussing types of telemetry data. Even if one disregards the fact that most malicious programs are not "viruses" in the narrow sense, the product landscape in IT security is too diverse to be subsumed under this term. A differentiation of all product types is hardly possible, especially because vendors regularly introduce new technologies, rename old approaches with exciting new names, or combine several existing products into new product bundles. Therefore, in the following we differentiate product categories only insofar as they illustrate the various telemetry data types.

File Scanner Computers of employees and private users are often referred to as endpoints or clients in the security industry. Most of these machines run programs that can be called—somewhat simplified—file scanners. These come with a database of more or less complex signatures, usually called virus definitions, to detect malicious files. From a telemetry point of view, it is irrelevant whether the file scanners run continuously and check every file before it is accessed, or run "on-demand" to scan the entire hard disk. In either case, almost all file scanners have the functionality to transmit data about detected malware to the vendor. This data includes at least the name of the signature, the hash and name of the detected file, the current time, and a computer-specific ID. Some manufacturers also transmit the IP address of the client, either completely or with the last octet zeroed out. Depending on the product and its configuration, the scanner may even upload the malicious file to the security company. For security reasons, vendors transmit files only if they are found on a number of different computers. This is to prevent legitimate user-specific documents from being transferred to the central database in case of false positives.

The user can deactivate the transmission of all data. During installation of the security software, the user is asked whether he or she agrees to submit information to optimize and improve the product. Often it is not transparent what type of data will be transferred in which conditions, so the consequences of agreeing to submitting data can often only be assessed with much effort.

Reputation Service For some product types, the entire functionality is based on user data being sent to a central database in order to be combined with data from other users. *Reputation services* were developed because signature-based scanners can no longer reliably detect new malware. Since signatures can only be generated after malware has already been distributed, there is always a critical period of time during which file scanners cannot detect the new samples. Reputation services are designed to remediate this challenge. The basic idea is that malware differs from legitimate files such as operating system drivers in that they are much rarer and newer. Therefore, in order to check whether a file is benign reputation services transfer the hash and the name of the file to a central database. It checks whether the hash is known to be benign (because it is listed as belonging to a legitimate software) or known malicious (because the file was already classified as malware). If the hash is unknown, it is checked how prevalent it is, and a reputation value is calculated. This ranges usually on a scale from -100 to 100, where the maximum value means that the file is known to be legitimate and the minimum value is given for known malware samples. The values in between are scaled based on the prevalence and age of the hash. If the calculated reputation value is below a threshold value, the user receives a warning or the security product automatically blocks the file. In any case, the data that the client has submitted is permanently stored in order to update the prevalence of the file.

Reputation can also be calculated for Internet addresses. If an endpoint attempts to access a URL, some reputation service products submit the URL, together with information on whether the Internet connection was initiated by a browser, a mail program, or a document viewer. Information about the application that opened the network connection can only be collected from products installed on the endpoints. If the reputation software runs centrally on the network perimeter, it can transmit only Internet addresses, ports, and a few meta-data such as the number of bytes transferred.

Products for Mail Servers Very rich telemetry data is generated by security products designed for mail servers. Several vendors offer solutions that automatically open mail attachments in dedicated sandboxes (see Chap. 3) and check whether any malicious actions are executed. If a mail attachment is detected as malicious, the sender, subject line, attachment name and hash can be sent to the vendor's database. The sandbox may even provide the complete analysis report, including the C&C addresses accessed by the malware, files created, and changes made on the system like registry keys being added. Similar to file scanners, some product offer the functionality to submit the entire malicious mail attachment to the vendor.

Behavior-Based Products While sandboxes only transfer data about malicious files, behavior-based products collect information about processes and activity. Like reputation services these products have been designed to overcome the weaknesses of signature-based approaches and attempt to detect attacker activity based on system behavior. For example, they may check whether a newly spawned process injects itself into the memory of another process, or whether unknown programs start PowerShell scripts. Put somewhat simplified they collect information from a normal computer as if it was a sandbox.

It is obvious that telemetry concerns privacy. Especially in Europe, and even more so in Germany, many users deactivate any functionality that is regarded as "phoning home". This hamstrings security approaches like reputation services. Therefore, some vendors offer special solutions to large companies at extra cost. With these "on-premise" installations the data is not transferred to the vendor's central database, but to databases operated by the customer. The vendor ensures that these on-premise databases are supplied with up-to-date information that is also available to other customers. This way, customers that pay extra can avoid the collection of telemetry while enjoying the security benefit of the product. Needless to say, this does not scale well. The more customers refrain from submitting telemetry, the worse is the reputation data.

Some security companies use telemetry data not only to improve the detection performance of their products. Instead, they process and enrich the data and sell it as Threat Intelligence. For example, C&C addresses obtained from customer sandboxes may be offered to other customers as blacklists or indicators of compromise. This way, customers can combine the information of several security companies without having to install different software products.

The quality of telemetry data also depends on the prevention strategy that the vendor pursues with its security products. For example, from a performance point of view it makes sense to cover several malware families with a single detection rule, if possible. For telemetry, however, this means that these different families cannot be differentiated anymore. And for security products for mail servers it may be effective to refuse mails if they originate from a sender address known to be malicious. But if spearphishing mails are refused before they are even sent, it is not possible to analyze the malicious attachments and collect additional information like the control servers of the malware. Therefore, there is a trade-off between the quality of telemetry data and the performance and prevention quality of the products.

7.3   Use-Cases for Telemetry Data

The main purpose of telemetry is not attribution, but to optimize the detection performance of security products. Given that approximately 390,000 new samples are distributed on the Internet every day, security companies must prioritize the malware families for which they develop signatures and detection methods. Telemetry was introduced for this purpose, as it provides information on how prevalent a malware family is, whether its usage is increasing, and in which regions and sector it is encountered (cf. [1] for a presentation from a vendor's perspective).

Also, many vendors of security software publish regular situation reports. An established part of these reports are statistics about the most common malware families and its regional distribution (e.g. [2–4]).

In the attribution process, telemetry data is useful in all analysis steps. However, they are most often used in the initial stages of attribution.

Prevalence The prevalence of a malware family can already give clues as to whether it belongs to a targeted or an untargeted criminal campaign. In the former case, significantly fewer people are affected and the infections are spread over fewer sectors or regions than in the latter case.

Regions and Sectors Telemetry can also provide input for the cui bono aspect of attribution, by giving an overview over the countries and sectors that the actors are targeting. Unfortunately, telemetry is always subject to certain limitations regarding its coverage and representativeness. For example, most vendors do not have a globally evenly distributed market share, but have different visibility in different countries and industries (see Sect. 3.2). This is commonly referred to as the collection bias, as it can lead to unexperienced analysts drawing wrong conclusions. The proportion of users who have activated the transmission of data also varies regionally depending on the awareness and appreciation of data privacy. And certain sectors such as government institutions and strongly regulated sectors also tend to be reluctant to transmit data to vendors. Also, analysts need to keep in mind that those telemetry types that are based on signatures will only yield insights into malware families and TTPs that are already known.

Reputation Reputation services can even generate data about malware that is not yet detected as being malicious, e.g. for lack of signatures. Every file that is written on a customer's computer is checked against the security company's databases. Even if it is not (yet) considered malicious, the associated telemetry data is stored. Analysts take advantage of this when they discover a new family of malware that has been used undetected for a long time. Provided that the attackers do not modify the samples' hash sum each time, analysts can check their reputation databases to assess where and when the malware has already been seen. This was how the spreading of the wormable NotPetya was investigated in 2017. This malware masqueraded as criminal ransomware and caused production downtimes in dozens of companies worldwide. Yet, analysts figured that NotPetya was not ransomware but a sabotage tool of a state-sponsored group. Real ransomware contains decryption routines so that the files of blackmailed victims can be restored once the ransom is paid. But NotPetya lacked such decryption routines. If it was in fact a sabotage tool, analysts needed to understand the motivation and targeting strategy of the attackers. Although the malware was not detected by security products in its early days, the reputation databases showed that the first infections occurred in the Ukraine—a country that had already been hit by targeted cyber-sabotage attacks in 2015 and 2016. Telemetry data also helped to identify the attack vector. It was initially unknown how NotPetya got onto the first victim machines, as no spearphishing emails or web-based exploits were found. Analysis of reputation data showed that the malware first appeared on systems that also contained files of the Ukrainian tax software M.E.Doc. This information allowed security researchers to find out that the perpetrators had added the malware to the installation archives of M.E.Doc. Based on these findings analysts concluded that the attackers had first and foremost targeted Ukrainian victims. The cui bono gave rise to the hypothesis that Russian actors were behind this campaign. This assessment was corroborated by publicly statements of the US and UK governments [5].

Co-occurrence Telemetry can be useful to analyze which malicious files are detected on the same machine. This can be droppers, downloaders, backdoors, and other tools. Assuming that they were placed there by the same attackers (cf. Sect. 2.5), the corresponding intrusion set can be enriched. WannaCry was another ransomware that caused havoc worldwide in 2017. Reputation data analysis showed that the first infections occurred on systems that had previously been compromised with backdoors from Lazarus, a likely state-sponsored North Korean group [6]. Subsequent investigations revealed that WannaCry had many code similarities with these backdoors. Within a few days after discovery of the first WannaCry samples, the attribution hypothesis was that members of the Lazarus group developed the ransomware as part of their self-financing (cf. Chap. 6): After they had installed backdoors on victims' computers for their espionage activity, they may have used WannaCry to supplement their finances [7]. The FBI came to the same conclusion [8]. This course of action is now included as a TTP in some intrusion set definitions for the Lazarus group.

Command Lines Feedback from behavior-based security products provides further insights into how attackers work. For example, some products collect the command line commands and even entire PowerShell scripts that the culprits execute on compromised machines. Since APT groups increasingly refrain from using malware and instead rely on legitimate tools like PowerShell, telemetry data about command lines becomes even more valuable. Just as incidents were clustered together because they involved the same malware families, now analysts can cluster them based on similar PowerShell commands. And just like malware usually contains C&C addresses, scripts and command lines contain URLs for downloading additional tools from control servers, that can be used as IoCs.

Malicious Mails Security products for mail servers provide similarly comprehensive data as behavior-based solutions. The meta-data of malicious mails can be queried, including sender email addresses, subject lines, attachment names, attachment hashes, and the names of the signatures that were triggered by the email. The real power of most telemetry data is that it can be correlated with other sources like samples from VirusTotal, log data from incident response cases, and telemetry from other product types. An illustrative use-case is that an analyst finds an exploit document on VirusTotal but lacks context, because the document was uploaded without the accompanying email. Since the same exploit document is usually sent to several targets, the analyst can try to search for the hash or even file name in the telemetry data. If an instance of the security product has been hit with that document, the analyst will find the meta-data of the malicious email that had the document attached. The sender addresses and the mail server can be used to compare the attack with other campaigns of the attackers. This not only further enriches the intrusion set, but also makes it possible to investigate in which industries and regions the attacks were carried out (see Chap. 6).

Timestamps Telemetry, especially that from behavior-based products, is very similar in form and quantity to log files that are collected during incident-handling on-site. For example, the timestamps of C&C connections provide clues about the perpetrators' working hours (see Chap. 5). It is important to distinguish between connections that the malware establishes itself automatically and those that result from manual interaction by the perpetrators. Examples for manual activity is establishing RDP connections, or executing commands on the command line, such as searching for document types or keywords. The exfiltration of data is also a manual process that provides information about the working hours of the attackers. In addition to network connections, it is also possible to collect the timestamps when the tools for lateral movement were written to disk—because this initiates requests to the reputation service. Timestamps from telemetry are very robust against attempts to forge them.

Samples Meta data is useful for analysis and correlation, but for generating new detection signatures, the samples of new malware are necessary. Therefore, many security products have the functionality to upload files from a customer computer if it was flagged as malicious (cf. e.g. [9]). The exact safeguards for this vary greatly from vendor to vendor. But for the detection quality this functionality is essential. From an attribution perspective the submitted samples feed into the collection phase in the 4 C model (cf. Sect. 2.4).

Intent Experienced analysts may even be able to deduce the intention of the perpetrators. Which systems did they attack first during lateral movement? Are they looking for databases or rather for mail servers? In the former case they are likely more interested in fundamental business data, in the latter they are more interested in current activities of the target. Are exfiltration archives created on development computers? Or on the file server? To answer such questions, analysts use the reputation data in a creative way that was not intended originally. Although there is usually no function in security products that explicitly queries the purpose of a system or the software installed on it, for each file on the system a reputation query was submitted, including the file name and hash. Thus, the vendor's database contains data about which executables, system drivers, and libraries are present on the system. By comparing hashes and file names to the known components of legitimate software, the analyst can determine whether the system runs database programs, banking software, office products, development environments, control systems, etc. Particularly unusual software can even betray the customer's industry, even if the customer has not or not accurately self-categorized itself. For instance, files of a software for X-ray systems are just as revealing as those for a tax consultancy software.

Telemetrybution—The Attacker as Customer The jackpot for attribution is if the perpetrators have installed a security product with activated telemetry on their own development or operator machines. According to some sources, the number of such cases has increased during the last years—in different countries and with APT groups of low to average sophistication. It is unclear what the reason is. Hypotheses range from attackers being afraid of being hacked by other groups, to testing samples for detection. In any case, each time the developers compile a new sample or operators save a new malware to their computer, the security software transmits hash and file name. To be more precise, this happens only if a file scanner type of software is equipped with a corresponding signature or if there is a reputation service installed on the machine. Up to now, security companies rarely detailed these cases publicly, because they did not want to inform the perpetrators. Yet, in 2019 it became public how analysts of Kaspersky Labs were able to identify the Uzbekistan's State Security Service (SSS) as being the likely actor behind activity of the group SandCat [9]. Employees of the intelligence service allegedly tested malware that they planned to use for operations by uploading them to VirusTotal. The analysts of Kaspersky Labs stumbled across those samples, generated detection signatures, and deployed them in their customer installations. They then noticed that all samples of this family were detected on a number of machines in the same IP range before they were used to target victims. This range was assigned to an organization with the unit designator "Military Unit 02616". Open Source analysis revealed this to be part of the SSS [9]. The case turned out to be an even bigger jackpot, as the SSS allegedly purchased the malware and exploits from an international contractor. With the insights collected from the SSS, Kaspersky Labs was able to track also the activities of other customers of that malware contractor.

For scenarios like this, the term *telemetrybution* was coined - attribution via telemetry. Findings based on it are regarded as high confidence evidence. Why are IP addresses in these scenarios reliable? How are they different from IPs of RDP connections that attackers obfuscate via C&C layers or VPNs? This is because developer machines are usually not used for conducting operations, so they do not run VPN software continuously. The security product may even ignore connections by some software products like TOR if TOR is configured to work only in a browser. And for sophisticated actors that are aware of telemetry, planting false flags by hacking other computers and placing malware there would have the drawback that the malware would then be known to the infosec community.

Apart from yielding source IPs directly from the attacker machines, telemetrybution provides detailed insights into their working habits. How dynamic is the perpetrators' development process? Are new samples generated several times a day? Or only at intervals of several weeks? Are version numbers specified in directory names, and how do the version numbers progress? Monitoring a developer machine is particularly useful if several malicious programs are developed on the same computer or if the perpetrator tests additional tools. This way the group's arsenal can be documented.

Still, telemetrybution is a rare situation. The vast majority of telemetry records is collected from benign machines, some of them affected by malware. But in general, telemetry data has the great advantage that perpetrators can hardly avoid it on the targeted machines. While attackers can practice good OpSec to prevent evidence from being left behind in malware or during registering C&C domains, telemetry is not based on the perpetrators' mistakes, but part of the target's environment. The biggest drawback of this technology, however, is that interesting data is often lost in the vast amounts of data, so that it never gets analyzed.

7.4   Overview of Relevant Information Types

Figure 7.1 lists typical types of information that can be analyzed in the aspect telemetry.

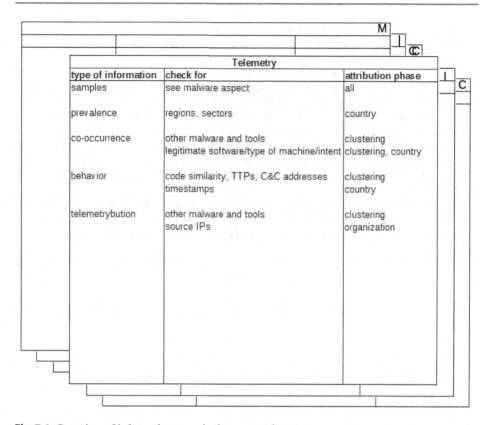

Fig. 7.1 Overview of information types in the aspect telemetry

References

1. Microsoft: Using Windows Defender telemetry to help mitigate malware attacks. In: MIcrosoft IT Showcase (2016). http://web.archive.org/web/20170901145212/https://www.microsoft.com/itshowcase/Article/Content/782/Using-Windows-Defender-telemetry-to-help-mitigate-malware-attacks. Accessed 1 Sept 2017
2. Symantec: Monatsbericht. In: Security Response-Veröffentlichungen. https://www.symantec.com/de/de/security_response/publications/monthlythreatreport.jsp. Accessed 3 Sept 2017
3. Gudkova, D., Vergelis, M., Demidova, N. and Shcherbakova, T.: Spam im Jahr 2016. In: Securelist (2017). https://de.securelist.com/kaspersky-security-bulletin-spam-and-phishing-in-2016/72383/. Accessed 3 Sept 2017
4. McAfee: McAfee Labs threats-report April 2017. In: McAfee Reports. https://www.mcafee.com/de/resources/reports/rp-quarterly-threats-mar-2017.pdf. Accessed 3 Sept 2017

5. Marsh, S.: US joins UK in blaming Russia for NotPetya cyber-attack. In: The Guardian (2017). https://www.theguardian.com/technology/2018/feb/15/uk-blames-russia-notpetya-cyber-attack-ukraine. Accessed 26 Dec 2019

6. Symantec Security Response: WannaCry-Ransomware attacks show strong links to Lazarus group. In: Symantec Offical Blog (2017). https://www.symantec.com/connect/blogs/wannacry-ransomware-attacks-show-strong-links-lazarus-group. Accessed 3 Sept 2017

7. Insikt Group: North Korea is not crazy. In: The RecordedFuture Blog (2017). http://web.archive.org/web/20170817185506/https://www.recordedfuture.com/north-korea-cyber-activity/. Accessed 2 Sept 2017

8. United States District Court for the Central District of California: United States of America v. Park Jin Hyok (2018). https://www.justice.gov/opa/press-release/file/1092091/download. Accessed 10 Dec 2019

9. Zetter, K.: Researchers say they uncovered Uzbekistan hacking operations due to spectacularly bad OPSEC. In: Motherboard (2019). https://www.vice.com/amp/en_us/article/3kx5y3/uzbekistan-hacking-operations-uncovered-due-to-spectacularly-bad-opsec. Accessed 28 Dec 2019

Methods of Intelligence Agencies

Much of the publicly available information about attribution methods and concrete cases originates from reports by security companies. Still, attribution statements by government agencies generate much more attention and are regarded as more reliable. Therefore it is worthwhile to examine what methods are available to intelligence agencies and whether they can provide a more complete picture than those of security companies. In this chapter, public sources are used to gain insights into the attribution methods of intelligence services.

8.1 Attacker Perspective: Countering Counter-Intelligence

The day-to-day work of APT groups requires a certain set of OpSec methods in order to stay under the radar of IT-security companies. Protecting against intelligence services takes fundamentally different techniques, though. The major concerns in this regard are being surveilled physically, associates being recruited by a foreign agency, or cyber-activity being monitored by passive or active eavesdropping.

How well APT groups can protect themselves against surveillance depends on their training and on their work situation. It can be assumed that hackers who work directly for a well-organized intelligence service receive a similar training as other employees of the agency. From their point of view, this serves the purpose of counter-intelligence. In the cyber-domain, this—of course—includes basic OpSec measures to hide one's own network addresses by anonymization services and several layers of control servers. Other OpSec rules may include using services such as WhoisGuard or DomainsByProxy to register C&C domains. The top-tier organizations provide extensive instructions for malware developers and operators, as illustrated by the Vault 7 leaks [1]. However, not all intelligence services are as professionally organized as the authors of the Vault 7 manuals.

In addition to OpSec in the cyber-domain, employees of intelligence services also receive training to protect themselves against recruitment or blackmail attempts by foreign

© Springer-Verlag GmbH Germany, part of Springer Nature 2020
T. Steffens, *Attribution of Advanced Persistent Threats*,
https://doi.org/10.1007/978-3-662-61313-9_8

agents [2]. This includes avoiding compromising situations and recognizing and countering recruitment attempts in the early stages. In Anglo-Saxon countries the acronym MICE has been coined for the basic motivations that can be exploited for recruitment: money, ideology, coercion, and ego [2]. There are also instructions for trips to foreign countries, in order to avoid being recruited or coerced while being abroad. Some members of APT groups may not even be allowed to leave their own country for the duration of their participation in cyber-operations.

Even more opaque, but likely more diverse, is how contractors, the so-called cyber-mercenaries, are trained in OpSec and counter-intelligence. Surprisingly, among the APT groups attributed as likely Chinese, those that are regarded as mercenaries are often known for very good OpSec in the cyber-domain. An example of this is the already cited group HiddenLynx [3]. Also the researcher Peter Mattis notes that the contractors allegedly hired by the MSS show particularly high OpSec postures [4]. One possible explanation is that mercenary groups are made up of people who taught themselves how to hack, were members of underground-forums, and honed their skills by staying under the radar of the authorities. It is unlikely though that the good OpSec posture from the cyber-domain extends to the physical aspects like recruiting or wiretapping.

Irrespective of the training in OpSec, working conditions are a crucial aspect of how vulnerable attackers are to foreign intelligence services. Dissatisfaction and overwork makes people more vulnerable to recruitment attempts via money or the attention and recognition of intelligence officers. In a (now deleted) online diary (the authenticity of which could never be established beyond doubt) a self-styled PLA hacker described his dissatisfaction very vividly. He complained about monotonous work, long working hours, and poor pay. According to the diary, the many hours of overtime made him isolated and lonely in his private life. These statements are at least in parts in contrast with the analysis of PwC who suggest that the presumably Chinese group APT10 does not work long overtime hours [5]. What is more, activity was only observed on weekdays from 8 to 18 o'clock with a two-hour lunch break. However, this contrast may be due to the fact that the lonely hacker claimed to work for the PLA, while APT10 is believed to be a group of contractors. It must therefore be assumed that the working conditions of groups from the same country can be very different. Ironically, the accepted lore among infosec analysts is that it is hackers-for-hire who work long into the night.

Military units and intelligence services conducting cyber espionage must take into account that their office buildings are under surveillance by foreign spies. For example, the security company Mandiant was apparently able to identify the office tower of APT1 in Shanghai [6]. By regularly commuting to these buildings, the risk of employees being identified as such is high. According to public statements by the Taiwanese secret service, another Chinese APT group therefore disguises itself by working on the campus of the University of Wuhan [7].

Of course, hackers being recruited as moles by enemy intelligence services is very unlikely. Much more relevant is the danger that their electronic communications are intercepted. This applies both to the C&C traffic of their malware and to their routine communication with clients or other units. An important basic OpSec rule here is that work infrastructure is not used for private purposes. As we have discussed in Chap. 5, using a wiretapped control server for private browsing can lead to disclosing the attacker's identity. The documented cases of members of even sophisticated APT groups using C&C infrastructure to visit social networks shows that these rules are not followed, or the control servers are regarded as secure. This is not the only OpSec rule that traditional intelligence services regard as fundamental and that most APT groups ignore nevertheless: Compartmentalization requires secret operations being planned and conducted in isolation from each other. If an operation is blown, this must not affect other operations. Yet, cyber-espionage operations are typically very strongly intertwined. If a security company discovers a malware being used against a target, it can usually develop detection mechanisms that will also thwart the attacks against other targets. This holds true even for the most professional campaigns that were allegedly carried out by Western intelligence agencies: When the telecommunications company Belgacom was targeted with Regin and when Russian agencies were compromised with RemSec the attackers only took care to isolate the infrastructure, by using victim-specific C&Cs. But they reused the same malware families in different operations [8, 9].

The reason for this violation of traditional OpSec rules is that developing espionage software is time-consuming, costly, and requires personnel with a certain skill-set. So not even well-funded intelligence agencies can afford to use a new malware family for each target. Even setting up target-specific control servers has been observed with only few groups. Granted, not all APT groups are directly embedded in intelligence services and might not be familiar with OpSec rules from the traditional tradecraft. For example, APT1 apparently was a unit in the military and not an intelligence service. Similarly, HangOver and Hidden Lynx are believed to be contractors (see Chap. 3). But APT28, which several governments claim to be part of the military intelligence service GRU, are known to use the same control servers against a variety of targets over a long period of time.

All these observations suggest that in many countries the cyber-espionage departments are not well integrated with the traditional intelligence departments, and are thus lacking decade-long experience with OpSec, camouflage, and plausible deniability.

Often this carelessness by APT groups is explained by the fact that they do not have to fear consequences because their governments will protect them from prosecution. Yet, they do not only lack OpSec against attribution, but also OpSec against detection and tracking by IT-security measures. For instance, the lack of separation between espionage operations does have very practical consequences; entire malware arsenals, infrastructures, and campaigns get unearthed and publicly disclosed. The large number of APT reports by security companies is proof of this. So the lack of basic OpSec in many APT groups is still surprising.

A particular challenge for the sponsors of APT groups in non-democratic countries is the danger of defectors. The greater the dissatisfaction with the political and economic situation, the greater the probability that persons with operational insight will use their information to seek asylum in other countries. While a number of cases from the Cold War are now publicly documented, publicly known examples from the cyber-domain are the exception. This is due to the fact that such cases are usually disclosed long after the fact—when defectors or intelligence officers share their experiences in interviews or books once they do not fear consequences for disclosure. Cyber-espionage is still too new and recent from the perspective of laws for handling confidential information. Nevertheless, defectors from Iran and North Korea have written about their insights into offensive cyber-programs. After his flight to South Korea a professor from Pyongyang reported that several of his computer science students were employed by Unit 180 of the Reconnaissance General Bureau (RGB) to procure foreign currency through cyber-operations [10]. The RGB is regarded as the main sponsor of North Korean cyber-espionage by analysts and American military personnel [11]. Lazarus was not explicitly mentioned by the professor, but their cyber-heists against international banks and the afore-mentioned links to Pyongyang come to mind. Much more nebulous is the case of the Iranian officer Mohammad Hussein Tajik. According to statements by a regime-critical journalist who was in contact with him, Tajik had been involved in setting up a center for cyber-espionage. After a while he had contemplated the idea of leaving Iran—it was unclear whether he wanted to disclose his knowledge abroad. He was arrested and died under unknown circumstances a few days before sentencing [12]. The journalist stresses that Tajik's death occurred shortly after the Iranian Supreme Religious Leader Ali Khamenei—one of the two major fiefdoms in Iran—had promised a pardon.

Another mysterious case in Iran may have involved a defector or a disgruntled insider. In 2019 a series of leaks provided detailed information about tools, infrastructure, and victims of the likely Iranian group OilRig [13]. The anonymous persons behind the leaks even claimed that the group worked for the Ministry of Intelligence (MOIS). The level of detail and nature of documents gave rise to the hypothesis that the leaker was a former member of the group [13]. Alternative hypotheses are that a foreign intelligence service hacked OilRig networks, or that the leaks were part of a turf war between the IRGC and MOIS. In any case, the effects for OilRig and MOIS were immense, both in terms of operational impact and reputation inside the Iranian hacker community.

8.2   OSINT—Open Source Intelligence

According to the former US National Security Advisor Michael Flynn, 90% of intelligence comes from open source. Only the remaining 10% are based on clandestine work [14]. While this statement was not explicitly about attribution or even the cyber-domain, it does document that intelligence agencies incorporate Open Source Intelligence (OSINT) into their assessments. While this type of information is available to anyone, intelligence services collect and analyze OSINT in a very structured and comprehensive manner. In comparison to Threat Intelligence vendors, government agencies do OSINT also irrespective of the cyber-domain and attribution. They systematically monitor foreign newspapers, television stations and websites, statements and announcements of politicians and officials worldwide.

This information is aggregated into situation assessments about regions, topics, and forthcoming events. For attribution, analysts can profit from this expertise in various specialist departments who are continuously on top of current events and situations.

All other information gathering methods are based indirectly on public information. OSINT can be used to identify which additional information is needed or in which areas there is an information gap. For example, most intelligence services seem to have been surprised by the detonation of a suspected hydrogen bomb in North Korea in September 2017 and only learned about it from public reports. It is safe to assume that these OSINT findings led to increased poring over satellite data and to intensified communication with human sources in the region.

In contrast to scientists and journalists who conduct geopolitical analysis (see Chap. 6), intelligence services have the advantage that they can complement public information with insights from confidential sources. Assume for example, that a conversation between foreign officials working in an agency with offensive cyber-capabilities is intercepted. If the officials vaguely mention that a contract is going to be awarded to a certain company, this can guide the collection of relevant OSINT. While company websites or their annual reports are usually overlooked in the vast amounts of available data, such confidential information can be the starting point to investigate current activities of the company. In the context of cyber-operations, analysts may start to check which skills have been listed in the company's job advertisements, whether the website lists services such as penetration testing or suspicious software development, and which tenders for government projects the company has won.

8.3   General Signals Intelligence—SIGINT

A unique capability of intelligence services compared to IT-security companies is to intercept electronic signals and Internet traffic. This method and the information it provides is called SIGINT (Signals Intelligence). SIGINT is much older than cyber-espionage and therefore not limited to the analysis of C&C traffic or other cyber-related activities. Instead, its original and still predominant purpose is reconnaissance in foreign countries via intercepting communication between persons of interest. Also domestic intelligence services can benefit for counter-espionage.

Findings obtained from SIGINT are classified as secret by default, as it might be possible to deduce how they were obtained and where interception equipment has been placed.

Therefore, it has not been publicly disclosed by what means US intelligence services have identified the GRU officials who allegedly directed the cyber-operations against the Democratic Party in 2016. While media reports suggest that the CIA had an informant close to Putin [15], it is possible that the operational details about GRU employees come from intercepted messages (or implants on smartphones) [16].

Another case is documented in an indictment against a Chinese citizen arrested in the USA. The investigators cite emails which the defendant allegedly exchanged with a client

[17]. These messages indicate that the hacker named 'GoldSun' obtained the malware Sakurel for his clients, compromised computers of several American companies, and stole defence-related data. Again, the details of how the US authorities got hold of the emails are not public. They may have been subpoenaed from email providers by law enforcement requests, or they may come from seized computers or from SIGINT. Since the Chinese citizen was arrested in the USA, it is likely that investigators forensically analyzed his smartphone, though.

Similarly, another indictment against another Chinese citizen who lived in Canada and is said to have exfiltrated confidential data from Boeing lists emails [18]. The quoted messages indicate that the defendant used an unnamed malware to identify which documents were on the victim's computer. He created lists of document names and sent them to his client. From these lists, the client selected the documents that he was interested in. These emails may have come from SIGINT.

It is noteworthy that even persons allegedly working for the Chinese foreign intelligence agency MSS used unencrypted communication to task their agents according to an US indictment [19].

Because intelligence services do not allow classified SIGINT to be used in quasi-public court proceedings, such findings are generally only used as starting points for law enforcement. The investigators then need to conduct 'parallel construction', meaning that SIGINT findings that have been used to identify a culprit are corroborated and then replaced by other (non-classified) investigation methods. This is often possible because classical police investigations can turn up substantial evidence once the perpetrator has been identified with a high degree of confidence. Only these traditional police investigation methods are then listed in the indictment. In the context of the DNC hack, the then White House press secretary, Josh Earnest, put it this way: 'And some of that evidence may not be something we want to show' [20]. While this decision is comprehensible, the vague documentation about sources and methods may undermine the credibility of indictments and attribution statements in general. Parallel construction needs to provide concrete, verifiable evidence, so that judges and the public will be convinced.

8.4   SIGINT About Cyber-Activity

Since the former NSA employee Edward Snowden had disclosed documents about the agency's vast SIGINT programmes, SIGINT is often connotated with the concept of mass surveillance. Yet, SIGINT can be used in a very targeted manner and specifically for the purpose of attribution. One of the documents published by Snowden shows that in some cases the NSA analysts monitored the activities of APT groups in real-time. Apparently they were able to filter and trace unencrypted C&C traffic and interactive RDP connections of the attackers. This is similar to Mandiant's approach for capturing the C&C traffic of APT1 (see Chap. 2). The difference is that—according to the Snowden documents—intelligence services like the NSA do not need to contact hosters to wiretap individual control servers. Instead, they monitor undersea cables and Internet exchange points (IX or IXP) where large amounts of Internet traffic converge [21]. With this level of access, intelligence services only need an IP address that was observed during an attack as a starting point (see [22]). The Internet traffic can then be filtered for connections from or to this IP address, revealing the attackers' infrastructure, victims, and origin. The challenge is to get and maintain access to enough trunk lines and IXPs. Traffic can only be monitored if it runs through a so-called listening post. It is safe to assume that only a few intelligence agencies have a visibility as comprehensive as described in the Snowden documents.

The importance of increasing the number of monitored networks is evidenced by the activities of Western intelligence services to compromise telecommunication providers—according to Snowden. The operation to compromise the Belgian telecommunications company Belgacom was referred to as *Operation Socialist* in leaked secret documents. According to a slide of the British intelligence agency GCHQ, the purpose of this operation was to gain access to mobile phone traffic in the network of the operator [23]. The intelligence agency allegedly used the malware Regin [24]. Attacks with the same backdoor against another GSM operator in Asia may have served a similar purpose [25]. German telecommunications providers were reported to be targets, too: Stellar provides Internet connectivity via satellite to customers in remote areas such as Africa, and was allegedly hacked by GCHQ [26]. These operations illustrate that access to undersea cables is not sufficient for visibility, as these do not carry local and satellite traffic. Thus, compromising regional providers such as Belgacom or satellite Internet operators such as Stellar is necessary to maximize SIGINT capabilities.

Not all Internet connections that are relevant for attribution can be detected automatically. An example is the case of Snake operators accessing their social networks via C&C servers (cf. Chap. 5). In the Snowden documents, Canadian intelligence analysts who were investigating a Snake campaign at the time explained their approach. They note that OpSec mistakes cannot be detected by signatures like C&C traffic. Lists of domains and IPs of sites that are candidates of divulging private data will never be complete, because the perpetrators can enter their billing address or credit card numbers at any small online store. Also content is hard to analyze automatically, as it may consist of photos, natural language, or alternative account names. Therefore, the connections to control servers must be manually checked for anomalies [27]. More precisely, the Canadians did not explicitly refer to control servers, but 'less attributable infrastructure', i.e. infrastructure that was particularly well camouflaged (in this case by satellite connections) and could only be assigned to Snake with some effort. It were such servers that intelligence analysts focused their attention on for manual analysis. This paid off, because they identified an unexpected anomaly in the network traffic: A development computer of the perpetrators was infected with a run-of-the-mill malware called Gumblar. This malware has keylogger functionalities and transmits this data to its own (Gumblar) control server. Since it uses the default Internet connection, the data was transmitted over the satellite connection via the (Snake) control server, which was monitored by the Canadian intelligence service. This way the analysts recorded the username and password for a LiveJournal account. The partially redacted slides do not mention whether this account provided information that helped to identify the perpetrator, though [27].

The NSA also conducts *4th party collection*. This involves monitoring C&C traffic of foreign APT groups and collecting the data that they exfiltrate. In a presentation contained in the Snowden leak, TAO employees reveal that they were able to collect documents that a Chinese group had stolen from the United Nations. These documents were so substantial that they resulted in three analysis reports disseminated to NSA clients [28].

For completeness' sake, it should be noted that 4th party collection does not necessarily require SIGINT. The IT-security company Symantec found evidence that Snake may have hacked the infrastructure of the likely Iranian group OilRig [29]. Apparently, Snake operators exploited vulnerabilities in the C&C panel of the PoisonFrog backdoor in order to get access to the victim network.

In another case, SIGINT apparently facilitated the attribution of cyber-incidents to the Democratic Party of Kurdistan. This is noteworthy, as IT-security companies have not yet reported any attacks of likely Kurdish origin. The NSA monitored C&C traffic from a family of keyloggers installed in Internet cafes in Iraq and Iran, as well as the Iraqi Ministry of Foreign Affairs. The exfiltrated keystroke data was sent to several email addresses under the control of the attackers. Through SIGINT, the NSA was able to observe how these mailboxes were accessed by computers apparently belonging to the Kurdish Democratic Party [30].

SIGINT is a powerful instrument for attribution if large parts of the Internet are covered. Unlike telemetry of security companies, it does not require software to be installed on end-points or customers opting into data transmission to the vendors. But it also has limitations: SIGINT is limited to network traffic. So it lacks information that is only available on the hard disks of computers and is not sent over the Internet. For example, installed samples and log data cannot be collected. Section 8.6 will explain which others methods intelligence services have to collect data from hard drives.

8.5   HUMINT—Human Intelligence

The President of the German counter-intelligence agency BfV Hans-Georg Maaßen talked about attribution methods in a panel at the 2017 annual meeting of the journalists' association 'Netzwerk Recherche'. According to him, analyzing technical artefacts will never result in a 100% certainty about the origin of an APT attack. Therefore, intelligence analysts assess the mission profiles of foreign intelligence services (see Chap. 6), and—according to Maaßen— the assessments of BfV were based on 'human sources of BND or foreign partners' [31] (author's translation).

Information from human sources is usually referred to as HUMINT (for Human Intelligence). From public sources it is hardly possible to assess the practical significance of HUMINT for attribution in comparison to SIGINT, since significantly fewer concrete cases are known that involved human sources. The protection of these sources has the highest priority, since they are difficult to obtain and their exposure can have serious consequences for the informants.

Generally, informants can be relevant for attribution in the following positions. Consumers of stolen data may be considered as sources that can be recruited with a realistic probability. If they work directly in an intelligence service, they are trained against recruitment attempts and are also embedded in strictly controlled work environments, though. Therefore, it is more feasible to recruit consumers who work in specialist agencies such as ministries of trade, foreign affairs or research. They do not have detailed information on how the information that was provided to them was obtained—due to the 'need-to-know' principle. But the attributing intelligence service can compare the information that is available to the consumer with that stolen in concrete cases. If they match and if other sources for this information are unlikely, there is a high probability that the information was sourced from APT groups.

Depending on how the APT group is organized, the feasibility of recruiting informants close to the perpetrators varies. If the group is directly integrated into an intelligence service, recruitment is significantly harder—as discussed above. But if the group has connections to the criminal underground, it is conceivable to recruit people who are in touch with the perpetrators. Potential candidates are other hackers who discuss attack techniques with the perpetrators in forums or even supply tools to the APT group. In China, for example, the personality cult around hackers often makes them interact with followers in forums [32]. For these actors, underground forums are part of their lifestyle, especially since many of them have acquired and honed their skills over the years in exactly these forums. For this reason, China has a huge online network of malware developers, criminals, counterfeiters and fences [33]. If an APT group is made up of (former) members of these forums, there is a high probability that the perpetrators will maintain contact with other hackers even during their APT jobs. So intelligence services do not necessarily target APT group members directly, but may try to recruit their contacts. Since many hackers only know each other online, it is also possible that intelligence service employees create their own covert persona in these forums and slowly gain the trust of relevant persons.

In countries whose intelligence services cooperate with universities for cyber-espionage, there are also opportunities for human informants. By their very nature, universities are not isolated institutions, but foster a constant exchange of students, scientists, and lecturers. Such environments are suitable for intelligence agencies to establish connections with informants. An example is the professor from North Korea, mentioned in Sect. 8.1, who was at least abstractly informed about the activities of Unit 180 by his graduates.

8.6   Offensive Cyber-Operations—Hacking Back

The drawback that SIGINT only covers network traffic and cannot collect so-called *data at rest* on machines, is compensated for by other methods. The NSA, for example, has a unit called Tailored Access Operations (TAO), whose job is to compromise computers and internal networks. By installing malware, also data-at-rest, i.e. data that is not sent over the Internet, can be collected. Although the main purpose of this team is likely espionage against foreign governments and terrorists, there are also indications that it supports attribution. This is ironic in that APT attacks are investigated by conducting APT attacks.

Often SIGINT provides the first starting points to identify targets for TAO. According to a slide from the Snowden leak, the NSA was able to trace back a network connection of a Chinese APT group called Byzantine Candor. Byzantine Candor is better known publicly as Titan Rain. The group is said to have stolen data from Lockheed Martin, NASA, and the US and British ministries of defense between 2003 and 2007 [34]. After tracing back a few hop-points, the NSA seems to have identified that the source IP address was assigned to a telecommunications provider but not to a specific customer or user. Therefore, the NSA operators compromised central routers of the provider and spread into the provider's internal network. Their goal was the database containing call records and billing data. Using these records the attackers' connection and source IP was linked to a customer—with the billing address of the 3PLA [28].

By analyzing the network connections that originated from the PLA network, the NSA was able to carry out one of its dreaded man-in-the-middle attacks [28]. These attacks are based on the idea that by having access to Internet routers, one can not only intercept but also insert or modify network traffic. When a member of Byzantine Candor uploaded data from a victim system to his own computer, NSA operators inserted their own malicious code into the traffic. This way they installed a backdoor on a computer in the PLA network. Apparently its owner was the head of the APT group. His computer contained information about compromised victims, but also plans for future attacks, as well as the source code of Chinese RATs. Also personal data of the PLA officer was collected, such as photos, forum nicknames, and emails.

This is not an isolated incident. Richard Ledgett, then deputy director of the NSA, stated that his staff was able to observe Russian perpetrators conducting an operation against the US State Department. The Dutch intelligence service AIVD—a partner of the US agency—had allegedly compromised surveillance cameras in a building that was used by APT29 operators. The faces of people entering and leaving the building could be identified [35]. According to sources paraphrased in media articles, the APT29 operators worked for the Russian SVR. It is not known which malware was used by AIVD. The Russian news agency TASS reported in 2016 that the FSB had discovered a network compromise that affected more than 20 Russian authorities and defence companies [36]. Shortly after, security companies published analyses of the malware RemSec, which had been found mainly in Russia and Russian embassies [9]. A connection between the hacked surveillance cameras, the attacks uncovered by the FSB, and RemSec has not been confirmed. Still, these cases show that extensive attacks on Russian government agencies are taking place. It can therefore be assumed that other governments suspected of conducting APT attacks are also targets of cyber-espionage. Even though the original motivation is usually general intelligence gathering, it is likely that occasionally information is collected which can be used for attribution. These findings do not necessarily have to be as concrete as the images from hacked surveillance cameras. For instance, even data from finance departments can be relevant if payments to a company that develops exploits or malware can be found. Similarly, backdoors on computers in specialist agencies may be used to determine where stolen documents are disseminated.

Offensive cyber-operations, or hacking-back as it is sometimes referred to, does not necessarily involve compromising the internal networks of APT groups. Useful information can also be gained from hacking control servers. When Dragonfly used Havex to collect information from industrial control networks in 2014, their C&Cs seem to have been hacked [37]. The control panel that they used to monitor and operate their backdoors was modified by an unknown third party. A tracking pixel was included that reported the source IP of the Dragonfly operators each time they logged into the panel. This source IP can be used as a starting point for SIGINT or for tracking and seizing hop points. Also, the timestamps of the operator logins can provide information about their patterns-of-life (cf. Chap. 3).

8.7 Requests to Providers

In most jurisdictions some government agencies have the mandate to request customer data from digital service providers. In the US, agencies can submit demands made under the Foreign Intelligence, Surveillance Act (FISA) and through National Security Letters (NSLs). Depending on the type of service they provide, companies are obliged to hand over user data like emails, login histories, chat histories, billing addresses etc.

Attribution of cyber-activities are believed to make up only a fraction of the requests that many companies report annually in transparency reports. But requests to providers for email communication did play a relevant role in some indictments against APT groups. When investigating the alleged developer of the Sakula malware, GoldSun, US agencies seized email histories for accounts that were used to register C&C domains (cf. [38]). The seized accounts—some of them at Google Mail—also contained communication between group members in which they discussed the use of Adobe Flash zero-days and which C&C domains to use in operations against US companies. This way, analysts can identify the roles that different individuals have in an APT group: e.g. developer, infrastructure admin, operator, or manager. It should be noted that such details will only be found in emails if the group members are only loosely interconnected. In contrast, it is unlikely that the individuals listed in the APT28 indictment communicated via external email addresses (or emails at all), since they allegedly worked in the same GRU unit [39].

Other useful data from providers are login logs. In the indictment against an alleged Lazarus member, US agencies requested source IPs from Facebook [40]. The source IPs

Table 8.1 Organization types that conduct attribution, their data sources, and their capabilities that are used extensively (+) or occasionally (o)

Capability	Foreign intelligence	Domestic-intelligence	Security company
Telemetry			+
On-site forensics			+
Reverse engineering	o	o	+
C&C-server forensics		+	+
Infrastructure analysis	+	+	+
Geopolitical analysis	+	+	+
Forum monitoring	+	o	o
HUMINT, SIGINT	+	o	
Offensive cyber-operations	+		

had been used to log into fake profiles in order to send spear phishing messages to Sony employees. Most times, the connections originated from North Korean address ranges.

8.8   Organizations Conducting Attribution

The examples presented in this chapter illustrate which attribution methods are applicable for intelligence agencies in general. However, only very few countries are technically and financially capable of using all these methods. Especially the extensive Internet monitoring via SIGINT and hack-backs against APT groups are likely only feasible for a few intelligence services besides the Five Eyes.

And even the NSA cannot cover all methods related to attribution. For example, (for all we know) it does not have telemetry databases and the vast databases of malware samples that security companies have at their disposal. As a result, the agency likely has no information from the millions of endpoints connected to the Internet worldwide. Another difference to security companies is that vendors run specialized infrastructure to automatically process malware samples on a large scale as part of their business model. A side-product of these automated processes (whose main purpose is to create detection signatures and optimize the performance of security products) is that they also provide information that can identify correlations between attacks and can thus enrich intrusion sets.

Therefore, it is worth to compare the capabilities of security companies and intelligence agencies in general. Does one have a more complete view than the other? Table 8.1 lists the methods available to security companies, foreign and domestic intelligence services.

Contrary to common belief, intelligence agencies do not cover all methods that security companies have at their disposal. But the same is true vice versa, infosec analysts lack access

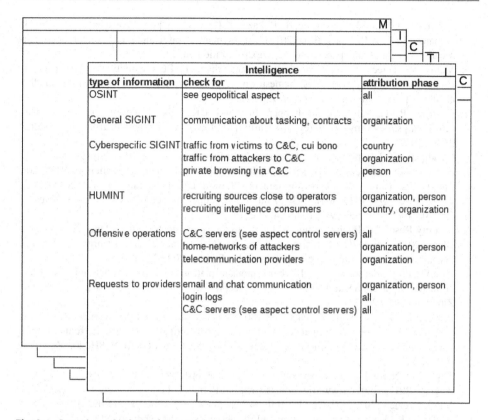

Fig. 8.1 Overview of information types in the aspect intelligence

to some data sources. The public and private sector can complement each other. So far, most of the public knowledge about APT groups has been provided by IT-security companies and their publications. Chapter 12 will examine in more detail under which circumstances and for which purposes the public sector can also communicate attribution findings publicly.

8.9   Overview of Relevant Information Types

Figure 8.1 lists typical types of information that can be analyzed in the aspect intelligence.

References

1. WikiLeaks: Development Tradecraft DOs and DON'Ts. In: Vault 7: CIA Hacking Tools Revealed (2017). http://web.archive.org/web/20170725092909/https://wikileaks.org/ciav7p1/cms/page_14587109.html. Zitiert am 25.7.2017
2. Petkus, D.A.: Ethics of human intelligence operations: of MICE and men. Int. J. Intell. Ethics 1(1) (2010)

3. Doherty, S., Gegeny, J., Spasojevic, B., Baltazar, J.: Hidden lynx-professional hackers for hire. In: Symantec Security Response Blog (2013). www.symantec.com/content/en/us/enterprise/media/security_response/whitepapers/hidden_lynx.pdf. Zitiert am 23.08.2017
4. Mattis, P.: Three scenarios for understanding changing PLA activity in cyberspace. In: China Brief **15**(23) (2015). https://jamestown.org/program/three-scenarios-for-understanding-changing-pla-activity-in-cyberspace/. Zitiert am 17.08.2017
5. Coopers, P.: Operation cloud hopper. In: PwC UK Cyber Security and Data Privacy (2017). https://www.pwc.co.uk/cyber-security/pdf/cloud-hopper-report-final-v4.pdf. Zitiert am 26.07.2017
6. Mandiant: APT1-Exposing One of China's Cyber Espionage Units (2013). https://www.fireeye.com/content/dam/fireeye-www/services/pdfs/mandiant-apt1-report.pdf. Zitiert am 21.07.2017
7. Tien-pin, L., Pan, J.: PLA cyberunit targeting Taiwan named. In: Taipei Times (2015). http://web.archive.org/web/20150311141017/http://www.taipeitimes.com/News/taiwan/archives/2015/03/10/2003613206. Zitiert am 04.09.2017
8. Security Response: Regin-top-tier espionage tool enables stealthy surveillance. In: Symantec Blog (2015). https://www.symantec.com/content/dam/symantec/docs/security-center/white-papers/regin-top-tier-espionage-tool-15-en.pdf. Zitiert am 09.09.2017
9. GReAT: ProjectSauron-top level cyber-espionage platform covertly extracts encrypted government comms. In: Securelist (2016). https://securelist.com/faq-the-projectsauron-apt/75533/. Zitiert am 09.09.2017
10. Park, J., Pearson, J.: North Korea's Unit 180, the cyber warfare cell that worries the West. In: Reuters (2017). http://uk.reuters.com/article/us-cyber-northkorea-exclusive/exclusive-north-koreas-unit-180-the-cyber-warfare-cell-that-worries-the-west-idUKKCN18H020. Zitiert am 09.09.2017
11. Tosi, S.J.: North Korean cyber support to combat operations. In: Military Review, July–August 2017. http://www.armyupress.army.mil/Portals/7/military-review/Archives/English/MilitaryReview_20170831_TOSI_North_Korean_Cyber.pdf. Zitiert am 11.09.2017
12. Al-Thani, R.: Khyber security station and the activities of the cyber armed forces of Iran. In: Al-Arabiya.net (2017). http://farsi.alarabiya.net/fa/iran/2017/01/15/%D9%82%D8%B1%D8%A7%D8%B1-%DA%AF%D8%A7%D9%87-%D8%A7%D9%85%D9%86%D9%8A%D8%AA%D9%89-%D8%AE%D9%8A%D8%A8%D8%B1-%D9%88-%D9%81%D8%B9%D8%A7%D9%84%D9%8A%D8%AA-%D9%87%D8%A7%D9%89-%D8%A7%D8%B1%D8%AA%D8%B4-%D8%B3%D8%A7%D9%8A%D8%A8%D8%B1%D9%89-%D8%A7%D9%8A%D8%B1%D8%A7%D9%86.html. Zitiert am 11.09.2017, Google-Übersetzung aus Farsi
13. Greenberg, A.: A mystery agent is Doxing Iran's hackers and dumping their code. In: Wired (2019). https://www.wired.com/story/iran-hackers-oilrig-read-my-lips/. Accessed 1 Jan 2020
14. Flynn, M.T., Pottinger, M., Batchelor, P.D.: Fixing intel-a blueprint for making intelligence relevant in Afghanistan. In: Voices from the Field (2010). https://online.wsj.com/public/resources/documents/AfghanistanMGFlynn_Jan2010.pdf. Accessed 1 Jan 2020
15. Sciutto, J.: US extracted top spy from inside Russia in 2017. In: CNN (2019). https://edition.cnn.com/2019/09/09/politics/russia-us-spy-extracted/index.html. Accessed 2 Jan 2020
16. Sanger, D.E.: Trump, mocking claim that Russia hacked election, at odds with G.O.P.. In: New York Times (2016). http://web.archive.org/web/20170831041630/https://www.nytimes.com/2016/12/10/us/politics/trump-mocking-claim-that-russia-hacked-election-at-odds-with-gop.html. Zitiert am 12.09.2017
17. United States District Court Southern District of California: Case 3:17-mj-02970-BGS. https://assets.documentcloud.org/documents/3955509/YuPinganComplaint.pdf. Zitiert am 12.09.2017
18. The US Department of Justice: Chinese National Pleads Guilty to Conspiring to Hack into U.S. Defense Contractors' Systems to Steal Sensitive Military Information. In: Justice News

(2016). http://web.archive.org/web/20160401055017/https://www.justice.gov/opa/pr/chinese-national-pleads-guilty-conspiring-hack-us-defense-contractors-systems-steal-sensitive. Zitiert am 12.09.2017

19. United States District Court Northern District of Illinois Eastern Division: United States of America v. Jichaoqun (2018). https://www.justice.gov/opa/press-release/file/1096411/download. Accessed 4 Jan 2020

20. Hosenball, M., Menn, J.: FBI trying to build legal cases against Russian hackers-sources. In: Reuters (2016). http://in.reuters.com/article/usa-cyber-russia/fbi-trying-to-build-legal-cases-against-russian-hackers-sources-idINKCN11M07U. Zitiert am 12.09.2017

21. Reissmann, O.: Flucht von Edward Snowden. In: Spiegel Online (2013). http://web.archive.org/web/20130626093238/http://www.spiegel.de/netzwelt/netzpolitik/edward-snowdens-flucht-rekonstruktion-a-907709.html. Accessed 13 Nov 2017

22. Greenwald, G., MacAskill, E.: Boundless informant: the NSA's secret tool to track global surveillance data. In: The Guardian (2013). http://web.archive.org/web/20130731051147/https://www.theguardian.com/world/2013/jun/08/nsa-boundless-informant-global-datamining. Accessed 13 Nov 2017

23. Spiegel Online: Britischer Geheimdienst hackte belgische Telefongesellschaft. In: Spiegel Online Netzwelt (2013). http://web.archive.org/web/20130921055633/http://www.spiegel.de/netzwelt/web/belgacom-geheimdienst-gchq-hackte-belgische-telefongesellschaft-a-923224.html. Accessed 12 Sept 2017

24. Marquis-Boire, M., Guarnieri, C., Gallagherm, R.: Secret malware in European union attack linked to U.S. and British intelligence. In: The Intercept (2014). http://web.archive.org/web/20170719231033/https://theintercept.com/2014/11/24/secret-regin-malware-belgacom-nsa-gchq/. Accessed 28 July 2017

25. GReAT: Regin-nation-state ownage of GSM networks. In: SecureList (2014). http://web.archive.org/web/20170802165138/https://securelist.com/regin-nation-state-ownage-of-gsm-networks/67741/. Accessed 10 Aug 2017

26. Spiegel Online: Ein deutsches Unternehmen erfährt, dass es gehackt wurde. In: Spiegel Online Netzwelt (2014). http://web.archive.org/web/20140915180305/http://www.spiegel.de/netzwelt/netzpolitik/stellar-gchq-hackte-rechnersystem-eines-deutschen-unternehmens-a-991486.html. Accessed 12 Sept 2017

27. Biddle, S.: White house says Russia's hackers are too good to be caught but NSA partner called them 'Morons'. In: The Intercept (2017). https://theintercept.com/2017/08/02/white-house-says-russias-hackers-are-too-good-to-be-caught-but-nsa-partner-called-them-morons/. Accessed 5 Aug 2017

28. NSA: Byzantine Hades-an evolution of collection. In: Spiegel Online (2015). http://web.archive.org/web/20150117190714/http://www.spiegel.de/media/media-35686.pdf. Accessed 14 Sept 2017

29. Symantec: Waterbug-Espionage group rolls out brand-new toolset in attacks against governments. In: Symantec Blogs (2019). https://www.symantec.com/blogs/threat-intelligence/waterbug-espionage-governments. Accessed 3 Jan 2020

30. NSA: '4th Party Collection': taking advantage of non-partner computer network exploitation activity. In: Spiegel Online (2015). http://www.spiegel.de/media/media-35680.pdf. Accessed 14 Sept 2017

31. Netzwerk Recherche: Hacker im Staatsauftrag (?)-Wie sie vorgehen und wie man sie enttarnen kann. In: YouTube (2017). https://www.youtube.com/watch?v=OfRb6hssfu8&feature=youtu.be. Zitiert am. Accessed 13 Sept 2017

32. Howlett, W.: The rise of China's hacking culture-defining Chinese hackers. Master's thesis. California State University (2016). http://scholarworks.lib.csusb.edu/cgi/viewcontent.cgi?article=1413&context=etd. Accessed 13 Sept 2017
33. Wong, E.: Hackers find China is land of opportunity. In: The New York Times (2013). http://www.nytimes.com/2013/05/23/world/asia/in-china-hacking-has-widespread-acceptance.html. Accessed 13 Sept 2017
34. Greenberg, A.: Cyberspies target silent victims. In: Forbes (2007). http://web.archive.org/web/20090929182530/https://www.forbes.com/2007/09/11/cyberspies-raytheon-lockheed-tech-cx_ag_0911cyberspies.html. Accessed 14 Sept 2017
35. Nakashima, E.: New details emerge about 2014 Russian hack of the State Department-It was 'hand to hand combat'. In: The Washington Post (2017). http://web.archive.org/web/20170912110914/https://www.washingtonpost.com/world/national-security/new-details-emerge-about-2014-russian-hack-of-the-state-department-it-was-hand-to-hand-combat/2017/04/03/d89168e0-124c-11e7-833c-503e1f6394c9_story.html. Zitiert am 12.09.2017
36. TASS: FSB finds cyber-spying virus in computer networks of 20 state authorities. In: TASS Russian Politics & Diplomacy (2016). http://web.archive.org/web/20170505015138/http://tass.com/politics/891681. Accessed 14 Sept 2017
37. Guerrero-Saade, J.A., Raiu, C.: Walking in your enemy's shadow- when fourth-party collection becomes attribution hell. In: Virus Bulletin (2017). https://media.kasperskycontenthub.com/wp-content/uploads/sites/43/2018/03/07170728/Guerrero-Saade-Raiu-VB2017.pdf. Accessed 3 Jan 2020
38. Attorneys for the United States: United States of America, Plaintiff v. YU PINGAN, a.k.a. 'GoldSun', Defendant. In: Politico (2017). https://www.politico.com/f/?id=0000015e-161b-df04-a5df-963f36840001. Accessed 10 Dec 2019
39. United States District Court for the District of Columbia: United States of America v. Viktor Borisovich Netyksho et al. (2018) https://www.justice.gov/file/1080281/download. Accessed 5 Nov 2019
40. United States District Court for the Central District of California: United States of America v. Park Jin Hyok (2018). https://www.justice.gov/opa/press-release/file/1092091/download. Accessed 10 Dec 2019

Doxing

The most impressive attribution results are those that identify specific individuals, ideally with their real names and even photos. Objectively speaking, the concrete individuals behind the espionage attacks are usually less relevant than the organization they work for. Nevertheless, at least on an intuitive level, the accountability of the actors becomes much more tangible when real people like 'UglyGorilla' are identified as the hackers behind an APT campaign and not just a faceless organization like the Third Department of the Chinese People's Liberation Army.

An important technique for identifying individuals is *doxing*, i.e. researching personal data in public sources. This chapter explains how analysts use doxing methods to uncover the identity of APT group members and which factors determine the validity of the results.

9.1   Attacker Perspective: The Online Identity

Doxing illustrates that cyber-espionage is not an abstract technique, but an activity that is conducted by real people. These people do not only exist as members of APT groups, but have a real life and a history before they started to work in cyber-espionage: they have acquired and honed their skills over a period of years, are integrated into social groups outside of their work life, and have a need for appreciation and companionship. When they start to work as hackers they do not get rid of these habits and needs. In their spare time they continue to exist as members of social groups and many of them continue to be active as more or less disguised alter egos in online forums.

Especially in China, forums play an important role for hackers. They are the place where hackers receive recognition for their technical skills and successful hacks. But even more important for a hacker's reputation is to share their knowledge and experience—sometimes leading to group structures that resemble a master-student relationship (cf. [1, 2]). It is therefore typical for Chinese hackers to acquire their very first skills in such forums. When

© Springer-Verlag GmbH Germany, part of Springer Nature 2020   147
T. Steffens, *Attribution of Advanced Persistent Threats*,
https://doi.org/10.1007/978-3-662-61313-9_9

they have proven their skills by developing new techniques or tools, they gradually switch to the master role and start to pass on their knowledge themselves. This way they are active in the same forums for years and consistently use the same usernames, because it is the anchor for their reputation. This reputation is important in order to gain access to the elite parts of forums, where the newest techniques are discussed, exploits are developed, or stolen credentials are traded.

As a result, hackers often use their nicknames and usernames, which they have used for many years, even for their APT jobs. These names have been found as strings in malware samples, in WHOIS data, and in emails used for work communication. It can be assumed that the boundaries between legal and illegal activities are defined differently in China than in Western cultures. This is certainly another reason why many Chinese hackers do not follow OpSec rules to separate their private identity from their job.

Also purely practical reasons lead to the fact that (regardless of regional origin) the same personas and identities are reused again and again. As a point in case, in previous chapters it was outlined that large numbers of control servers are needed to conduct large-scale APT campaigns. Creating new contact email addresses and personas for each C&C domain is likely regarded as a nuisance to many perpetrators, so that they reuse them for long periods of time.

9.2   Researching Persons Online

The term *doxing* originates from the English abbreviation 'dox' for 'docs' or 'documents'. It refers to the search for publicly available resources containing personal data. These are not necessarily documents in the strict sense, but in most cases they are profiles in forums or social networks. This research method was not invented for attribution, but used to be a pastime for young people who wanted to expose supposedly anonymous profiles of their peer groups in underground forums.

So not surprisingly, from a technical or analytical perspective doxing is relatively simple. It is based on using general Internet search engines and some specialized online databases. Examples for the latter are reverse phone lookup sites or services to check the creditworthiness of business partners. Such databases are widespread in the USA, where data protection is much more lax than in Europe. But for attribution of APT attacks these special databases do not play a relevant role, anyway.

The different doxing methods are illustrated in this chapter using two example cases. The first case was published by CrowdStrike and is about the group PutterPanda [2]. This group has compromised companies that develop technology for satellites and earth observation. In their report, the analysts describe how they identified a Chinese citizen named Chen Ping who apparently managed the group's control servers. From private photos that Chen Ping posted on the Internet, they deduced that he is most likely working for the 12th Bureau of 3PLA. The second case is about Ge Xing, who likely is a member of the Naikon group according to a report by ThreatConnect [3]. This group has targeted government officials, military personnel, and corporations in Southeast Asia. The report presents evidence that suggests that Ge Xing was responsible for managing the C&C infrastructure. Through information he posted on personal blogs, ThreatConnect analysts hypothesized with high confidence that he worked for the Technical Reconnaissance Bureau in Kunming.

Personally identifiable data as starting point The starting point for doxing is always personally identifiable data. An example for applicable data types are email addresses from Whois data of C&C domains. Email addresses are particularly suitable, as they are typically only accessible for one person and are often used as registration handles for blogs or social networks.

Other starting points are user names from PDB paths if they are characteristic enough or contain personal and company names (as documented in the case of the company Appin, see Chap. 3).

Also network traffic captured on control servers can contain useful personal data if the perpetrators use social networks or shop online via their attack infrastructure (see Chap. 5).

It is no coincidence that both in the PutterPanda and the Naikon example the identified persons managed control servers. It is also typical that doxing was based on rather old registration data of C&C domains from 2009 and 2010. During this time, detailed reports about APTs were still rare. As a result, many groups paid little attention to OpSec and sometimes registered C&C domains with email addresses that they also used for private purposes.

Unambiguous links Similar to infrastructure research, doxing is based on pivoting from one data point to new ones. While for investigating C&C infrastructure passive DNS- or reverse Whois databases are used, doxing uses general search engines like Google or Bing to find web pages that contain specific strings of personal data. If these web pages contain new personally identifiable data, it is used as an additional search term. This way, networks of web pages and profiles emerge where the nodes are connected via search terms of personal data.

Nodes in these networks are strongly connected if they are linked by search terms that represent unambiguous data. Email addresses are the best and most common examples of this. If two profiles have been registered with the same email address, this almost certainly means that they were created by the same person.

In our case, Chen Ping registered the domains ctable[.]org and gamemuster[.]com, which were used by PutterPanda as C&C, and the website cpyy[.]net using the email address cpyy.chen[@]gmail.com [2]. Thus, these domains are unambiguously linked to each other.

Telephone numbers and account names for online messengers are also unique, but they are less common to be found, as they are rarely used as confirmation method for domain registration. Still, in the investigation of the perpetrators behind Naikon, a unique number of the Chinese QQ messenger was used to link several profiles of Ge Xing [3]. His private profile qun.594sgk.com/qq/15689281.html lists the QQ number 42113496, just like an ad for selling a bike in a local forum in the Chinese city of Kunming.

Weak links Data types that lead to weaker links are nicknames in forums or even real names. Profiles with the same names on different social networks or forums might belong to the same person, but not necessarily so. Butterfly77 on Instagram might be a different person than Butterfly77 on Twitter. Also real names are not unique at all and may even have different transliterations between scripts.

In both cases of Naikon and PutterPanda, the crucial data types that link APT activities to personal profiles are technically weak—if taken in isolation. In the infrastructure of Putter-Panda, the nickname 'cppy' stands out in several email addresses hat were used to register C&C domains [2]: cppy.chen@gmail[.]com, cppy@qq[.]com and cppy@sina[.]com. Using this string as search term, the analysts found a private blog that used this nickname, and also used the string in a slightly modified form in its hostname: cpiyy.blog.163[.]com

Thus, when doxing with weak data types analysts must assess the likelihood that a link is due to random people using the same names or strings. Part of this assessment can be determining the number of results for the search term. For example, during the writing of this book (two years after the publication of the PutterPanda report), a search engine found 113,000 web pages containing the string 'cppy'. Given the short length of the name, this is not surprising. Therefore, a purely accidental match between the strings in the registration addresses and the blog must be regarded as very likely if there had been no additional data.

Plausibility checks and corroboration Therefore, it is crucial to conduct plausibility checks in order to determine whether the additional resources (in our cases: profiles) refer to the same person. This may involve all information contained on the profile or website being compared with already known data. For instance, the full name of the blog owner was listed as Chen Ping. This was consistent with the already known email address cppy.chen@gmail[.]com. The initials 'CP' are also consistent with the nickname cppy. From a methodological point of view, such plausibility checks are susceptible to confirmation bias, i.e. focusing on information that confirms the assumptions of the analyst: The fact that Chen Pings's blog indicates 'military' or 'police' as employer can be interpreted either as a plausibility check or as confirmation bias. In Chap. 10 an analysis method is described which is intended to prevent such psychological effects.

Somewhat stronger is the link between the attack infrastructure of Naikon to private profiles. One of the C&C domains was greensky27.vicp[.]net. Searching for 'greensky27' turns up a profile of the Chinese messenger service QQ: t.qq.com/GreenSky27, which lists Ge Xing as name of the user. The character string 'greensky27' is better suited as a search criterion than 'cppy'. In October 2017, a search for this string returned only 843 hits. If you also filter out those websites that refer to the APT report about Naikon, only 349 hits remain. So the probability that this string on the QQ profile matches the C&C domain by chance is much lower than in the case of 'cppy'. Another plausibility check is that the C&C domain was very often located on servers that were hosted in the Chinese city of Kunming. This is consistent with the QQ profile which lists this city as home town.

The likelihood that the owner of this QQ-profile and the operator of the control server are the same person was strengthened by further information on the profile. The user reported the birth of his child in November 2012. During the following 8 days there was a period of inactivity for the domain greensky27.vcip.net.

The profiles of Ge Xing and Chen Ping also contain a large number of personal photos.

Analyzing photos Photos that potential APT group members post on their personal profiles can be revealing, even though they usually do not provide links to the technical data observed in APT activities. But under the assumption that the person who took the photos is a member of an APT group, visual clues about locations and organizations can help attribute the group.

Ge Xing—or the user behind the identified profiles—published a private photo that also showed his car [3]. Analysts identified the license plate as having been registered in the city of Kunming. (While in principle even concrete individuals can be identified by their license plates, this requires access to government databases. Since the perpetrators typically come from a different country than the analysts or victims, this access is denied even for law enforcement officers working on such cases.)

Further photos by Ge Xing provide clear evidence of a connection to the People's Liberation Army according to the analysis of ThreatConnect. Some of the photos show celebrations of a PLA anniversary in the Yunnan province, others were taken on the campus of a university of the PLA. This is consistent with scientific publications by an author named Ge Xing, who stated his employer as PLA unit 78020 [3], which is the designator for the Kunming Technical Reconnaissance Bureau. Several photos on the private blog were most likely taken on the grounds of this facility.

Also in the PutterPanda investigation photos turned out to be relevant. A Picasa profile assigned to Chen Ping (the presumed member of PutterPanda) shows photos that associate the user with the PLA [2]. One of them apparently shows Chen Ping during military exercises, others were most likely taken inside rooms in barracks. The CrowdStrike report is famous for showing that a uniform hat that can be seen on one of the photos shows insignia of a PLA unit. Also legendary are the image analyses in which satellite photos from Google Maps were used to reproduce the camera angle of photos that Chen Ping shot out of buildings. These analyses suggest that the photos were taken from inside an office building of Unit 61486. The analyses appear robust, since the photos show very characteristic arrangements of huge satellite dishes and office buildings. Unit 61486 belongs to the 12th Bureau of the 3PLA. Among other things, it was responsible for satellite and space technology, which were a consistent feature of the victims of PutterPanda.

The analyses regarding Chen Ping and Ge Xing are good examples of the strengths and weaknesses of doxing. They both impressively illustrate the methods that link the owners of private blogs to Units 78020 and 61486 respectively. However, the links of these blogs to the APT groups Naikon or PutterPanda are weaker, so that they needed to be corroborated with additional information.

Top-down doxing A combination of doxing and methods from geopolitical analysis was used by the anonymous group IntrusionTruth for identifying front companies in the Chinese province Hainan [4]. The analysts applied the assumption that the Chinese MSS used front companies to conduct cyber-espionage. So IntrusionTruth looked for job advertisements in the city of Hainan and picked those that listed pentesting skills or experience in developing trojans as requirement. 12 companies were found that were linked to each other by the same contact email addresses, business addresses, or even CEO. The analysts were able to show that these businesses were in fact front companies for an APT group.

While the personally identifiable information necessary for doxing often comes from technical artefacts, the approach of IntrusionTruth shows that it can also be acquired in a top-down matter by OSINT analysis.

References

1. Howlett, W.: The Rise of China's Hacking Culture-Defining Chinese Hackers. Master's thesis. California State University (2016). http://scholarworks.lib.csusb.edu/cgi/viewcontent.cgi?article=1413&context=etd. Accessed 13 Sep 2017
2. CrowdStrike: Hat-tribution to PLA Unit 61486. In: CrowdStrike Blog (2014). S. 14. https://cdn0.vox-cdn.com/assets/4589853/crowdstrike-intelligence-report-putter-panda.original.pdf. Accessed 8 Oct 2017
3. ThreatConnect: Camerashy-Closing the aperture on China's Unit 78020. In: ThreatConnect Blog (2015). http://cdn2.hubspot.net/hubfs/454298/Project_CAMERASHY_ThreatConnect_Copyright_2015.pdf. Accessed 9 Oct 2017
4. IntrusionTruth: What is the Hainan Xiandun Technology Development Company? (2020). https://intrusiontruth.wordpress.com/2020/01/09/what-is-the-hainan-xiandun-technology-development-company/. Accessed 9 Jan 2020

False Flags

The biggest challenge for attribution are clues and apparent evidence that were left behind intentionally. Following the tradition of using military terms in cyber-security, these planted clues are called *false flags*. In practice, it is often not the actual tricks of the culprits that make life difficult for analysts. Rather, even the abstract possibility that any clue might not be based on an actual mistake of the attackers, but was intentionally created to frame another actor, is the greatest Achilles' heel for any attribution analysis. Considering the fact that cyber-espionage is often conducted by intelligence services, such tricks are definitely worth keeping an eye for; after all, for centuries espionage and counterespionage in the physical world have led to the development of complex methods of deception. In this chapter, real cases of false flags are discussed, and methods are introduced to identify the tricks of APT groups.

10.1 Attacker Perspective: Planting False Flags

Even if APT groups are state-sponsored, they need to manage their personnel and time resources. This is true for developers, infrastructure administrators, and operators. They need to determine the best trade-off between efficiency of completing their missions and maintaining OpSec against detection and against attribution. If their attacks are not detected, they will not have to worry about attribution. In contrast, if they implement elaborate processes to plant consistent false flags, this will not prevent IT-security companies from detecting their cyber-operations.

Thus, the priority of APT groups is to avoid being detected, not to misdirect attribution after detection. This may explain why analysts regularly discover new techniques that attackers apply to stay under the radar of security products. New methods to plant false flags are significantly rarer.

© Springer-Verlag GmbH Germany, part of Springer Nature 2020
T. Steffens, *Attribution of Advanced Persistent Threats*,
https://doi.org/10.1007/978-3-662-61313-9_10

Two intrusion sets that are regarded as particularly advanced and stealthy are the creators of Regin [1] and RemSec [2]. Both malware families are famous for their sophisticated techniques to hide from file scanners. They persist themselves after the allocatable parts of disk partitions or hide themselves in undocumented data structures of the file system. However, there is no evidence whatsoever to suggest that they contain false flags. On the contrary, they are masterpieces that lack any clues about their developers at all. Technical analyses have found no evidence that can be used for attribution—besides the level of sophistication itself. In the case of Regin, an attribution to the British GCHQ was only brought up by documents in the Snowden leak. But the origin of RemSec is completely unclear publicly, and speculation about attribution is solely based on the cui-bono and the technical sophistication. Thus, both cases illustrate that the most advanced actors invest into OpSec against detection and attribution altogether, and apparently saw no need for planting false flags.

Similarly, the Vault 7 documents published by WikiLeaks contain instructions on how to prevent attribution—interestingly, covering several phases of the analysis process described in Chap. 2. For example, during the development of malware care is taken to ensure that it cannot be clustered into intrusion sets by source code similarity: The MARBLE framework provides a whole library of obfuscation functions so that different functions can be used for every operation [7]. There are also instructions to prevent clustering and country-attribution based on strings, PDB paths, and timestamps [10]. But there is no documentation about planting false flags. The editors of WikiLeaks reported that the CIA reused code parts of foreign APT groups in the project UMBRAGE and inserted foreign language strings with the WARBLE framework [11]. However, the original documents for UMBRAGE state practical efficiency reasons for using foreign code instead [9]. Software development is much more efficient if functionalities do not have to be developed anew. Similarly, the documentation for WARBLE does not mention planting false clues. Instead, the foreign-language character strings mentioned by the WikiLeaks editors are likely used to test obfuscation functions for different codepages [8].

And yet: Even though false flags are less common than widely assumed, there are a number of examples where they have been planted (and identified). These cases will be discussed in the following.

From an epistemic and scientific perspective, it cannot be ruled out that false flags are much more frequent and have simply not been recognized as such. If this was true, these faked clues would result in a corpus of wrongly attributed groups, which in turn would negatively impact the attribution of new attacks. Such a phenomenon is known from art history: At the beginning of the 20th century Han van Meegeren painted several paintings in the style of the Dutch painter Jan Vermeer [13]. He presented them to auction houses and galleries as previously unknown, i.e. newly discovered works by the famous master. After the paintings were wrongly certified as authentic by art experts, they were included into the canon of reference works for Vermeer. Subsequently, it was much easier for van Meegeren to make up completely new Vermeer paintings, as he only needed to make them look similar to his own forgeries. Such a Vermeer effect is also conceivable for APTs.

False flags can be planted in all aspects of an attack. The methods can be categorized by effort as follows.

Minimal Effort APT groups know that many of the existing attribution methods are based on (apparent) mistakes made by the perpetrators. Since real mistakes happen only now and then and inconsistently, with little effort the culprits can plant a few isolated clues that look as if they happened due to sloppiness, stress, or fatigue.

These clues may be strings in a foreign language that are inserted into the malware. In a campaign targeting Palestine the perpetrators used several German words in the malware Micropsia [14]. They were used as parameters in the C&C communication. The value for "betriebssystem" (German for "operating system") specified the Windows version and the value for "anwendung" (German for "application") was the version of Micropsia itself. Section 10.2 explains why these words were very likely chosen to misdirect attribution.

Strings in several different languages were used by the CloudAtlas group. It is unclear why they did not use only one foreign language consistently in order to frame a specific country. A plausible hypothesis is that they aimed to undermine attribution as a discipline in general, by generating confusion. This is in line with the observation that the group went to relatively great lengths to make attribution difficult. In addition to the multilingual strings, they manipulated an exploit document by including Spanish language resources [4] (cf. Chap. 3). In a malware for iPhone devices, they left an English PDB path with the user name 'JohnClerk'. These two methods could have been considered moderately sophisticated if the perpetrators consistently used intentionally configured development environments. The computer that was used to create the exploit documents would have run Spanish language settings and the development environment would have used the account name 'JohnClerk'. But since the traces were only found in a few samples, it can be assumed that the attackers added these false flags manually.

Very easy to fake is the contact data when registering C&C domains. The name and address of the registrant are usually not even checked for existence or correct format by the registrar (cf. Chap. 4). Fake Whois data has become so widespread that analysts did not use them for attribution to countries or organizations even before GDPR came into effect, but only as a means of grouping domains into intrusion sets.

A method that uses established analyst lore against the analysts themselves was used by Snake. When they noticed that they had been detected in a victim's network, they downloaded a malware called Quarian onto an infected system [4]. They knew that security companies had attributed Quarian as likely Chinese. Luckily, the analysts noticed that the Snake operators did not use this planted sample, made no effort to configure it to fit into their own operation, and did not even execute it. This gave rise to the hypothesis that Snake had copied a Quarian sample from a different incident or even a malware database.

Moderate Effort More complex are false flags which are not generated at random and manually, but are based on a consistent workflow or configuration.

For example, APT groups can run their development computers with a consistently shifted system time. This would result in the timestamps in the compiled malware matching a different time zone. Alternatively, this can also be achieved by inserting a step into the development process that systematically modifies the timestamps after compilation.

Likewise, language resources can be consistently set to a foreign language. These configurations do not even affect the probability of detection.

The risk is different with some methods that leave false clues in the control server infrastructure. The fact that CloudAtlas operated a large part of its C&C servers in South Korea [4] could lead inexperienced analysts to conclude that this is the group's origin. However, due to the high concentration of their control servers in South Korea, the perpetrators also run the risk of losing almost their entire infrastructure through a coordinated takedown by the Korean authorities.

Similarly risky is to exploit the fact that C&C domains expire after a time if the owners do not renew the registration. Attackers might spot such domains of other APT groups. Registering them and then using them for own operations would be a quite effective false flag. This illustrates that OpSec against attribution can be at odds with OpSec against detection: In order to make analysts link the stolen domain to the intrusion set covering the old owner, the C&C domain must already have been known and attributed. But this increases the risk of detection. A viable way for the perpetrators would therefore be to store the known C&C domain only in their malware, but not to use it so that it does not trigger an alarm in network traffic. If the attack is detected by other means, a superficial analysis would possibly misclassify the domain as an actually used control server and assign the attack to an incorrect intrusion set.

Maximal Effort The most convincing false flags are those that are planted together with fake clues from several MICTIC aspects to consistently frame a different country or group. Assuming that different people or even subteams are responsible for the different aspects of a cyber-operation, planting consistent false flags requires coordination between them as well as different methods for each aspect.

Such a deceptive tactic also requires continuous effort, especially for clues that are not based on (apparent) OpSec mistakes but on systematic patterns. For example, the analysis of the Patterns of Life needs to be misdirected. This requires timestamps to match a different timezone—in at least the MICTIC aspects malware, telemetry, and control servers. Some of the systems generating timestamps are not under the control of the culprits and cannot be faked. So in order to shift the time stamps consistently to another time zone, the perpetrators would either have to set their working hours to untypical hours or actually work from another country.

Even more elaborate are scenarios like the attack of the purported Islamist hacktivists on the French television channel TV5 Monde in 2015. The goal of the attackers was to sabotage the broadcasting infrastructure, but this activity was accompanied by hacking the corporate websites and social network accounts and posting propaganda messages with references to the Islamic State. Even a fake analysis blog was created, which pretended to be authored by a person involved in the investigation [5]. The blog described in detail and quite plausibly (only actually incorrectly) that a trojan was found in the TV5Monde network which was rather common for APT groups from the Middle East. Later, however, French governmental authorities debunked this claim and reported that in fact the malware Sofacy had been found [6]—the signature trojan of APT28.

In theory the deception tactics in the TV5Monde incident could even be an attempt to misdirect the geopolitical cui bono analysis regarding APT28. A sabotage attack on a French media institution would be quite plausible for the Islamic State, since France had sent soldiers to fight in Syria. A motivation for the presumed Russian APT28 is less obvious. There are no reports about APT groups attacking targets that are clearly not relevant for them just to plant false flags. This is not surprising, since conducting an attack consumes resources and each additional attack increases the probability of being detected. In order for an APT28 operation against a non-relevant target to be attributed to the same intrusion set (and thus dilute the cui-bono analysis), important TTPs must match. Yet this would mean that a detected attack on a diversionary target will endanger operations against real targets.

Theoretically speaking, under certain circumstances an intelligence service might want to invest some effort to create an intrusion set that is completely isolated from its other cyber-operations. This would involve using publicly available tools, set up a new control server infrastructure, and use generic TTPs. With such an intrusion set it would be possible to target networks that are of no relevance for the intelligence service itself, but misdirect the cui bono to another country. Such a campaign would be of little use for intelligence collection, but could be used as an information operation to discredit another country. This would be a new dimension of cyber-activities. After the publication of stolen documents by APT28 it has become obvious that influence operations are tools in the method arsenal of intelligence services. However, up to now there are no indications that intrusion sets have been created with the sole purpose of framing another country. Still, in the early days attribution results were second-guessed by suggesting similar hypothetical scenarios.

Another point that is often used against attribution is that perpetrators could use the signature malware of other groups. Since malware is an important component of TTPs and intrusion sets, this would indeed be a very effective false flag. For many years, there were no indications of APT groups doing so. As mentioned above, it was only observed that samples of other groups were downloaded without using them. Also the already discussed UMBRAGE project from the Vault 7 documents was apparently not intended to frame other groups, but to speed up malware development by reusing foreign code. Only in 2019, the NCSC-UK and NSA published a joint analysis that suggested that Snake extensively used malware stolen from an Iranian group [23]. According to these two government agencies, Snake operators had compromised Iranian control servers and found source code on one of them. Apparently they found the malware Neuron and Nautilus useful and subsequently used them in their own operations. Ironically, if this was intended as a false flag, it never worked out. Before Snake had stolen the source code, the malware families had not been attributed to Iran. And from then on, Neuron and Nautilus were only observed together with other Snake malware. So analysts never even got the idea that the malware was developed by Iranian groups. All incidents involving Neuron and Nautilus had been (correctly) attributed to Snake. It is therefore likely that Snake acted opportunistically and saw the value in the source code and decided to use it for efficiency. This also shows that nowadays attribution is not limited to the analysis of malware, but uses clues from all MICTIC aspects.

For the sake of completeness it should be noted that some analysts are skeptical about the analysis of NCSC-UK and NSA. Neuron and Nautilus are more sophisticated than any known Iranian malware and have never been observed together with Iranian tools. These observations contradict the hypothesis that the two malware families were developed and used by Iranian APT groups.

10.2 Analyzing False Flags

In a milestone essay Thomas Rid, then professor at the King's College in London, and Ben Buchanan stated that the attribution of cyber-attacks was an art, not a science [17]. According to them, the intuition and experience of an analyst are crucial. This is particularly true when analysts need to assess whether evidence is genuine or a false flag. Nevertheless, several systematic methods for assessing the confidence in evidence exist.

From an academic point of view, attribution must be based on data that the perpetrators cannot control or influence [18]. In practice, however, this requirement can hardly be met. Most of the evidence described in this book can be manipulated by the perpetrators. Compiler timestamps, language settings, and strings can be modified easily. So, most of the attribution results of security companies do not measure up to such a strict academic requirement. But even many of the methods available to intelligence services are not immune to deception. HUMINT, for example, is generally considered to be only weakly reliable, since human sources often tune their information to please the intelligence officer. Even more so, there is always the risk that the agent is deliberately given false information by the enemy or that the agent is even a double agent. SIGINT can also collect fake information, for example, if people know they are being tapped and stage a conversation.

So what types of evidence stand up to this strict academic scrutiny? Basically none. In general, certain types of SIGINT are considered irrefutable [18]. For example, every interactive connection of an attacker after any number of hop-points must eventually lead to the computer of the operator. And an offensive cyber-operation for attribution (hackback) can plant a backdoor on this computer to monitor the attackers. But from a strictly theoretical point of view, even then it cannot be ruled out that the intelligence service behind the APT group has bribed an employee of a foreign agency to carry out an attack from the network of his or her employer.

That sounds like a death sentence for attribution.

However, in practice attribution is about assessing the likelihood of different hypotheses. If we assumed that APT1 was not part of the PLA, would it be likely that a bribed PLA employee targeted dozens of organizations with APT1 malware from the military's networks without his superiors noticing? Or is it more plausible that Mandiant's statement is correct and that the PLA itself controlled APT1? Or more general: How much effort will APT groups invest to create false flags?

Therefore, the challenge for analysts is to collect evidence from as many different sources (i.e. MICTIC aspects) as possible and to generate the most probable hypothesis. To this end, they carry out the following steps.

Assess Validity Each evidence that is turned up must be checked for validity. In Sect. 10.1 it was mentioned that the malware Micropsia contained several German words. This in principle gives rise to the hypothesis that German might be the native language of the developers. However, one of these words was "ausfahrt", which the culprits apparently believed to mean "exit", as in terminating the malware process. But while the German "ausfahrt" can be translated as "exit", it refers to a "highway exit", not the termination of a process. It is obvious that a native German speaker would not have used this word in this context. Therefore, it is likely that the perpetrators translated expressions from another language into German to plant a false flag.

Micropsia is not the only example for APT groups inserting words in a foreign language that a native speaker would not have used. In samples attributed to the North Korean group Lazarus, several Russian words were found that had been used in grammatically wrong contexts. Other Russian terms were apparently transcribed into the Latin alphabet by people who did not know how to pronounce the words [19].

Not every type of evidence has to be assessed each time to be regarded as not convincing. For example, analysts usually ignore the postal addresses in Whois data of C&C domains because they are easily (and commonly) forged.

Check Consistency An important step is to combine all the different types of evidence into an attribution hypothesis and then check them for consistency.

An illustrative, if hypothetical example arises from the fact that source code of X-Agent, the signature backdoor of APT28, was found on a control server [16]. Parts of it were even published in a code repository. What would it mean for attribution if another group used X-Agent in its operations? Analysts would find samples of that backdoor in an incident, together with a lot of other evidence, like C&C domains, other tools, and TTPs. Since X-Agent is regarded as typical for APT28, a first hypothesis would indicate that this group was behind the attack. Now analysts can apply several methods to verify this hypothesis. For example, most malware is subject to continuous development and improvements. Samples based on source code that has been released once will not match new versions of the original developers after a period of time. Therefore, samples must not only be classified into a malware family, but also into the different versions and development branches. So analysts can check whether the sample used in an incident is consistent with samples from other incidents. Furthermore, if a new group starts to use X-Agent they will likely apply their own routine TTPs, resulting in analysts noting inconsistencies between using X-Agent and the other aspects of the attack. The confidence in the attribution of the incident to APT28 would therefore be low.

But what if there is not yet much prior knowledge about a campaign or group? Even for an isolated and new incident the different types of evidence can be checked for consistency. If, for example, the perpetrators' actions are very professional and characterized by high OpSec, all alleged mistakes that indicate sloppiness or disorganized teamwork should be regarded with skepticism.

The actors behind the attack on the Olympic Games ceremony in South Korea applied a very creative, novel method of planting false evidence—but were found out nevertheless. They copied the Rich header from samples of the Lazarus group into their own malware binaries [22]. The Rich header contains information about the development environment that was used to compile the binaries (cf. Chap. 3). In the case of the Olympic Destroyer and Lazarus samples, the header indicated that they were compiled using Visual Studio 6—a very old versions, dating from no later than 2004. However, Kaspersky analysts noticed an inconsistency between the code part of the Olympic Destroyer samples and their Rich header. The binaries referenced a library named "mscoree.dll" that did not exist at the time of Visual Studio 6. So obviously the Rich header was inserted after compilation to pretend a link to Lazarus. This method is unusual in that it did not fake clues for the country-attribution phase of the analysis, but for the clustering phase. In this sense, it is similar to the Vermeer effect that is based on establishing similarities between a real and a forged object.

A prime example of lacking consistency are the clues from the CloudAtlas campaign [3]. Their malware contained strings of characters from a variety of languages, including Arabic and Hindi. This was at odds with the username in the PDB path, which was "JohnClerk" and was more in line with English-speaking actors. And the language resource in an exploit document was Spanish. Finally, the culprits even downloaded a malware attributed as Chinese.

Weight Evidence Types Apparently, CloudAtlas assumed that so many inconsistent false flags would undermine any formal analysis process because no consistent hypothesis could be generated. Yet, analysts did not attempt to find hypotheses that were consistent with all clues. Instead, they weighted the types of evidence depending on how easy they are to fake.

For example, the selection of targets was very similar to that of the Red October campaign [20]. This group was already publicly known and almost unanimously attributed by security companies as probably Russian-speaking at the time of the CloudAtlas attacks. As discussed before, planting a false flag by targeting irrelevant victims would be a comparably large effort. Also, the similarities between the exploits and malware of the two campaigns would have been very difficult to generate if the perpetrators were not the same. Finally, the temporal patterns from the manual activity, which is difficult to fake as discussed above, pointed to the time zone UTC+2, which covers parts of Russia and the partly Russian-speaking Ukraine [20].

Table 10.1 Types of evidence in the CloudAtlas campaign and their weighting

Evidence	Hypothesis about origin	Effort of faking
Arabian strings	Middle East	Low
Hindi strings	India	Low
JohnClerk in PDB path	English-speaking	Low
Spanish language resource	Spanish-speaking	Low
Many C&C servers in South Korea	South Korea	Medium
Code-similarity with Red October	Russian-speaking	Large
Similar targets as Red October	Russian-speaking	Large
Manual activity in UTC+2	Russian-speaking	Large

Table 10.1 lists the types of evidence, the corresponding hypotheses, and the effort required for a false flag.

An analysis based on the weighting evidence requires additional assumptions to generate a robust hypothesis. In the case of Cloud Atlas the additional premise that the perpetrators invest not more than medium effort for false flags yields the consistent hypothesis that the culprits are Russian-speaking.

However, this additional premise must be communicated if the attribution result is presented (see Chap. 12). Since two evidence types are based on the origin of Red October, the analysis depends on the validity of this prior attribution. If that attribution was wrong, it would cause a Vermeer effect.

Analysis of Competing Hypotheses In a more formalized way, similar analysis steps are conducted in a classic methodology called *Analysis of Competing Hypotheses* (ACH) [21]. This is an approach developed by the CIA in the 1970s, which has been used by intelligence services in Anglo-Saxon countries ever since. Its actual purpose is not to uncover false flags but to evaluate incomplete and contradictory information which is typical for intelligence analysis, especially when dealing with HUMINT. ACH is used to keep the analysis of such information as free of cognitive bias and assumptions as possible. It is no coincidence that the methodology was introduced in a book about the psychology of intelligence analysis.

ACH is a very structured and practical methodology. All possible hypotheses are entered into a matrix together with the available evidence. The analysis is evidence-centered, i.e. for each evidence it is examined which hypotheses are consistent with it, and to which extent. This is to avoid focusing too much on favored hypotheses and thereby laying too much importance on evidence that fits them. The matrix also allows to check the sensitivity of the hypotheses to changing evidence, i.e. assuming that some of the listed evidence may be false or incomplete. Finally, the analyst selects the most likely and robust hypothesis.

Table 10.2 shows ACH applied to the Cloud Atlas campaign. The hypotheses are as follows: H1 states that the actors are Russian-speaking. H2 states that the actors are from the Middle East. H3 states that the actors are Spanish-speaking. H4 states that the actors are from South Korea. H5 states that the actors are English native speakers. H6 states that the actors are from India. H7 is the null hypothesis that the actors are from a different country or region. To calculate the score of each hypothesis, each matching evidence is added as 1, each inconsistent evidence as −1, and neutral evidence as 0. The effort to fake the evidence is multiplied using a value of 0.33 for low, 0.66 for medium, and 1 for high effort.

By far the most valid hypothesis according to ACH is H1 stating that the actors are Russian-speaking. Sensitivity analysis shows that H1 is strong, the three consistent evidence entries are from three different MICTIC aspects (malware, cui bono, and telemetry). Yet, it is also dependent on the assumption that the prior attribution of Red October is correct. If the two evidence entries involving Red October were removed (if the attribution statements were retracted), the score of H1 would be down to 0.7. But H2 and other hypotheses would only be increased to −1.7, making no difference in the overall result. So H1 would be the most sound hypothesis to communicate.

Table 10.2 Analysis of Competing Hypotheses applied to the Cloud Atlas campaign. + denotes that the hypothesis is consistent with the evidence, − denotes inconsistency, and o denotes neutral evidence

Evidence	Effort	H1	H2	H3	H4	H5	H6	H7
Arabian strings	Low	−	+	−	−	−	−	−
Hindi strings	Low	−	−	−	−	−	+	−
JohnClerk in PDB	Low	−	−	−	−	+	−	−
Spanish lang. res.	Low	−	−	+	−	−	−	−
C&C servers in SK	Med	o	o	o	+	o	o	o
code-sim RedOct.	High	+	−	−	−	−	−	−
targets like RedOct.	High	+	−	−	−	−	−	−
activity in UTC+2	High	+	−	−	−	−	−	−
	Score	2.7	−3.7	−3.7	−3.7	−3.7	−3.7	−4.3

The discussed examples of identified false flags and the existence of systematic analysis approaches are cause for optimism. Nevertheless, false flags will remain the Achilles' heel of attribution.

References

1. GReAT: Regin-nation-state ownage of GSM networks. In: SecureList (2014). http://web.archive.org/web/20170802165138/https://securelist.com/regin-nation-state-ownage-of-gsm-networks/67741/. Accessed 8 Oct 2017
2. GReAT: ProjectSauron-top level cyber-espionage platform covertly extracts encrypted government comms. In: Securelist (2016). https://securelist.com/faq-the-projectsauron-apt/75533/. Accessed 9 Sep 2017
3. Grange, W., Fagerland, S.: Blue Coat Exposes 'The Inception Framework'-Very Sophisticated, Layered Malware Attack Targeted at Military, Diplomats, and Business Execs. https://www.symantec.com/connect/blogs/blue-coat-exposes-inception-framework-very-sophisticated-layered-malware-attack-targeted-milit. Accessed 22 Sep 2017
4. Bartholomew, B., Guerrero-Saade, J.A.: Wave your false flags! Deception tactics muddying attribution in targeted attacks. In: SecureList (2016). https://securelist.com/files/2016/10/Bartholomew-GuerreroSaade-VB2016.pdf. Accessed 22 Sep 2017
5. Paganini, P.: A new hypothesis on the attack that compromised the French TV station TV5Monde: Hackers of the Cyber Caliphate team used the Kjw0rm Remote Access Trojan. In: SecurityAffairs (2015). http://web.archive.org/web/20150522100008/http://securityaffairs.co/wordpress/35864/hacking/tv5monde-hacked-kjw0rm-rat.html. Accessed 22 Sep 2017
6. Jones, S.: Russia mobilises an elite band of cyber warriors. In: Financial Times (2017). https://www.ft.com/content/f41e1dc4-ef83-11e6-ba01-119a44939bb6. Accessed 26 Sep 2017
7. WikiLeaks: the marble framework. In: Vault7 (2017). http://web.archive.org/web/20170307165659/https://wikileaks.org/ciav7p1/cms/page_14588467.html. Accessed 22 Sep 2017
8. Cimpanu, C.: WikiLeaks dumps source code of CIA tool called marble. In: BleepingComputer (2017). http://web.archive.org/web/20170401112838/https://www.bleepingcomputer.com/news/government/wikileaks-dumps-source-code-of-cia-tool-called-marble/. Accessed 22 Sep 2017
9. WikiLeaks: umbrage-component library. In: Vault7 (2017). http://web.archive.org/web/20170307164812/https://wikileaks.org/ciav7p1/cms/page_2621753.html. Accessed 22 Sep 2017
10. WikiLeaks: development tradecraft DOs and DON'Ts. In: Vault (2017). http://web.archive.org/web/20170307164813/https://wikileaks.org/ciav7p1/cms/page_14587109.html. Accessed 23 Sep 2017
11. WikiLeaks: press release. In: Vault7 (2017). http://web.archive.org/web/20170307133856/https://wikileaks.org/ciav7p1/. Accessed 23 Sep 2017
12. WikiLeaks: marble framework. In: Vault7 (2017). http://web.archive.org/web/20170331151813/https://wikileaks.org/vault7/. Accessed 23 Sep 2017
13. Goodman, N.: Languages of Art. Bobbs-Merrill, Indianapolis (1968)
14. Rascagneres, P., Mercer, W.: Delphi used to score against Palestine. In: Talos Intelligence Blog (2017). http://web.archive.org/web/20170619170458/http://blog.talosintelligence.com/2017/06/palestine-delphi.html. Accessed 24 Sep 2017

15. Kling, B.: Cyberkriminelle nutzen Open-Source-Software zur Spionage. In: ZDNet (2016). http://www.zdnet.de/88268761/cyberkriminelle-nutzen-open-source-software-zur-spionage/. Accessed 26 Sep 2017
16. Tanriverdi, H.: Was der Code russischer Elite-Hacker verrät. In: Süddeutsche Zeitung (2017). http://www.sueddeutsche.de/digital/it-sicherheit-was-der-code-russischer-elite-hacker-verraet-1.3379915. Accessed 26 Sep 2017
17. Rid, T., Buchanan, B.: Attributing cyber attacks. J. Strateg. Stud. **38**(1–2) (2015)
18. thegrugq: cyber attribution in cyber conflicts. In: Underground Tradecraft (2014). http://web.archive.org/web/20141231182131/https://grugq.tumblr.com/post/106516121088/cyber-attribution-in-cyber-conflicts-cyber. Accessed 16 Sep 2017
19. Shevchenko, S., Nish, A.: Lazarus' false flag malware. In: BAe Systems Threat Research Blog (2017). http://web.archive.org/web/20170929152617/http://baesystemsai.blogspot.de/2017/02/lazarus-false-flag-malware.html. Accessed 29 Sep 2017
20. GReAT: Cloud Atlas-RedOctober APT is back in style. In: SecureList (2014). http://web.archive.org/web/20170718181955/https://securelist.com/cloud-atlas-redoctober-apt-is-back-in-style/68083/. Accessed 29 Sep 2017
21. Heuer, Jr. R.: Chapter 8-analysis of competing hypotheses. In: Psychology of Intelligence Analysis, Center for the Study of Intelligence, Central Intelligence Agency (1999)
22. GReAT: the devil is in the Rich header. In: Securelist (2018). https://securelist.com/the-devils-in-the-rich-header/84348/. Accessed 15 Nov 2019
23. NCSC-UK and NSA: Turla group exploits Iranian APT to expand coverage of victims (2019). https://www.ncsc.gov.uk/news/turla-group-exploits-iran-apt-to-expand-coverage-of-victims. Accessed 10 Jan 2020

Group Set-Ups

What constitutes an APT group? Is it about the individual members of the APT group and their particular skills and traits? Or is it the agency unit that the hackers work for? Who owns tools and infrastructure? What happens to the hackers and the source code if a group is disbanded after disclosure? When is it advisable for analysts to discontinue using a group name and define a new one? Does the group stop to exist in its known form if a malware developer leaves? Maybe not, but what if a malware developer and two operators leave? What if the group loses a contract with a government agency and starts to work for another customer? What if this customer enforces the use of infrastructure that it manages itself?

The infosec community has avoided to give clear answers to these questions—for good reasons. The APT landscape is diverse and the way groups are organized differs from country to country. Even within the same jurisdiction APT groups may be set up differently. So there will not be one and only one definition of what constitutes a group. Yet, many published reports seem to assume that most intrusion sets correspond to a canonical team of hackers.

Indictments and Threat Intelligence reports suggest that many APT groups are not monolithic teams. They purchase malware from contractors [1], cooperate with freelance operators [2], or may even be set up dynamically for each campaign [3]. This is a major challenge for analysts that attempt to cluster incidents into intrusion sets while assuming a fix team of hackers that covers all aspects of the cyber-operations (cf. Sect. 2.5).

This chapter aims to provide an analytical approach to tackle the challenge of non-monolithic APT groups.

11.1 Pattern-Based Approach

Attribution is an abductive reasoning process that attempts to find the best fitting explanation for observations. In Sect. 2.5 we outlined that this approach is used to generate hypotheses about the likely country, organization, or persons behind cyber-operations. The same general concept can be applied to reason about the set-up of the hacker group.

© Springer-Verlag GmbH Germany, part of Springer Nature 2020
T. Steffens, *Attribution of Advanced Persistent Threats*,
https://doi.org/10.1007/978-3-662-61313-9_11

How an APT group is organized internally will have an effect on the traces and evidence that will be left behind. If malware is purchased from an international contractor, samples from the same family will be found in disparate victim networks that cannot be explained with a consistent cui bono. If several units use infrastructure that is managed by the same quartermaster-like entity, there will be intrusion sets that differ in malware and TTPs, but will be similar in the configuration of the infrastructure. If a sponsor hires several freelancers, there will be a high variety of malware and TTPs targeting similar organizations, with malware correlating strongly with certain TTPs.

Just like programmers choose from a set of software design patterns the one that is best-suited for a task, analysts may select from a set of group patterns that best fits the available data. In the next section, a catalog of such patterns is presented, together with a description how they will manifest in observable data.

In the end, the exact internal group structure will only be revealed by methods of intelligence agencies and law enforcement. Unfortunately, these findings will only be published in detail in rare cases. The majority of Threat Intel consumers and infosec analysts will have to approximate the most likely group set-ups from technical data.

11.2 Group Templates Based on MICTIC Aspects

Theoretically, group set-ups can be defined by any subset of the MICTIC aspects malware (developers), infrastructure (procurement manager), control servers (administrators), telemetry (operators), and sponsors (cui bono). But here we cover only those set-ups that either correspond to findings in reports and indictments, or that are consistent with the current lore in infosec.

Needless to say that the following set of patterns is not exhaustive. Researchers may already have found evidence for additional set-ups, or future revelations will uncover more. Even more so, more empirical research is needed to more clearly define the data characteristics that result from the different group set-ups.

A consequence of using more fine-grained group set-ups is that campaigns or even incidents may involve several teams. This makes sense intuitively if one considers a hypothetical attack that involves malware developeded by an international contractor, that was used by freelance operators in a job for a government agency.

In the following, each pattern is presented along with its MICTIC profile, with those aspects that are covered by the pattern designated in capital letters. This also characterizes how the corresponding cyber-operations will turn out in clustering: Those aspects that are covered by the group will be more consistent than those that are purchased or conducted externally.

Monolithic Team—MICTIC Any catalog of group set-up patterns would be incomplete without the concept of a fix team that covers all aspects of cyber-operations itself. Examples include the Tailored Access Operations unit of the NSA and the likely Chinese APT3 [4].

Both seem to work rather autarkic, developing exploits and malware themselves, managing infrastructure, and conducting operations.

The technical data about their operations will result in comparatively clear-cut clusters of intrusion sets. The correlations between exploits, malware, infrastructure, and TTPs will only become inconsistent by the group changing its techniques over time.

Malware Freeriders and Malware Purchasers—mICTIC Another common and oft-reported phenomenon are groups that do not have malware developers at their disposal. These come in two variations. Freeriders make use of publicly available frameworks like Powershell Empire or Poison Ivy. Malware purchasers buy tools from contractors—either non-exclusive like the Uzbekistan SSS (according to [1]), or by specifying concrete requirements to out-sourced developers (an approach that may be at work in the APT29 complex).

In technical data the exclusive-purchase scenario will be nearly indistinguishable from the monolithic-team set-up, as the usage of the malware will strongly correlate with all other aspects of the group.

The freerider- and non-exclusive-purchaser scenario will lead to the same malware families being part of several otherwise disparate clusters of infrastructure and TTPs—to a larger or smaller extent, respectively.

Of course, researchers may use OSINT to confirm that the source code of a malware family is publicly available. Or they can monitor underground forums for malware developers offering their products.

Public APT reports suggest that the non-exclusive purchase scenario may cover the cyber-operations of countries that are at the beginning of their cyber-activities. Exclusive development of malware appears plausible for Western groups, while also likely for some Russian operations.

The Orchestrator—MictiC The indictment about cyber-espionage against manufacturers of aerospace turbines suggests a pattern that was previously unknown in the general infosec community. According to US investigators, an intelligence officer at the MSS hired individual freelancers to steal the intellectual property that he needed [5]. Some of these contractors used malware from their own arsenal (such as Winnti), others were given trojans that were provided by members of the conspiracy (such as Sakula). Apparently, the individual hackers were not part of a fix team, but nevertheless cooperated closely in the campaign: The indictment describes how operators were instructed to use a specific control server and specific malware against a target.

From the perspective of analysts poring over technical data, this is one of the most difficult set-ups to handle. It is not even intuitively clear how such a structure should be reflected by intrusion sets, even if complete and perfect technical data would be available. Should all operations managed by the MSS officer be handled as one group? Or should the campaign-specific cooperation between the individual freelancers be covered by a (temporal) intrusion set? Or would it make more sense to define an intrusion set for each freelancer?

The data that such a set-up will produce will show a set of targets within a specific sector or region (reflecting the current interest of the intelligence officer). The other aspects will be rather inhomogenous, showing diverse malware families and disparate infrastructure. At least certain malware samples will correlate with specific TTPs, as each freelancer uses his malware and has his individual operator style. Also, samples of different freelancers might turn up in the same victim networks around the same time or be configured to use the same C&C (as ordered by the orchestrator).

According to current knowledge, this set-up might be typical for operations run by the Chinese MSS. Research by Recorded Future suggests that the Iranian IRGC organizes its cyber-campaigns following the same pattern, with the clear intent to undermine attribution [3]. Each operation is contracted to two different contractors who need to cooperate for the time being. The combination gets more or less randomized using up to 50 teams, according to the report.

The Freelance Operator—mICTic The orchestrator pattern suggests the existence of individual hackers-for-hire. In the scenario described by the turbine-indictment the freelancers do not develop their own malware, but may configure backdoors, register C&C domains, and install control servers. In general, such activities can generate enough data that a consistent intrusion set can be defined—but only if analysts specifically consider this set-up as an option. If researchers assume the existence of a monolithic team, they will be distracted by co-occurrence of samples from other freelancers in the same network, or by the changing victimology if the contractor is hired by another customer.

Malware Developers—Mictic The pendant to the malware-purchaser is the malware developer. Obvious examples from public sources include the Hacking Team and NSO. The less obvious cases are of course even more interesting. According to some analysts, APT29 may in fact be an amalgam of one or more malware developer contractors that sell their product to several government agencies.

For this pattern, only the malware aspect is relevant (the consequences of malware being used by different operators are handled in the purchase-pattern). All evidence types discussed in Chap. 3 can help to attribute the developers.

The Infrastructure Quartermaster—mIctic The indictment against several GRU officers gives rise to hypothesize that their may be units that are specialized to procure and manage infrastructure for several partner units [6]. Unit 74455 allegedly provides infrastructure for APT28 (or at least the subteam that uses X-Agent) and to units that conduct information operations. Analyses by security companies suggest that also Sandworm may benefit from the service of Unit 74455.

In this set-up there will be several links between different intrusion sets based on overlapping infrastructure or infrastructure characteristics like registration habits or preferred hosters and registrars. The intrusion sets may differ in the malware they use, TTPs, and even targets.

The quartermaster may stockpile domains and hand them out on a case to case basis. So a phenomenon to be expected in the data is that there will be C&C domains that will be registered and maybe even assigned to IP addresses long before any malware samples will connect to them.

The Infrastructure Guests—MiCTIC Analogously to the infrastructure quartermaster there will be groups that use the provisioned servers for their malware and their operations. Their activities will be reflected in technical data that is consistent in most MICTIC aspects, but will generate infrastructure links to other intrusion sets.

Sharing Groups and Super Threat Actors—mICTIC Juan Andres Guerrero-Saade and Silas Cutler suggest a pattern on a higher abstraction level than the templates mentioned above [7]. In their research they coin the term *Supra Threat Actors* for organizations that cooperate on malware source code internationally. According to them, the GCHQ's DARE-DEVIL and the NSA's UNITEDRAKE were designed to work together. While both agencies correspond to the monolithic pattern, they cooperate on a more abstract level. Without additional input from other sources (like the Snowden leaks in this case), such a scenario is almost impossible to distinguish from the non-exclusive-purchase pattern or from groups that share malware domestically.

Up to now, Supra Threat Actors are considered to be limited to Western countries.

11.3 Group Templates Based on Killchain Phases

Just like MICTIC, also the killchain is a simplified abstraction of the real world. Some APT groups might specialize and limit their activity to certain phases of the killchain, cooperating with other teams that cover the other phases. The existing literature suggests the existence of three set-ups.

Full Killchain This is the standard model for APT groups that conduct a cyber-operation from start to end.

Access Teams Some groups may specialize in getting a foothold in a target network. This involves reconnaissance of vulnerable servers or suitable target persons, delivering exploit-documents, compromising servers in the DMZ, or using social engineering to infect a workstation. Once they have gained access to network, they hand it over to another team.

The activity of access teams will lead to a plethora of technical data about exploit documents in malware repositories. They may generate their malicious lure documents using a proprietary framework, and they may reuse infrastructure for different campaigns. This may result in a rather consistent intrusion set. However, this intrusion set will lack backdoors, rootkits, and TTPs related to lateral movement or exfiltration.

Interestingly, the access team may cooperate with different teams for the later stages of the killchain. If analysts assume a monolithic team, they will include all of the other teams in the intrusion set, wondering that the group has several distinct approaches to lateral movement and exfiltration.

Marauders The marauders take over from the access team. They make either be provided with credentials or they may be given access to a control server that a backdoor connects to from within the victim network.

The crucial point is that technical data will show many links between the access team and the marauder. Samples from both teams may be found on the same computer or at least in the same network. Even worse, the marauders may configure their later-stage backdoors to use the same control server that they were handed by the access team.

Unraveling a set of teams that work together in this way will only be possible if analysts check the available data against the different group set-up patterns.

References

1. Zetter, K.: Researchers say they uncovered Uzbekistan hacking operations due to spectacularly bad OPSEC. In: Motherboard (2019). https://www.vice.com/amp/en_us/article/3kx5y3/uzbekistan-hacking-operations-uncovered-due-to-spectacularly-bad-opsec. Accessed 28 Dec 2019
2. Attorneys for the United States: United States of America, Plaintiff v. Yu Pingan, a.k.a. 'Gold-Sun', Defendant. In: Politico (2017). https://www.politico.com/f/?id=0000015e-161b-df04-a5df-963f36840001. Accessed 10 Dec 2019
3. Gundert, L., Chohan, S., Lesnewich, G.: Iran's hacker hierarchy exposed. In: Recorded Future Blog (2018). https://www.recordedfuture.com/iran-hacker-hierarchy/. Accessed 26 Jan 2020
4. The US Department of Justice: United States of America v. Wu Yingzhuo, Dong Hao, Xia Lei (2017). https://www.justice.gov/opa/press-release/file/1013866/download. Accessed 13 Dec 2019
5. United States District Court Southern District of New York: Unites States of America vs. Zhang Zhang-GUI, Zha Rong, Chai Meng et al. (2017). https://www.justice.gov/opa/press-release/file/1106491/download. Accessed 4 Nov 2019
6. United States District COURTFOR the District of Columbia: United States of America v. Viktor Borisovich Netyksho et al. (2018)
7. Chronicle: who is GOSSIPGIRL? In: Chronicle Blog (2019). https://medium.com/chronicle-blog/who-is-gossipgirl-3b4170f846c0. Accessed 26 Jan 2020

Part III

Strategical Aspects

Attribution is not an end in itself, but a prerequisite for IT-security, legal, or political purposes. These include allocating administrator resources, exerting diplomatic pressure on the nation-state sponsors, informing the public about influence operations, or even sentencing the culprits. In all these cases it is essential that the attribution statement and the analysis are comprehensible and convincing. Therefore, the communication of the results must meet a number of requirements. This chapter looks at what these requirements are and how the various institutions that conduct attribution can implement them.

12.1   Audience and Purpose

Every public attribution statement is an intentional communication and serves a purpose. For the majority of known APT groups, security companies and government agencies have a more or less robust hypothesis about their originator, at least at the level of the country of origin. Only very few groups are completely unattributed (the same is not necessarily true for individual incidents, though). Nevertheless, not all attribution results are published. One reason is that for a public statement the hypotheses must be more robust than for internal working hypotheses. Another is that not all sources, evidence types, and methods are suited for publication. And from a tactical perspective, any public communication is a signal to the opponent, i.e. the attributing institution puts its cards on the table. This may help the culprits to deduce which detection capabilities and sources the analysts have, which malware, infrastructure, and victims they have discovered. These insights can be used to adapt future operations accordingly. Therefore, the publication of an attribution analysis is only advisable if it pursues a specific purpose and accomplishing the purpose is likely. The following purposes may motivate a public disclosure.

© Springer-Verlag GmbH Germany, part of Springer Nature 2020   173
T. Steffens, *Attribution of Advanced Persistent Threats*,
https://doi.org/10.1007/978-3-662-61313-9_12

Network Defense One of the first paragraphs of Mandiant's APT1 report sounded almost like a vindication for publishing the analysis. The analysts explained why they deviated from their previous habit of not publishing information about the origin and sponsors of APT groups. Their motivation for the report was to "arm and prepare security professionals to combat that threat effectively" [1, p. 6]. According to Mandiant, only by understanding the landscape of cyber-espionage coordinated action to counter APT operations is possible. Also, IoCs were published to facilitate detection of attacks. Finally, the report argues that disclosing the activities of APT1 leads to the perpetrators incurring high costs for developing new malware, procuring infrastructure, and applying new techniques.

Mandiant admitted that publishing their results risked losing their visibility into the operations of APT1. If the perpetrators change their TTPs and IoCs, analysts have to adapt their own tracking methods. Therefore, disclosure always is a trade-off between *information gain* and *information loss*.

Of course network defense is also possible if the perpetrators behind the attacks are not named. Technical indicators and signatures for intrusion detection systems, firewalls, and file scanners are actor-agnostic. In practice, however, the decision as to which security measures are implemented depends not only on technical feasibility, but also on an assessment of the risk of attacks against the network. Therefore, intelligence about the identity and collection interests of APT groups are essential to assess one's own cyber-security risk (see Chap. 2).

In contrast to security companies, government agencies need an official mandate to publish attribution statements. The Computer Emergency Response Team of the US government (US-CERT), for example, regularly shares campaign-specific IoCs and recommendations with US companies. But as an agency with a purely technical focus it avoided naming intrusion sets and APT groups for a long time (e.g. [2, 3]). Apparently, they followed the actor-agnostic approach which made their reports lack some context. However, nowadays US-CERT alerts at least contain web links to reports about named groups from security companies (e.g. [4]), so that network defenders can better assess the relevance of IoCs for their own systems.

Court Proceedings The most convincing and transparent attribution results are those that lead to the conviction of the perpetrators. If the evidence is not convincing or if its source is unclear, this can lead to the rejection of the indictment. Examples of successful indictments are the cases against the PLA officers of APT1 [5] and of the Chinese citizen who stole data from Boeing [6] (cf. Chap. 8).

But as Thomas Rid of King's College in London remarked in an academic essay, the evidence that was made available to the public was not detailed at all [7]. The law enforcement officers and judges apparently had additional evidence, but the unsealed indictments contained only abstract statements about malware, control servers, and the exfiltration of data. Most important, for many types of evidence it was not stated how the information was obtained.

Since Rid's essay several more indictments have been unsealed. For example, the indictment against the alleged X-Agent developer of APT28 contained many details about the internal roles in the GRU department, but almost no information about investigation methods and sources. The indictment against the alleged member of Lazarus, Park, was significantly longer and listed a lot of evidence that was obtained by requesting them from providers and social media companies. Obviously, the level of detail and transparency varies greatly between indictments, showing that up to now there is no established format and process to write them. But this variety in details is likely also due to the fact that methods and sources vary in confidentiality from investigation to investigation.

Diplomacy In academia, the diplomatic consequences and ramifications of public statements about the actors behind cyber-operations are the most active sub-topic of attribution. There is a vast corpus of literature, which cannot be discussed comprehensively in this book. We focus on current developments in multilateral joint attribution, sanctions, and deterrence.

In 2016 the White House publicly accused the Russian government of being responsible for compromising the network of the DNC [8]. In the following year, WannaCry was attributed to North Korea by the US and Canadian governments [9]. In 2018, the United States and the British governments publicly blamed Russia for the NotPetya ransomware attacks [10].

For government agencies, public statements about the actors behind APT attacks are painstaking decisions that primarily serve signaling. At first, allegations and requests to cease cyber-operations are communicated via diplomatic, i.e. non-public, channels. A public statement about attribution can therefore be regarded as an escalating step after more discreet negotiations have not led to a concession. The pressure on the accused government is increased by public statements, and the consequences can be manifold. Private companies might want to reconsider investing in the respective country if its intellectual property cannot be guaranteed to remain safe. Other counties may become aware of the accused country's cyber-operations and can in turn increase diplomatic pressure. Multi-national sanctions are another option, depending on the severity of the cyber-operations, as illustrated by the sanctions regime of the European Union [11].

The crucial point is that the public is usually not the intended audience. Instead, the statements of governmental institutions are meant for the sponsors of the APT campaigns. This explains why the authorities have hardly presented any details in the cases documented so far. After all, the purpose is not to inform the public or to convince doubting experts, but to send a signal to the other side (which does not need details to know whether the accusations are correct or not). One of the few example that is at odds with this fact is the much-cited Grizzley Steppe Report, in which the US government publicly accused the Russian government of influencing the 2016 US presidential election [12]. A criticism in the infosec community was that no evidence was presented at all. This lack of details would have been understandable if the purpose had not been to also convince the public, but only to warn the Russian government against further meddling in US domestic politics. Yet, before the Grizzley Steppe report was published, the US media and the public in particular had demanded that the government issue a clear and unambiguous statement about the perpetrators behind the DNC hack. Therefore, many experts were surprised that the report stated a clear responsibility by Russia, but did not contain any evidence. It is therefore reasonable to assume that the authorities used information from sources that they did not want to reveal.

Apparently, they also considered themselves regarded as trustworthy and competent by the public, so that a joint statement by several US intelligence agencies would be sufficient to convince the media and citizens.

However, this self-perception of the US intelligence community did not take into account that the attribution of hacker attacks overlaps with the field of information technology with a large technical community. And this infosec community values checking and reproducing technical claims. Several infosec experts are well-connected with journalists. So if the attribution evidence presented by the government is not technically convincing, public opinion can easily turn against the credibility of the agencies. This must be considered when attributing information operations, since trust in the attribution is all the more important if it concerns political, particularly democratic, processes.

If the activity in question is not an influence operation, public attribution by governments is only diplomatically sustainable if it also entails consequences. If this is not the case, attribution statements can have the opposite effect: The perpetrators learn that no punitive measures are to be expected, so they can continue their cyber-activities without restraint.

A possible consequence of identifying a government as sponsoring cyber-espionage can be sanctions against companies that likely benefited from the stolen intellectual property, against individuals that were part of the operations, or even whole sectors of the country's industry [13]. A successful example are the potential sanctions against Chinese companies (cf. Chap. 2), that the Obama administration prepared in the run-up to a summit meeting in 2015 [14]. Presumably, these threats were one of the reasons why Xi Jinping reached an agreement with the USA that prohibited cyber-espionage against companies. In hindsight from 2020 it can be argued whether this agreement really had a lasting effect. Reports from various security companies did observe less activity from likely Chinese APT groups following the agreement. But US indictments later suggested that Chinese cyber-espionage against US companies did continue (e.g. [15]).

Real sanctions were imposed by the US government against Russian individuals and companies, after the White House had attributed hack-and-leak campaigns during the presidential election to Russia. In an official statement the White House announced that officials of the FSB and GRU, as well as three companies and several civilian individuals were no longer allowed to enter the USA and were not allowed to have business relations with US organizations. In addition, 35 Russian diplomats were expelled and two properties of Russian foreign missions in the USA were closed.

Such measures arguably also have the side-effect of serving as a deterrent against the activities of other groups and states. They demonstrate the attribution capabilities of the US intelligence services and the determination to make use of sanctions against sponsors of APT groups. It can be expected that perpetrators will try to test the limits now: Which activities are considered acceptable or negligible, and which lead to diplomatic consequences? After all, not all cyber-activities can be investigated with the same effort. Particularly, official law enforcement investigations bind resources over a long period of time, as sub-poenas or requests to providers need to be in accordance with the rule of law, which involves time-consuming paper-work. Thus, also in the future only those campaigns will be selected for official attribution that cause the greatest damage or pose the greatest risk [7]. In this sense, a period of norm-building is to be expected.

A consequence of the necessity to select cyber-operations for public attribution is that there is a skewed coverage of actor countries [16]. Public attribution runs the risk of being exploited as a tool for propaganda during bilateral conflicts—or at least making it appear so (cf. [16]). This may be the reason why in the last years governments have increasingly decided to publish joint attribution statements. Such an approach has the potential to increase the credibility of accusations without the need of presenting more details—but only if the governments that join in on an attribution are not regarded as strategic partners anyway.

In this context, a statement of the Dutch government may be symptomatic for the attitude of several governments: The Dutch Minister of Foreign Affairs stated that for public attribution it is not required to set forth the basis on which a government attributes a cyber operation—only if that operation is assessed by an international tribunal [17].

The USA can be regarded as a pioneer in using attribution for foreign policy purposes. But also other countries have prepared for public attribution. For instance, Estonia and Norway established inter-agency processes for coming up with an attribution result and assessing the potential consequences of publishing it (cf. [18]). These processes even allow to fine-tune the political impact by communicating the attribution either by an agency director, minister, or head of government.

Maybe inspired by the US, the European Union has agreed on a sanctions regime [11] that allows joint measures against individuals responsible for cyber attacks, and subjects that provide financial, technical or material support. This regime does not entail a process for joint attribution, though, but relies on the member states to implement their own attribution processes.

Reputation for Security Companies The overwhelming majority of public attribution cases are from IT security companies. Their business model is certainly not to provide companies with free information for assessing their risk of being targeted by an APT group—especially since this very information is also offered as commercial Threat Intelligence. Their paying customers receive IoCs and attribution for significantly more APT groups than are even known publicly. Therefore, it is safe to assume that publishing APT reports and the perpetrators behind them also serves marketing and reputation-building purposes. Technical details about new espionage-backdoors do demonstrate a security company's technical skills, but it is attribution results that will gain attention of the media and the public.

Companies such as Kaspersky, Symantec, CrowdStrike or FireEye are filling the gap that intelligence agencies do not cover. This led to the fact that attribution is no longer regarded as a monopoly of government authorities. Nowadays, not only the public sector is targeted by cyber-espionage and has a need for attribution, but also the private sector has a constant need for information about relevant APT groups—if only to justify investments in IT security. This is documented by the long-standing popularity of commercial Threat Intelligence.

Thus, Threat Intelligence and public APT reports shape the public perception of cyber-attacks. It is important to note that these reports are written by technical analysts and then revised by marketing departments. Unlike journalists in established media, these authors are not bound by a universally accepted standard or a code of conduct. Although these publications can have far-reaching political consequences and sometimes name individuals as perpetrators, there are no industry-wide processes for fact-checking or established ethical guidelines. (The ethical aspects of attribution are discussed in more detail in Chap. 13). In academia, for contrast, many universities have adopted rules for good scientific practice. Similarly, scientific publications almost always undergo a peer review, i.e. an (anonymous) assessment by other scientists. This is to ensure that only relevant and correct results are published. Such processes and structures do not exist for the publication of attribution results. The security companies themselves decide what they publish and in what form. At least, a clear incentive to publish only verified and reliable results is that false statements can lead to a considerable loss of reputation. Since no security company has exclusive visibility into the activities of APT groups, it is very likely that other security researchers will discover and publicly point out any errors in the analysis. Still, this did not prevent a number of half-baked attribution statements being published in the last few years—mostly by newly founded security companies that may have had a need for publicity. In many cases the shortcomings of their analyses were identified and documented by the infosec community.

Just like government agencies, security companies are free to cherry-pick APT groups to be attributed. This also results in a skewed distribution of actor countries, as the vendors will choose APT groups that are relevant for their customer-base. And they might be tempted to avoid attribution to governments that they have business relations with.

12.2   Presentation of Results

If a public attribution statement is not meant as a mere signal to the perpetrators, the results must be transparent and credible (see [7, 13]). This includes explaining analysis methods, presenting evidence, and describing the offenses and motives of the culprits.

However, currently there is no standardized and generally accepted analysis methodology. Therefore, presentations of attribution results vary from case to case and are of varying quality. While some studies call for standardization of the attribution methodology [13], others emphasize that there cannot be a systematic one-size-fits-all approach to attribution [7].

Still, looking at the analysis reports available to date, those that appear convincing share a number of features. It should be noted that not all of these features will be required for all purposes and audiences. But they define the best-in-class approach to communication of attribution results. Agencies and security companies that regularly publish attribution results should consider adopting an attribution policy, defining the analysis objectives, which levels of attribution are covered, which sources and methods are at the analysts disposal, and the ethical rules that the analysts adhere to.

Object of Attribution First of all, it must be defined which activity is the object of the analysis. Is a malware family analyzed to identify its developers? Or did the analysts identify individuals that manage a C&C infrastructure? Or does the analysis cover a set of incidents at several organizations?

Level of Attribution It should be made explicit on which level the attribution was conducted. Is it about assigning an incident to an already known (and possibly attributed) intrusion set? Or is the attribution about linking activity to a country, a person or an organization? And if the attribution statement is about the native language of the perpetrators, it should be made explicit whether the analysts conclude that it is state-sponsored, or whether this question was not within the scope of the analysis. The 4C model introduced in Sect. 2.4 can serve as a reference for the levels of attribution.

Level of Detail Reports are particularly transparent and credible if they can be reproduced and verified by third parties. This will remain one of the biggest challenges, though, as attribution heavily depends on access to data—and some of this data will always be confidential for privacy, intellectual property, or national security reasons. But methodologically, documenting evidence in reproducible detail increases the credibility of any analysis. For example, instead of a summarized description that strings of a certain language were found, these strings should be explicitly listed, if possible together with the hashes of the samples. A similar procedure can be applied to most of the other types of evidence.

Diversity of Evidence The more MICTIC aspects of a campaign or APT group are covered by evidence, the more reliable is the resulting hypothesis. Thus, the documented clues should come from malware samples, C&C infrastructure, forensic data from control servers, and from telemetry. These technical investigations should be complemented by geopolitical analysis, in particular the cui bono. If no useful information was found for an aspect, this should be documented explicitly.

Premises and Assumptions As discussed in Sect. 2.5 many conclusions depend on assumptions and premises. If the attribution depends strongly on some of them, they should be made explicit.

Inconsistent Evidence For objectivity and to avoid cognitive bias, evidence that does not support the resulting hypothesis and was assessed as irrelevant should be documented and discussed.

Potential False Flags Chapter 10 noted that the existence of false flags can never be ruled out, but can only be assessed with varying confidence. Therefore, for each evidence the report should estimate the effort that would be necessary to plant a false flag.

Alternative Hypotheses If there are alternative hypotheses with a relevant confidence, they should be discussed. Even if they are significantly less robust than the favored hypothesis, a discussion may illustrate why the analysts arrived at the published conclusion.

Confidence Level Intelligence agencies use different levels of confidence for conclusions based on imperfect knowledge and uncertain sources [19]. There are no internationally standardized confidence levels and no definition of the conditions under which a certain confidence is justified. Nevertheless, even rough gradations of confidence such as 'low', 'medium' and 'high' are intuitively understandable for most audiences. The purpose of the attribution has an impact on acceptable confidence levels. If documents about a government's negotiation position for a multilateral summit was stolen, a medium confidence about who now knows about this position is already helpful—at least better than guessing. In contrast, legal or foreign policy measures such as sanctions can only be justified with high confidence levels. The media can decide for themselves whether they want to cover results with low confidence. If a confidence level is stated in the original analysis, it should be good practice to indicate it appropriately in the media. Attribution is still young as a discipline so that even single incorrect or methodologically flawed reports can cause lasting damage to its reputation. In this respect, beat journalists are an important filter for attribution statements by security companies and intelligence services, at least until standardized processes and criteria are established.

Audience Public attribution statements are received by a heterogeneous public. Thus, good presentations cover different information needs. For decision-makers, strategic assessments should outline the motivation of the perpetrators, their targeting profile, and the regions and sectors in which they are active. In contrast, TTPs and IoCs are of greater value for the technical audience, e.g. IT-security teams. For the non-technical public, the cyber-operations should be put into context politically and economically.

Most reports of security companies already fulfill many of these features. In particular, Mandiant's APT1 report, CrowdStrike's report about PutterPanda, and the Naikon report by ThreatConnect were milestones in attribution. These reports have been instrumental in convincing the media and the public that the perpetrators behind APT attacks can be identified. However, the fact that attribution is now more or less accepted as a discipline can lead to more lax analysis, as attribution statements will have to stand up against less skepticism. For instance, during the WannaCry ransomware campaign in 2016, it took only a few days for security companies to link it to North Korean perpetrators due to code similarities. This statement has not proven false apparently. But it is questionable whether all aspects of the campaign had been investigated and all the assessments that are part of a full-fledged attribution process had been conducted in this short time.

12.3   Reaction to Disclosure

Although the academic literature treats public attribution as a means to form cyber-space
and to define cyber-norms, there is not much empiric research about the actual and mea-
surable reactions of APT groups that were publicly disclosed. It is generally accepted that
perpetrators have reacted in various manners to APT reports in the past. Saher Naumaan, an
infosec researcher, categorized the reactions and provided examples (cf. [20]). APT1 seems
to have disbanded after being described in great detail and being attributed by Mandiant.
The likely Iranian group OilRig apparently invested a year to develop new tools and stand
up new infrastructure after they were outed in 2014. In contrast, APT28 continues its activities almost unimpressed by a constant flurry of reports about its campaigns—the group
just slightly adapts its malware and procures additional control servers (while continuing
using existing ones). Another observation is that some APT groups strike back against the
analysts that outed them, often in almost childish manners. For instance, Snake and APT10
inserted derogatory strings about a German researcher or the Japanese CERT, respectively,
into their malware. Naumaan relates an anecdote about CharmingKitten that set up a fake
website mimicking the security company ClearSky after their researchers had published a
report about the likely Iranian APT group.

There is no framework for predicting the reaction of APT groups to disclosure. More
empirical work is needed. But there are some patterns that seem to effect the decision of
the groups or their sponsors. In general, the reaction seems to depend on characteristics
of the disclosure itself. One factor is whether the report is limited to technical details or
contains attribution results on the organization or person level. If the attribution is only
about a country of origin the respective government can plausibly deny its responsibility by
framing criminals (e.g. [21]). Also the publication venue plays a role—a technical blog is
less visible than a story that gets covered by international media.

The difference between APT1 (which apparently disbanded) and APT28 (which continued its operations) after being attributed to the PLA or GRU in international media, shows
that the reaction also depends on the group itself. A relevant factor is likely the level of
accountability that applies to the government sponsor. A democratic government is more
likely to order a break in cyber-operations after an embarassing news article than an author-
itarian regime that does not have to fear critical oversight. Another important aspect is the
level of OpSec that the group has shown beforehand. This is often correlated with technical
sophistication. According to public reports, the Regin malware underwent a major development jump after media covered the Belgacom incident. Finally, the type of targets that a
group is after influences the necessity of retooling. If targets have a high security posture,
they will be aware of the APT reports and will implement counter-measures. In contrast,
groups that are known to target individual activists with low security skills have often been
rather unimpressed by being reported about.

On the diplomatic level, in the last years, several sanctions have been issued, often after the unsealing of indictments. It is difficult to assess the impact of these diplomatic measures, as they have targeted Russia, Iran, and North Korea, who were already under diplomatic pressure for non-cyber conflicts. If a country is already accused of invading another country, violating human rights, or financing terror organizations, sanctions for cyber-operations will be of a much lower priority.

To conclude this chapter optimistically, several countries have asserted their interpretation that according to international law reactions to cyber-attacks have to be proportionate (e.g. [17]). This interpretation also entails that use of force will only be admissible as a response if the cyber-attack itself was equivalent to an armed attack.

References

1. Mandiant: APT1—Exposing one of China's cyber espionage units (2013). https://www.fireeye. com/content/dam/fireeye-www/services/pdfs/mandiant-apt1-report.pdf. Accessed 21 July 2017
2. US-CERT: Alert (TA14-353A) Targeted destructive malware. Official website of the Department of Homeland Security (2014). https://www.us-cert.gov/ncas/alerts/TA14-353A. Accessed 25 Oct 2017
3. US-CERT: Alert (TA15-213A) recent email phishing campaigns—mitigation and response recommendations. Official website of the Department of Homeland Security (2015). https://www.us-cert.gov/ncas/alerts/TA15-213A. Accessed 25 Oct 2017
4. US-CERT: Alert (TA17-117A) intrusions affecting multiple victims across multiple sectors. Official website of the Department of Homeland Security (2017). https://www.us-cert.gov/ncas/alerts/TA17-117A. Accessed 25 Oct 2017
5. United States Department of Justice: U.S. charges five Chinese military hackers for cyber espionage against U.S. corporations and a labor organization for commercial advantage (2014). https://www.fbi.gov/contact-us/field-offices/pittsburgh/news/press-releases/u.s.-charges-five-chinese-military-hackers-with-cyber-espionage-against-u.s.-corporations-and-a-labor-organization-for-commercial-advantage. Accessed 18 July 2017
6. The US Department of Justice: Chinese national pleads guilty to conspiring to hack into U.S. defense contractors' systems to steal sensitive military information. Justice News (2016). http://web.archive.org/web/20160401055017/https://www.justice.gov/opa/pr/chinese-national-pleads-guilty-conspiring-hack-us-defense-contractors-systems-steal-sensitive. Accessed 12 Sept 2017
7. Rid, T., Buchanan, B.: Attributing cyber attacks. J. Strat. Stud. **38**(1–2) (2015)
8. The White House: FACT SHEET: Actions in response to Russian malicious cyber activity and harassment. White House Briefing Room (2016). https://obamawhitehouse.archives.gov/the-press-office/2016/12/29/fact-sheet-actions-response-russian-malicious-cyber-activity-and. Accessed 18 July 2017
9. Press Briefing on the Attribution of the WannaCry Malware Attack to North Korea. James S. Brady Press Briefing Room (2017). https://www.whitehouse.gov/briefings-statements/press-briefing-on-the-attribution-of-the-wannacry-malware-attack-to-north-korea-121917/. Accessed 13 Jan 2020
10. Marsh, S.: US joins UK in blaming Russia for NotPetya cyber-attack. The Guardian (2017). https://www.theguardian.com/technology/2018/feb/15/uk-blames-russia-notpetya-cyber-attack-ukraine. Accessed 26 Dec 2019

11. https://ccdcoe.org/library/publications/european-union-establishes-a-sanction-regime-for-cyber-attacks/ . Accessed 13 Jan 2020
12. Department of Homeland Security: Joint statement from the Department Of Homeland Security and Office of the Director of National Intelligence on Election Security. Official Website of the Department of Homeland Security (2016). https://www.dhs.gov/news/2016/10/07/joint-statement-department-homeland-security-and-office-director-national. Accessed 25 Oct 2017
13. Davis II, J.S., Boudreaux, B.A., Welburn, J.W., Aguirre, J., Ogletree, C., McGovern, G., Chase, M.: Stateless Attribution—Toward International Accountability in Cyberspace. RAND Corporation (2017). https://www.rand.org/pubs/research_reports/RR2081.html. Accessed 19 Sept 2017
14. Kopan, T.: White House readies cyber sanctions against China ahead of state visit. CNN Politics (2015). http://web.archive.org/web/20170718181028/http://edition.cnn.com/2015/08/31/politics/china-sanctions-cybersecurity-president-obama/. Accessed 18 July 2017
15. United States District Court Southern District of New York: Unites States of America vs. Zhu Hua, Zhang Shilong (2018)
16. Egloff, F.J., Wenger, A.: Public attribution of cyber incidents. CSS Analyses in Security Policy, No. 244, May 2019
17. Schmitt, M.: The Netherlands releases a Tour de Force on International Law in Cyberspace—analysis. Just Security (2019). https://www.justsecurity.org/66562/the-netherlands-releases-a-tour-de-force-on-international-law-in-cyberspace-analysis/. Accessed 14 Jan 2020
18. Kaminska, M., Robert C., Smeets, M.: A transatlantic dialogue on military cyber operations. Workshop Report, University of Texas at Austin, Amsterdam, 13 August 2019. https://www.strausscenter.org/images/pdf/Amsterdam-Workshop-Report-Final-Oct-1.pdf. Accessed 14 Jan 2020
19. Office of the Director of National Intelligence: Background to 'Assessing Russian activities and intentions in recent US elections': the analytic process and cyber incident attribution (2017). https://www.dni.gov/files/documents/ICA_2017_01.pdf. Accessed 23 July 2017
20. Lemos, R.: Disclosure does little to dissuade cyber spies. Dark Reading (2019). https://www.darkreading.com/threat-intelligence/disclosure-does-little-to-dissuade-cyber-spies/d/d-id/1336273. Accessed 15 Jan 2020
21. RFE/RL: Putin compares hackers to 'Artists,' says they could target Russia's critics for 'Patriotic' reasons. Radio Free Europe Radio Liberty (2017). https://www.rferl.org/a/russia-putin-patriotic-hackers-target-critics-not-state/28522639.html. Accessed 15 Jan 2020

Ethics of Attribution

A public attribution statement is an accusation against a state, an organization, or a person. It is usually accompanied by the exposure of an APT group and its tools and techniques, as well as its targets. Since cyber-operations have become an established instrument for a variety of purposes, the targets may be governments or companies, but also journalists, opposition members, drug dealers, or even terrorists. Intuitively, some of these might be legitimate targets for law enforcement or counter-terrorism agencies. Even political cyber-espionage against a war-mongering or repressive regime might serve a greater good. In each of these scenarios, ethical questions need to be considered by those who wish to expose these operations. Another painstaking decision is whether it is justifiable to name individuals as likely perpetrators, particularly if the confidence in their involvement is only medium.

There are no general answers or solutions to these questions. This chapter discusses the various aspects that analysts have to consider before disclosure.

13.1 Neutrality

Most of the reports published by security companies cover groups that are assessed as being likely either Chinese, Russian, Iranian or North Korean. In contrast, analyses of cyber-operations of presumably Western origin are extremely rare. This skewed coverage might lead to the suspicion that Western security companies are biased or even intentionally turn a blind eye to malware from their own hemisphere. Such behavior would be plausible because of economic interests—a security company might be ill-advised to publicly disclose an operation of an agency that is one of its customers. Also, ideological or political reasons may lead to a selective bias for exposing APT groups. Will a security company invest great effort for attributing an intelligence operation that serves the good of its own country?

These questions are not limited to attribution, but also arise for the detection strategy of security products. Following the publication of the Snowden documents, 25 privacy- and

© Springer-Verlag GmbH Germany, part of Springer Nature 2020
T. Steffens, *Attribution of Advanced Persistent Threats*,
https://doi.org/10.1007/978-3-662-61313-9_13

human rights-organizations signed an open letter in which they asked anti-virus vendors about their handling of so-called government malware for surveillance [1]. They wanted to know whether the companies had already detected such software and whether they had been asked by authorities to suppress detection alerts. In December 2013, six security companies responded to the letter [2]. All of them essentially stated that the companies' policy was to detect malware irrespective of its origin and that they had never been asked by authorities to ignore specific families or samples. (Also note the focus on malware instead of general hacking-activity and TTPs, which was typical at that time.)

These actor-agnostic detection policies could be ethically motivated, but purely economic interests cannot be ruled out either. The reputation of a security company certainly benefits from such statements. After all, most security companies operate internationally and publicly favoring certain governments could be detrimental to economic success. It seems plausible that no company can afford to deliberately configure its security products to intentionally ignore certain samples. Also for technical reasons, explicitly whitelisting malware families or samples does not appear feasible. But a totally different question is whether the analysts that develop detection signatures spend the same effort for all APT groups. It is safe to assume that the allocation of analysis resources is skewed—for one reason or another.

The same skewed allocation of resources likely applies to attribution. Attribution in a quality suited for publication does not happen by chance, but requires considerable effort that must be allocated intentionally. Some companies that were pressed about not having published reports about Western APT groups pointed out that they focus on campaigns that target their own customers. This policy is certainly legitimate. Still, as long as a company has not publicly attributed APT groups by some set of countries, it will have to face some reservations.

For international security companies the political domain is full of similar reputation risks. Even a policy to not expose campaigns targeting terrorists may be hard to motivate under certain circumstances. Whether a group is regarded as a terrorist organization can be subject to political ideologies. For instance, in 2019 the United States classified the Islamic Revolutionary Guards Corps as a terrorist organization—whereas from the Iranian perspective it is a branch of the Armed Forces with a personnel of 125,000 and an essential social, political, military, and economic role.

Ignoring APT groups or malware that target terrorists would be hard to adhere to consistently, as the vendor would have to rely on authorities separating their campaigns sincerely into espionage against governmental institutions versus operations against terrorists (cf. [8, 9]). Even if this separation was adhered to generally, there would be a strong temptation to use such whitelisted malware families for a few high-value targets outside of anti-terror operations every now and then.

13.2 Consequences of Attribution

Attribution statements can have far-reaching consequences—even if they were not published by government agencies but by security companies. The diplomatic pressure exerted by the Obama administration on China in 2015 [3] was likely in part based on the many reports about Chinese cyber-espionage against US companies. Publications by security companies can corroborate government findings and thereby support allegations. But publications can also put a government under pressure to act—even at inconvenient times. In diplomacy and foreign policy the timing of raising an issue is crucial. Relations between states are about constant trade-offs, balancing requests and pressure, giving and taking, compromising. Media reports about attribution results by security companies may force a government to raise issues at inopportune times. Companies might even be tempted to publish a previously private Threat Intelligence report during international conflicts to maximize media attention.

In contrast, if the attribution was conducted by a government agency, it can coordinate with the foreign policy authorities.

Another potential consequence of attribution reports is that an APT campaign is aborted. If the group had targeted commercial enterprises for intellectual property, this may be a welcome effect. However, if it was an anti-terror operation or an investigation against drug dealers, the criminals may be alerted and go into hiding.

Journalists face similar dilemmas—though not necessarily in the cyber-domain (cf. [8]). In the United States it has become common practice for media representatives to discuss planned articles concerning national security or ongoing intelligence operations with government officials prior to publication. This way officials have the chance to explain the context and try to convince the journalists that some information is too sensitive for publication (cf. [4], p. 85 f.), or that disclosure should be postponed (e.g. [6], p. 85). A similar approach was suggested for the field of cyber-espionage [10]. But it is questionable whether this is practically feasible. Hacker attacks, unlike operations by special units or human spies, are usually not isolated individual events. Instead, they are linked to each other by malware or infrastructure and may be tracked as intrusion sets. If a security company publishes details of a malware that was detected during an attack, many other attacks and operations may be exposed as well. A prime example of this is a report about APT29 by the Finnish company F-Secure. While the main focus was on espionage-operations against embassies and other government agencies, the report also covered campaigns apparently aimed at monitoring the smuggling of illegal substances [5]. Also, as security researcher Collin Anderson pointed out, security companies and analysts have an international audience and would have to establish trusted contacts to a multitude of government agencies [8].

13.3 Outing Individuals

Another ethical question is whether individuals should be named in public reports, maybe even together with photos. On the one hand concrete individuals make an attribution tangible, the report will attract much more attention, and it will appear more substantial. On the other hand, the person in question is very likely just a pawn in the overall system. As alluded to earlier, the individuals that were identified in APT research where often those that procured servers—usually not the masterminds of the group. They might not even have much insight into operations and do not steal data themselves. Additionally, for members of APT groups the cyber-operations are their daily work, which they carry out for a commercial or government customer. Depending on the legal system of their country, they may not even violate laws from their point of view. In some countries, working in APT groups is a way to be exempted from military service. So depending on the respective army, one's own physical condition or family situation, opting for service in a cyber-unit may be an understandable decision.

If one changes the perspective, the ethical dimension becomes even more apparent. From a Western perspective, show trials of spies convicted abroad or the display of prisoners of war are considered degrading. In a sense, the situation is similar to naming and showing individuals in APT reports.

A putative solution could be to avoid attribution on the person level and focus on the organization level—after all, this is the politically and operationally more relevant result. Unfortunately, it is often not possible to present evidence for the involvement of an organization without naming persons. In most published cases, the military unit or agency was identified by their employment of individual perpetrators (see [7], p. 12). For instance, the investigations described in Chap. 9 used photos and information from personal blogs to infer the two PLA units. If the personal information is omitted in the reports, the attribution to the organization is no longer convincing.

Similar considerations lead to the inclusion of names in this book. To illustrate certain methods it was indispensable to show how certain individuals could be linked to military units or government agencies. The ethical ramifications were deemed justifiable as the persons had already been named in public reports, and omitting their names was pointless as the original reports had to be referenced anyway.

A challenging question is whether the victims of APT attacks should be named. It is often possible to present the geopolitical analysis in a comprehensible manner even if the victims are only named abstractly by their industry and region. However, there may be cases where the cui-bono analysis is only transparent enough if the victim is named explicitly. The attribution of the GhostNet campaign is much more convincing if the Dalai Lama and his staff are named as targets—instead of an 'Asian religious organization'. Even more important was disclosing the DNC as an APT28 victim in 2016. In both cases both effected organizations had agreed to be named in the reports anyway.

For this ethical question there is no universal solution. The right to privacy of perpetrators and victims must be balanced with the public's interest and the relevance for the attribution in each individual case.

13.4   Possibility of Mistakes

In addition to the fundamental ethical questions discussed above, there is also the possibility of errors in attribution research. These may be methodological errors or misinterpretations, or false flags may lead to wrong conclusions. In such cases, there is the risk that the consequences mentioned in Sect. 13.2 are initiated unprovoked.

To minimize the likelihood of taking measures based on wrong attribution results, confidence levels need to be stated explicitly (see Chap. 12). Still, just like mistakes by the perpetrators are possible and will facilitate attribution, the same holds true for analysts. Mistakes can never be ruled out. Therefore, before publishing attribution hypotheses, potential consequences need to be considered. The more grave the potential consequences, the more reliable and robust the attribution must be.

References

1. Multiple authors: Your policy on the use of software for the purpose of state surveillance. In: Open Letter (2013). https://www.bof.nl/live/wp-content/uploads/Letter-to-antivirus-companies-.pdf. Accessed 16 Oct 2017
2. Schwart, M.J.: Do Antivirus Companies Whitelist NSA Malware? DARK Reading (2013). http://web.archive.org/web/20171016164108https://www.darkreading.com/vulnerabilities-and-threats/do-anti-virus-companies-whitelist-nsa-malware/a/d-id/1112911. Accessed 16 Oct 2017
3. Kopan, T.: White House Readies Cyber Sanctions Against China Ahead of State Visit. CNN Politics (2015). http://web.archive.org/web/20170718181028/http://edition.cnn.com/2015/08/31/politics/china-sanctions-cybersecurity-president-obama/. Accessed 18 October 2017
4. Greenwald, G.: Die globale Überwachung, S. 85. Droemer Verlag (2014)
5. F-Secure Labs: The Dukes—7 years of Espionage (2015). https://www.f-secure.com/documents/996508/1030745/dukes_whitepaper.pdf. Accessed 19 Oct 2017
6. Sanger, D.E.: Confront and Conceal, S. 85. Broadway Paperbacks (2012)
7. Rid, T., Buchanan, B.: Attributing cyber attacks. J. Strat. Stud. **38**(1–2) (2015)
8. Anderson, C.: When Indicators of Compromise Become Indicators of Counterterrorism. Personal blog (2018). https://cda.io/notes/indicators-of-compromise-counterterrorism/. Accessed 18 Jan 2020
9. Guerrero-Saade, J.A.: The ethics and perils of apt research: an unexpected transition into intelligence brokerage. In: Virus Bulletin Conference Proceedings (2015). https://media.kaspersky.com/pdf/Guerrero-Saade-VB2015.pdf. Accessed 18 Jan 2020
10. Lotrionte, C.: Threat Intelligence Threatening Intel Operations. Security Analyst Summit (2017). https://www.youtube.com/watch?v=0DsEd8M6-Go. Accessed 18 Jan 2020

Conclusion and Outlook

In the German version of this book which was published two years ago, the conclusion stated that attribution cannot be organized like a project and that there exist no checklists for conducting the analysis. While this statement may still be true to some extent, it needs to be refined in a more nuanced way. Framing attribution as if it depended on some strokes of luck that turn up evidence underestimates the state of the art and does not do justice to the analysts that documented their findings about the perpetrators behind attribution in many reports. It is certainly true that nobody can plan attribution as a project that is guaranteed to come up with results after completing milestone by milestone. And there is indeed no magic checklist that will cover all possible analysis methods. But nobody has to start from scratch to conduct a structured attribution analysis. If a security company or government agency is given the task to attribute a certain set of incidents, there are some best practices that can be followed, and a set of analysis methods that should be conducted as a minimum.

14.1   Attribution as a Process

Therefore, in this book, attribution has been presented by covering the aspects of the MICTIC framework in separate chapters. The aspects were chosen in a way that they allow a research team to partition the investigation into work packages for malware, infrastructure, control servers, telemetry, intelligence, and cui bono. Each chapter concludes with a list of various evidence types. While these lists are not exhaustive and should be extended with findings from future research or ideas from analysts more knowledgeable than this author, they form a basic guideline that any organization that wants to conduct attribution can follow. Just like police investigations, attribution is never guaranteed to succeed in identifying a country, organization, or individuals as the perpetrators. But after checking for the evidence types mentioned in each chapter, there is a good chance that analysts will be able to formulate some plausible hypotheses.

© Springer-Verlag GmbH Germany, part of Springer Nature 2020   191
T. Steffens, *Attribution of Advanced Persistent Threats*,
https://doi.org/10.1007/978-3-662-61313-9_14

Attribution remains hard—but not necessarily intellectually or technically. While it requires a set of very diverse and specific skills, the main challenge is access to data. Some evidence types require large quantities of data to discover patterns (like timestamp analysis or cui bono), other evidence types will be present only in confidential data from incidents, servers, mail accounts, or network traffic. It is no coincidence that in most cases the organizations that published convincing attribution results are security companies with access to sample databases and telemetry, or government agencies that can subpoena data or have SIGINT capabilities. Still, even if all necessary analytical skills are available and access to data is granted, some APT groups may be so stealthy that attribution will fail.

Nevertheless, throughout the chapters several examples were discussed where attribution with high confidence was possible. Although the analyses differed in details from case to case, they lead to an overall picture of how APT campaigns can be investigated. Figure 14.1 illustrates the flow of evidence types and analysis steps in a simplified form.

A characteristic feature of the attribution process is that many analysis activities run in parallel. Reverse engineers may work on samples while threat intelligence analysts unravel the actor's infrastructure. Therefore, Fig. 14.1 should not be interpreted as a strictly sequential process. Also, the analysis steps often loop back to previous steps. Most types of evidence can be fed into scan or search queries in order to discover related samples, servers, or person identifiable data that can in turn provide new search queries.

Some of the steps in the depicted analysis process are not necessarily conducted to identify perpetrators. Instead, the analysis steps in the upper part are necessary for improving detection signatures and network defense measures. They are part of the day-to-day business of IT security companies. Only the analysis methods in the lower area are explicitly conducted for attribution and usually do not generate output for security software products.

14.2   Outlook

It has been a recurring prediction of security companies that it will become more difficult to distinguish intrusion sets from one another in the future. Some years ago, the use of Dynamic DNS providers was considered an obstacle to analysis because it prevented the use of Whois data. Since the GDPR took effect, Whois is even less useful. And the current trend for perpetrators to use publicly available tools indeed makes it more difficult to distinguish between the various groups. But contrary to most predictions, such trends have never led to the complete disappearance of old methods. APT groups continue to register their own C&C domains and develop their own malware. These findings show that perpetrators cherish flexibility and therefore often resort to supposedly old methods in addition to following new trends. Also, analysts constantly develop new analysis methods and tools: For instance, the lack of useful Whois data has led to security companies now proactively scanning for control servers or using other features such as SSL certificates to discover malicious servers.

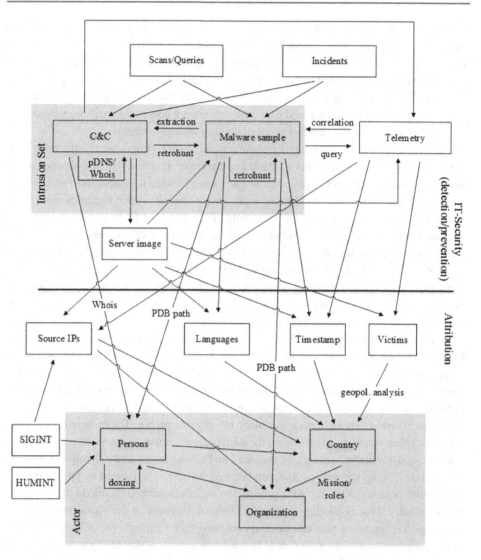

Fig. 14.1 Overall picture of evidence types and attribution steps. Data is depicted by rectangles, arrows depict analysis methods. The process should not be interpreted as strictly linear and sequential

While the OpSec of most APT groups has matured significantly since the beginnings of cyber-espionage, only very few perpetrators managed to avoid mistakes completely, be it systematic patterns or random slip ups. Only very few groups seem to follow OpSec-by-design, and only adapt their processes and techniques after reports document how analysts are able to discover and track them.

Nowadays there exists a large corpus of attribution results. This is both a blessing and a curse. On the one hand, not every incident has to be investigated from scratch. In many cases it is common practice to assign new campaigns to an already attributed group. This allows efficient attribution analysis. On the other hand, this makes investigations susceptible to the Vermeer effect. Clustering attacks of different actors into the same intrusion set will lead to even more incidents being assigned to it—either foiling a consistent attribution hypothesis on the organization level or leading to incriminating wrong governments.

Clustering, i.e. generating meaningful definitions of APT groups, will be the main challenge in the next few years. This is illustrated by the observation that few disagreements between security companies or government agencies exist when it comes to attributing established APT groups to countries. But agreeing on clusters, i.e. which incidents were likely conducted by the same perpetrators, is a totally different matter. Each analysis team has its own interpretation—often due to different data, rarely because of different methods.

Another, more fundamental challenge for attribution will remain false flags. Less so the cases of actually planted red herrings, but the ever-lingering doubt that any evidence could be a cunning false flag. Structured analysis techniques like ACH may help analysts to uncover them, and explaining the necessary effort of generating consistent false flags may help to establish a pragmatic assessment of their likelihood.

Attribution as a discipline will also benefit from making implicit premises explicit, so that they can be questioned and adapted if necessary. This can be motivated by another comparison with art history. In some cases, the authorship of paintings was contested because there was too much variation in the details of the craft, or the number of paintings for individual artists was too high. Thus, ascription to an artist had to fail as long as the art historians assumed that each work was made by only one person. The essential insight that led to a solution was that—at least since the Renaissance—artists ran workshops. The master limited his involvement to designing the motif and overall layout and painting central parts of a picture. Filling the tedious and standardized parts were delegated to journeymen. A similar phenomenon exists for APT groups that are not directly embedded into an agency or the military. Just as painting became a common business in the Renaissance, cyber-espionage has become a product. Several companies offer exploits or backdoors for sale, or even conduct operations for clients. These developments make APT groups even more complex than art workshops. While apprentices worked for the same master artist over a long period of time, it is possible for hacking contractors to work for several clients. Their employees may even take tools and techniques with them when moving to another job, making attribution even more difficult. The state of the art in attribution has so far been mostly based on the assumption of monolithic, fixed teams that share tools only with groups nationally. These assumptions were justified as long as cyber-operations were observed only from a few countries, that have had offensive cyber-capabilities for a decade or more. But nowadays other actors are entering the stage, some of which make use of international contractors to jump-start their cyber-operations.

Apart from the existence of international contractors, also other insights call for a more flexible understanding of the group concept. A side effect of the unsealed US indictments is that the infosec community gained profound insights into different set-ups of running cyber-espionage operations. For example, in-house development in a Russian agency, front companies in North Korea, and contracting individuals in China were among the documented cases. This serves as an important reminder that APT groups are not always monolithic teams that work together on a floor in a government agency.

Although there have been some outstanding examples where security companies have succeeded in attributing APT groups to specific military units, these remain the exception. For the majority of APT groups there are hypotheses only about their country of origin. For attribution on the organization or person level, often intelligence methods such as HUMINT or SIGINT or at least subpoenas for accounts or servers are necessary. This illustrates an opportunity for government agencies and IT-security companies to complement each other. The latter have a high level of competence in detecting new attacks and clustering them into campaigns and intrusion sets. Using telemetry data from hundreds of thousands of computers, they can also determine the relevance and regional impact. Even the most likely country of origin can often be derived with some certainty. This commercial or public Threat Intelligence may enable intelligence agencies to select APT groups that are relevant to their own area of responsibility. Applying SIGINT on control servers or malware characteristics in Internet traffic, as well as human informants in the suspected country of origin, can drive the attribution further to also identify the organizations or even persons behind the attacks.

For governments, fostering its agencies' attribution capabilities is an opportunity to create a strategic instrument for international cyber-security policy. Without attribution, cyber-espionage and—sabotage provide an attractive risk-benefit ratio for actor states, which leads many countries to develop their offensive capabilities. Worldwide, government agencies, commercial enterprises, and critical infrastructures are currently defended primarily by technical measures rather than by diplomacy or foreign policy pressure. Only countries that master attribution demonstrate their analysis competence and develop a strategy for dealing with actor states can add diplomatic measures to their defensive toolbox against cyber-operations.

Until then, the only certainty is a bon mot by Thomas Rid: "There is always someone who knows whether the attribution is correct" [1].

Reference

1. Thomas Rid. Personal communication. Bonn, January 2017

Glossary

APK Installation file for Android.

APT Advanced Persistent Threat—State-sponsored hacker group.

Attribution Process of identifying the actors behind cyber-operations.

Backdoor Software used to access a computer while bypassing security controls.

Banking trojan Software for stealing credentials to online-banking.

Confirmation bias Psychological effect causing the selection or preference of evidence that is consistent with one's favored hypotheses.

Library Compiled code that can be used in own software for standard functions.

Command-and-control server (C&C) Server used by hackers to communicate with their backdoors.

Compiler Software that translates source code into object code.

Content Management Software Software that is used by website owners to maintain their websites.

Debugging Process of finding programming mistakes in source code.

Deep packet inspection Method to filter network packets based on their content.

Diamond model Model to assess cyber-operations based on features from their capabilities, infrastructure, victims, and adversary.

Domain Name System (DNS) System for assigning IP addresses to domain names.

Domain Controller Server that stores credentials of all users and systems in a network (domain).

Doxing Methodology to research individuals by public person identifiable data.

Dropper Small malware used to write a payload onto the hard drive.

Influence operation Operation to manipulate the public opinion in a foreign country.

Exfiltration Process of stealing data from a network.

Exploit Malicious code that uses a vulnerability in a software.

Family Group of malware samples that contain similar code and are referred to by the same name.

Framework Program design and code to develop malware with shared characteristics.

Graphical User Interface (GUI) Visual components that allow to work with a program.

GSM Telecommunication standard for 2G mobile.

Hacktivism Ideologically motivated cyber-attack meant to promote a political message.

Hash Cryptographic value used as fingerprint for strings or files.

Hoster Company operating servers to be rent.

HTTP(S) Protocol developed for WWW browsing. HTTPS is the encrypted version of HTTP.

HUMINT Human Intelligence, information from (typically clandestine) human sources.

Indicator, IoC Also Indicator of Compromise, technical feature that can be used to detect cyber-attacks.

Industrial Control Systems (ICS) Systems used to run and control physical processes.

Intrusion set Indicators and TTPs characterizing several incidents by the same actors.

Keylogger Malware that captures keyboard input.

Killchain Idealized model for describing the phases of an APT attack.

Lateral movement Techniques used by hackers to move from one computer to the next in a network.

Leak Unauthorized publication of confidential information.

Linker Software that merges object code and libraries into an executable file.

Loader Malware that starts a payload.

Man-in-the-middle Attack based on an attacker having access to a network connection of a target.

Operational Security (OpSec) Methods to avoid being discovered.

OSINT Open Source Intelligence, Information from public sources.

Patient zero The first computer that was compromised in an incident.

Pass-the-hash Most frequent method of lateral movement, collecting cryptographically hashed credentials from memory and using it to authenticate to other computers.

Password dumper Tools extracting credentials from memory.

Passive DNS (pDNS) Method to store IP resolutions for domains.

Portable Executable (PE) File format for executables under Windows.

Privilege escalation Attack, usually by exploiting a software vulnerability, that grants extended access rights.

Program database (PDB) File with debug information generated by development environments.

Ransomware Malware that encrypts files on an infected computer and drops instructions for paying a ransom in exchange of the decryption key.

Registrar Service to register domain names.

Remote Administration Tool (RAT) Malware that grants full administrative access to the attacker.

Remote Desktop Protocol Protocol used for logging into the graphical user interface of a computer over the network.

Reputation service Software that assesses the legitimacy of files or internet addresses by their frequency of occurence.

Reverse engineering Translating compiled code into source code.

Rootkit Malware that hides at lower levels than the operating system to avoid detection.

Root server Also dedicated server. Rented server for exclusive use by the customer.

Data at rest Data that is stored on a medium, in contrast to data that is sent over a network.

Sample Manifestation of a malware in form of a file.

Sandbox Prepared system for executing software in a controlled environment and logging its activity.

Malicious code Commands and software that was developed by an attacker, usually exploits or malware.

Malware Malicious software developed by an attacker such as a backdoor, keylogger or dropper.

Vulnerability Programming or design mistake in a software, that allows to circumvent security controls.

Shared hosting Business model of hosters, running webservers of several customers on the same physical machine.

Secure Sockets Layer (SSL) Encryption protocol for network traffic, now replaced by the Transport Layer Security (TLS) protocol.

SIGINT Collection of electronic signals from radiocommunication, telephony or Internet.

Social engineering Non-technical approach of manipulating people into conducting steps that lower their security posture.

SQL injection Attack technique that exploits programming mistakes that lead to input data being interpreted as database commands.

SSH Software used for securely logging into computers over the network.

Staging server Server in the internal network of a compromised organization, used to store collected data before exfiltration.

Telemetry Collecting and transmitting data from security products to the vendor.

Transport Layer Security (TLS) Successor of the Secure Sockets Layer protocol.

Trojaner Nowadays very common term for malware.

TTP Techniques, Tactics and procedures of attackers.

User agent Header field in HTTP-request that denotes the software that initiated the request.

Watering hole Website with malicious code planted by an attacker, because his targets are likely to visit the website.

Webshell Tiny script that is placed on servers that are reachable from the Internet and that allows attackers to execute commands.

Whois Internet protocol to query contact data of domain owners.

Zero-day Exploit for a vulnerability for which no security update exists yet.

Index

© Springer-Verlag GmbH Germany, part of Springer Nature 2020
T. Steffens, *Attribution of Advanced Persistent Threats*,
https://doi.org/10.1007/978-3-662-61313-9